BLACK ENTERPRISE GUIDE TO INVESTING

BLACK ENTERPRISE GUIDE TO INVESTING

James A. Anderson

John Wiley & Sons, Inc.

New York • Chichester • Weinheim • Brisbane • Singapore • Toronto

Published by John Wiley & Sons, Inc.

Published simultaneously in Canada.

Library of Congress Cataloging-in-Publication Data:

Anderson, James A. (James Albert), 1961–
    Black enterprise guide to investing / James A. Anderson.
        p. cm.
    ISBN 0-471-38184-5 (pbk. : alk. paper)
    1. Investments—United States.   2. Afro-Americans—Finance, Personal.   I. Title.

    HG4910 .A715 2000
    332.6'089'96073—dc21
                                                                                00-043362

Printed in the United States of America.

10 9 8 7 6 5 4 3 2 1

CONTENTS

Introduction

AFRICAN AMERICAN INVESTORS AND OUR INVESTMENT BOOM

Arriving a Little Late Is Better Than Never!

A new century has begun and African Americans reflecting on the past 50, 75, even 100 years have much to celebrate. We are richer and more comfortable financially than ever before. We are better educated. We have more political clout.

Blacks indeed can be proud. Statistics gathered since World War II, show a sizable and growing number of African Americans are college graduates, are enjoying a life of middle- and upper-class stability and comforts, and have a longer live expectancy than ever before. African Americans are being elected to office in steadily increasing numbers. New fields of employment and higher wages are allowing many to stake a claim on the promises that are part and parcel of the American dream.

In 1998, a burgeoning black middle class, numbering as many as 6 million households, wielded whopping purchasing clout—$500 billion in annual expenditures by some counts. There are even signs that during the 1990s the chasm between the earnings of African Americans and whites reached its narrowest point in history.

Although this hardly seems like a time of missed opportunities, in some ways it is because the African American community has yet to fulfill its financial potential. Behind the scenes, a problem festers—a gremlin that could be called the wealth gap, the investment divide, or the coming black middle-class shortfall. Not only are the consequences being felt right now, they're guaranteed to linger for some time.

Despite employment gains and rising incomes, African Americans remain woefully underinvested in the stock market and in bonds compared with other groups in the United States. Many of us have settled on savings accounts and other investments that have failed to increase wealth as much as other options could. Many of us have remained on the sidelines during one of the greatest bull markets of all time, effectively missing out on a critical way to improve our lives, our futures, and the lives of our children.

Some of us think that it won't make much of a difference today, tomorrow, or next week. We can probably make do, as we always have. In fact, many of us could remain blissfully ignorant of the disparity between what we have and what we *could* have, and at the same time live relatively comfortable lives, furnishing our homes, buying new automobiles, and taking vacations.

Make no mistake, though. As small as the problem may seem now, it has jarring implications down the road. For starters, it's an indication that many of us won't retire as soon as we'd like or live as comfortably as we would have wished once we leave our jobs. It's also a sign that we might have to shortchange our children's education because we did not stow away enough to fund their tuition, something which would allow our kids and not financial aid officers to choose where they attend university. It also means we're starving ourselves and our communities of an economy's life force: capital.

The purpose of this book is to help you to take control of your financial future through investing. As you make your way into the financial markets, you'll learn how to stake your own claim to our nation's economic power. The following chapters guide you through some of the trickier concepts behind investing and then show you how to make stocks, bonds, and mutual funds work for you. There is even a chapter of tips to help you pass your knowledge of the markets on to your kids.

In that way, a community of overachieving under-investors can become a community of overachievers who are invested. Read on, go forth, and build wealth.

THE INVESTING BOOM

Call it a craze, a boom, or mania—your neighbors, your friends, and probably many of your enemies as well have taken to stocks, bonds, and mutual funds like never before. In a 1999 study, the Securities Industry Association (SIA—a trade organization representing brokerage firms across the country) and the Investment Company Institute (ICI—a Washington group that represents the mutual fund industry) found out that almost 50 percent of all American households have a stake in the stock market, up from a mere 19 percent in 1983. Back almost 20 years ago, just over 42 million people owned stocks or were invested in mutual funds that owned stocks. By 1999, that figure had almost doubled to 79 million people (see Figure I.1).

Figure I.1   Everybody into the Pool

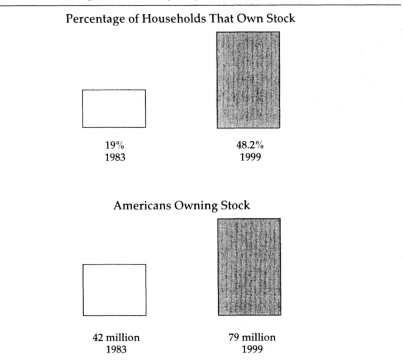

Percentage of Households That Own Stock

19%
1983

48.2%
1999

Americans Owning Stock

42 million
1983

79 million
1999

Source: Securities Industry Association, the Investment Company Institute.

Most stock market investors weren't Johnny-come-lately sorts who had picked up the phone and called a broker in the past year. A surprising 54 percent of all stockholders made their first purchase prior to 1990; 28 percent entered the stock market between 1990 and 1995; and only 18 percent took the plunge in 1995 or later. Also, the SIA-ICI study found that the average household held $50,000 in equities or stocks and stock mutual funds.

These statistics show that during the biggest bull market in history—an unprecedented climb of stock values over the past 10, 15, even 20 years—nearly 50 percent of all Americans have decided to get in and take advantage of a great opportunity. They took funds they were saving for retirement, for education, for all sorts of dreams and wishes and put them to work in stocks. They invested.

While the joint SIA-ICI study doesn't isolate and examine investing patterns of African Americans or any other ethnic group, it serves as an indicator of the country at large. The basis for saying that African Americans trail their peers stems from a distinguishable pattern that has cropped up again and again in a few recent studies.

Private and public sector fact finders show that some African Americans don't understand the financial markets, and feel intimidated by stocks, bonds, and other investments. If and when African Americans learn about investing, it tends to be at a later age than other Americans. And once blacks do start investing, their choices tend to be conservative and often inadequate for the financial demands they may face in life.

Consider a 1999 survey of African American and other investors prepared by Ariel Mutual Funds, an African American investment firm in Chicago, and Charles Schwab & Company, a brokerage firm located in San Francisco, California. The main aim of the study was to determine differences between African American and white investors with comparable incomes. The results showed that more black investors felt like beginners than their whites counterparts, and this lack of knowledge kept them out of the market. They were more mistrusting of the market, according to survey findings, and were more prone to abandon investments if the market went down. Another disturbing finding: African Americans saved less money than whites.

Instead, blacks who put money aside gravitated toward conservative investment vehicles such as insurance policies and bank accounts. Fewer had brokerage accounts than whites and, predictably, blacks trailed in ownership of mutual funds, stocks, and money market accounts. The Ariel-Schwab survey found that just 57 percent of blacks owned any stocks at all, compared to 81 percent of whites. It showed that just 56 percent of the blacks polled had a brokerage account, compared to 71 percent of the whites that

Figure I.2   African Americans and the Market

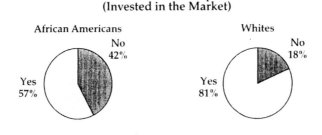

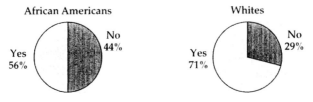

Note: Nearly 75% of African Americans say their lack of knowledge about investing deters them from saving or investing more.
Source: The Ariel Mutual Funds/Charles Schwab & Co. Inc. Black Investor Survey, 1998.

participated in the study. And when asked where they keep "most of their assets," 44 percent of the blacks pointed to the bank, compared to just 31 percent of whites in the survey (see Figure I.2).

Why were African Americans behind? A possible reason is that only 36 percent of the blacks in the survey had opened their first savings account before they entered high school compared with 54 percent of the white participants. African Americans were also unfamiliar with stocks growing up; 24 percent said their families had stocks when they were children, compared with 46 percent of whites. And in fact, the majority of blacks in the survey felt investing in stocks to be tantamount to gambling, playing the lotto, or betting on the horses.

There were glimmers of hope among the numbers gathered up by Ariel and Schwab. They show that a larger percentage of African Americans than whites read books about saving and investing, had gone to investment seminars, or belonged to investment clubs. In fact, the number one New Year's resolution of blacks was to save or invest.

WHY THIS BOOK

You've taken the first step toward changing all the statistics by buying this book. Whether you're a novice to investing or have already started working with stocks, bonds, and mutual funds, the chapters ahead are sure to be well worth your while.

If you've picked this guide up, chances are you're feeling somewhat comfortable. You've got food on the table, a roof over your head, a car or two in the garage. Your kids are in good schools, and happy. No doubt, you have some possessions—a stereo, big-screen television, cellular phones—that your parents couldn't have dreamed of when they were your age.

At the same time, just like everyone else, you have needs to fill and a future you want to secure.

As great as the good life may now be, there's that fateful day ahead when you'll have to box up the stuff in your cubicle, say goodbye to your office chums, and retire. You'll need something to cover the 20-, 30-, maybe 40-year stretch that many folks say could be the best years of your life.

Or, your kids will be starting college before you know it. Most of us can't count on lottery winnings to cover the bill. So what's to do when the spunky tike you've showered in toys and tennis shoes comes to you with a tuition bill in hand and a hopeful look on his or her face?

Maybe the time has come to pack up the moving van and scoot along to the home of your dreams. But, if you've been following the real-estate ads in the classified pages, you've seen how prices have continued to climb year after year. You probably want to start thinking about how to make that dream home a reality.

Those are valid concerns. Take retirement, for example. The experts say you'll need to bring in about 75 percent of your salary to live comfortably once you leave your job. Not only that, but you can expect—and should plan—to be around and leading an active life a good 20 years after you reach the age of 65. Medicine is slowly stretching life expectancy further and further. What the good doctors and lab technicians haven't found is a medicine to make your money grow to cover the many more years you'll need to finance. That's up to you.

Medical science is equally unlikely to discover a way to keep prices in place. We all know that our groceries, car note, or electricity bill have a mysterious way of creeping ever upward. That gradual, yet steady rise in prices—inflation, in other words—isn't making your task of building retirement funds any easier. Prices have tended to rise 3 percent or so annually over the past 75 years. At that pace, money you have put aside in the bank, in a savings account that pays say 2 percent interest is losing value over time—1 percent annually to be exact. Keep $1,000 in the bank under those circumstances, and in 10 years' time, its purchasing power will have slid to the equivalent of $904.38 in today's money. All that is to point out that your plans for retirement need all the help they can get. The money you set aside needs a boost to stretch it as far as possible as well as a push strong enough to get it past inflation's clutches.

Recent statistics about tuition underscore your need to start investing as well. To get your son or daughter through one year at a state university in 1999—including room, board, tuition, books, and an occasional visit to a fast-food restaurant—required an outlay of $20,000. And by current estimates, the cost of a college education is going up perhaps 6 percent a year. At that rate, the new bundle of love that graced your life in 1999 is slated to cost $57,086 a year in 2018. Gulp.

Take heart. Investing can help you in both endeavors, if only for one simple reason: unbeatable returns. Statistics show that stocks have an enviable track record of producing wealth for investors for instance. Depending on which study you read, the market has delivered an annual average return of 10 percent to 13 percent. That means investors in stocks and mutual funds have put their money to work in holdings that in many cases could double their money in under 8 years. Bonds and bond mutual funds are another investment winner. They've returned investors an average 5 percent to 6 percent a year. That's enough to double an investment every 12 years.

That's more than enough reason to get going. But at Black Enterprise, we also want to make sure that you get started *right*. If you've leafed through the financial pages of the local paper occasionally, you've no doubt read about hapless investors whose stocks or mutual funds hit a rough spot and went into a nose dive. Stock and bond investments, as sterling as their record may be, carry a certain risk as well. Investors will sometimes see good, solid, even spectacular gains. At other times, their holdings will decrease in value. If they invest in good stocks, mutual funds, or bonds and stick by their selection, however, they stand an excellent chance of benefiting from the long-term returns.

LET'S GET TO WORK

Your job as an investor is a matter of taking the future into your own hands. Better yet, the sooner you get started, the more time you have.

What You'll Find Here

In this book, you'll learn what you're getting into when you put your money to work. We'll explain stocks, bonds, and mutual funds, and how they go together in a well-focused strategy. You'll see what risks you can and should incur, and learn to avoid risks you shouldn't dabble in. Each company, each individual you choose to work with stands to gain from your investments— you will know what fees they'll pocket and how much you should expect to pay. That way, you'll be able to keep an eye on costs and save as much of your money as possible for investing instead of paying for someone else's retirement dreams or kids' tuition.

Each step of the way starts with an overview of a specific investment tool or concept—stocks, mutual funds, asset allocation, or even ways to teach your kids about investing. We follow up with details on each facet and give you a bird's-eye view of the landscape of the financial markets as well as information about some of the best investments and strategies used by professionals. To help make abstract investing concepts clear, there are true-life examples of people who have faced the same questions and challenges you do right now.

And to help clarify things even further, the following sections are designed to brush away any excuses you may still have for not investing.

Beginners' Luck

Are you just now scraping together enough to even begin to think about investing? Are you worried that you just can't get in on the fun for another few years?

Keep your chin up; that's not always the case. We've scouted around for opportunities to start investing with as small a sum as possible, and have found stocks and mutual funds aplenty that sometimes require no more than

$50, $100, or $250 to start. These recommendations are sprinkled throughout this guide under the heading "Beginner's Luck."

Numerology

Numbers, numbers everywhere but not an explanation to help. CNBC and the financial pages of the newspaper often seem to present an avalanche of statistics and insider "speak"—terms about numbers that are too complicated for novice investors.

A special section in most chapters of this guide is devoted to deciphering the numbers and to telling you what's important and what you can skip over. You'll find the lowdown on the mathematics under the heading "Numerology."

The Black Market

African Americans are now making strides in money management, and portfolio managers have brought a slew of mutual funds to market. Blacks are finally beginning to break through the corporate glass ceiling on their way to the boardroom or the CEO's corner office. Financial markets now list stocks of African American companies. Stock markets are springing up on the African continent.

Not only are these development investment opportunities, they're a chance to lend your financial support to the larger community. The financial markets for African American opportunities are included under the heading "The Black Market."

Web Sightings

The computer is here to stay. The Internet is having a profound change on every facet of life. And together, they are giving investors access to information and new-found power.

Some of the things you can now do online are astonishing. You can monitor the activity of each one of the stocks and mutual funds you own from trading day to trading day. You can calculate how much money you'll need for goals in the years ahead and whether your current budget is on track to meet targets or fall short. You can hunt near and far for mutual funds and stocks, look up as much information on them as you could ever want, and buy new investments for your portfolio.

Throughout this book, listings and brief descriptions for the many wonders on the Web appear under the heading "Web Sightings."

THE MOST IMPORTANT POINT

All together, this package of information and steps to get started can help keep you investing wisely for life. To sum up the rest of what you need to know, we offer the thoughts of Robert Crenshaw, an African American medical device salesperson from Redmond, California, who's been an avid investor for 17 years: "If you're in the market you have a 50 percent chance or greater of succeeding over the long-term despite whatever ups and downs there are," he says. "If you stay on the sidelines, you have a 100 percent chance of failure."

Wise words, indeed.

1

GETTING READY
TO INVEST

Dealing with Debt, Setting Up a Safety Fund, Online Resources, and More

You should be aching to invest by now. After all, putting your money to work in stocks, bonds, and mutual funds is a good way to realize dreams and ambitions, from a new car to a college education, or an early retirement. No doubt, you have bought this book to learn how to get into the stock market and how to set up an investment portfolio to help attain goals that will make your life better.

Excited? Ready to get online and start a brokerage account? Before you charge onward, let's call a quick time-out. No matter how revved up you might be at this point, you need to take a few preliminary steps before you start shoveling money into company shares or mutual funds. The two most important things on your agenda now *sound* like relatively simple jobs. They are creating a stream of money to invest, and then keeping that cash tucked away in investments where it can grow over time. As easy as they both sound, though, you should take enough time to look them over and plan them out correctly.

ON YOUR MARK

Task 1—freeing up some money, any money, to invest—sounds easier than it is. Sure, most of us have a job that reels in an income and secures money for our efforts. Alas, things get a lot more complicated from there. Heap on real-life responsibilities and obligations. The bills, the mortgage, and the car are sure to sap whatever salary you're bringing in. Then, there are frivolous little items you might pick up here and there, impulse buying that creeps into the monthly budget and settles on credit card bills. Add it al! up, and it's little wonder that cash tends to leave the household bank account at practically the speed of light.

Debt is one of the biggest demons you'll need to conquer before you can get started. The funny thing about credit is that everyone has to borrow, and some of that debt is simply unavoidable. That said, many of us could stand to lose a credit line or shred up a credit card or two and still manage to live quite well.

The pages ahead shed some light on the difference between necessary and unnecessary credit. By examining the two in your budget, you can determine how to free up some money to put into stocks and bonds. After all, if you're carrying a huge debt load, the money you invest might actually be a burden in your day-to-day struggle to pay the mortgage, cover the car note, and maybe even put a few steaks on the table. Cut debt down to size, and suddenly you may find not only that your life has become more manageable, but that you have extra money to set aside and save.

You'll also need a way to ensure that the money you invest stays invested. Too often, it is easy to start putting money away with the best intentions. Soon, though, temptations start popping up. How about tapping your savings just a little bit for a Tahitian getaway? Then there's the birthday party for Aunt Doris, and the hot leather jacket you just saw at the department store. . . .

The problem is that those wonderful returns stocks and bonds provide only work if you keep your money safe and snug in place. Over time, the market's historical returns will help build your portfolio, but only if you leave your money alone and allow it and the gains you make to snowball until they're transformed into a truly monumental sum. Shift money in and out, and you sabotage the big scheme. For the short term, that might mean a chance to buy a new car. Over a longer term, however, those items along the way can hijack your goal to create wealth.

Another reason it's a bad idea to dip into your investment accounts is that wishy-washy investing often costs you more money than the market makes for you. You can get slapped with a long list of fees or high penalties for jumping in and out of investments. Remember, there's a commission to pay when you buy stocks and when you sell them as well. Bond market investments, too, may lose value when you sell them before they mature.

To ward off the temptation to cash out of investments and lose money to boot, you need a safety fund, a store of cash to tap for unexpected expenses. Emergencies, after all, have an odd way of cropping up whenever you're strapped. Stash away a contingency fund, and you'll have money to cushion any blow your finances might take in the future.

Just how much is enough, especially when your aim is to earmark funds for the stock market and bonds? Your "safety" account should include your mortgage or rent and other expenses for 3 to 6 months. That's not all, though. While your money is parked in a safety account, it should bring you a bit of interest, preferably more than the measly 1 or 2 percent your bank savings account parcels out. And, to top it all off, you should be able to tap that financial cushion quickly and at no cost.

REALITY CHECK

Lois Hasan learned firsthand that debt and investing don't mix very well.

Nine years ago, she found herself in a jam. Her husband had just died, and suddenly Hasan, a manager for an outpatient medical center in Columbia, South Carolina, had to find a way to not only support herself and three daughters, but come up with a savings plan that would help foot college tuition for all three. Soon after Hasan met with Deborah Breedlove, a financial planner for American Express, she received a candid evaluation: she simply could not continue dragging along a $3,500 balance on three credit cards—four if you included a gas card issued by a major oil company.

Hasan, mind you, hadn't been a slouch. "I'd regularly pay 10 percent or so above the minimum monthly required for each," she recalls. "It just didn't seem to be making much headway, though."

Breedlove's advice was to up the ante. She suggested that Hasan aim for 50 percent above the lowest required monthly payment on the card with the highest interest rate. "We looked at all the bills that I could pay off to free up some money to invest," Hasan says. Breedlove also suggested that Hasan start making regular investments of $300 a month in a money market mutual fund to build up a reserve in case of an emergency.

Hasan kept to the straight and narrow, and within a year found that she had freed up enough cash to put away $600 a month. "The higher payments really started to make a difference within a year and a half or two years," she said.

So much so, in fact, that Hasan was able to help her eldest, Rasheeda, 22, pay much of her tuition and fees at Florida A&M, and foot a large portion of her 20-year-old daughter Ayesha's expenses at the University of South Carolina. Her efforts will also help when Sakeenah, now 17, decides on school (she's currently looking at the state university).

We may spend a good portion of this chapter preaching the benefits of frugality. Nevertheless, there's one purchase we recommend that you make: the new millennium's version of the investor's best friend—a trusty home computer. These days, you can't really be an efficient financial manager without one. Careful, though. Just any old box with a few microchips and a plug won't quite do. Whatever personal computer you buy should be equipped with up-to-date financial software and a hookup to the Internet. Don't fret. That's not such a tall order. A package including all three—computer, software, and Internet access—can be had for less than $1,000.

Why bother with all that technology? Well, when it comes to mapping out, planning, and calculating your expenses, income, and investments, you can get overwhelmed in a hurry. Record keeping can get messy, confusing, and discouraging. And investment research is nothing short of frightening without a little help. A computer can conquer those phobias and more. Your local electronics store is stocked with software packages that tame the algebra. Cyberspace is chock-full of Web sites that warehouse thousands of statistics and bushels of information on companies the world over and investments from bonds to blue-chip stocks. You can even open a brokerage account online, and trade and invest to your heart's content.

So, before you set up an E*TRADE account or rush to find stocks to invest in, you need to slow down for a second. Investing methodically works to your advantage for several reasons. First, you'll make better choices by accessing information and documents to help you make sound decisions. Second, you'll be in better financial shape. And once your house is in order, you can weather the ups and downs of financial markets and keep to a sound plan—the only way to go about investing.

STEP 1: TACKLING DEBT

Debt comes in three flavors—the good, the so-so, and the downright objectionable.

Yes, a lot of investment books will tell you to avoid the evils of indebtedness at all costs. Good luck. The words, "Never a borrower, nor a lender be," sounded great on the Shakespearean stage. *Hamlet,* however, was written a few hundred years ago. As anyone who has had to juggle utility bills, grocery shopping, and insurance deductibles knows, there's little if any way to get around debt in the twenty-first century. Cash flow—the income coming in from work—seems so limited, practically pinched. Cash outflow—what must go out to keep creditors at bay—seems infinite and drains away faster by the minute.

"I don't know a single person personally who doesn't have some sort of debt, or who has managed without borrowing a cent," says Los Angeles financial planner Percy Bolton. He's right. Show us someone who's paid for a home in cash, and we'll show you the eight-figure contract that same person recently signed with an NBA club or a talent scout for Def Jam records.

All the same, credit card payments, mortgages, and car notes sap the money you bring in, diverting it from any lofty investing goals and making anything you buy much more expensive than its purchase price. Consider a $20,000 car note at 8 percent interest, stretched over a 5-year period. That shiny new four-door is going to wind up costing $24,331, or in essence a car and what might well amount to another used sedan to boot. And to make that thought all the more bothersome, consider this harrowing truth: that car loses a good chunk of its value on its way off the dealer's lot. Its worth might as well spew out of its exhaust pipe.

Many families can blame the plastic demon of credit card debt for the trouble they have scraping together money to invest. According to data compiled by RAM Research, a Frederick, Maryland, company that monitors the credit card industry, the average family lugs a $7,000 credit card debt and services that mountain of debt by paying out $1,000 a year in interest.

To make investing possible, you need to sketch out some sort of blueprint for handling debt and savings simultaneously. Otherwise, you could be doomed to pass an eternity on a treadmill of monthly minimum payments, with nothing left over to save.

Good Debt

The category we label as good debt, is limited to money you've borrowed to pay for absolute necessities. Another stipulation is that good debt should be linked to things that tend to increase in value over time.

There's your mortgage, for instance. Shelter is a basic human need; a house note is a certain way to fix a roof above you and your favorite chair. What's more, interest on the house note is tax deductible. And, as a winning stroke, your home stands a pretty good chance of appreciating in value over time.

Student loan payments fit in the good-debt grouping, too. More often than not, strapping on a considerable debt load to get a diploma is the most effective way to move up the ranks of job applicants. Just as a mortgage is attached to an asset that could increase in value, an education has as its payoff a marked increase in earning power over the course of a working career. In the job market, academic credentials normally increase in worth with each additional degree an applicant has completed.

So-So Debt

Next in line is so-so, or "okay," debt. This category includes any borrowing you take on for needed items, but would do better off to limit or avoid.

For the single most widespread example of so-so debt, look no further than the garage. In a country of vast expanses traversed by a system of mighty highways, and where mass transit is often inadequate, an automobile makes life easy. It's there for trips to the store, outings at the amusement park, or a Saturday night on the town.

The problem: Four wheels often cost well into the five figures. That's a sum so large, it's enough to swallow up many peoples' savings, and then some. While borrowing for a car racks up sizable interest (8 percent to 10 percent annually when we went to press), it's done in the name of buying an object whose value decreases at an alarmingly rapid rate. Essentially, you've entered a contract to pay a sum that exceeds a car's sticker price, while watching the value of your trusty station wagon steadily dwindle.

"If there's any rule folks should follow on debt it's this: Never borrow to pay for something that's decreasing in value over time," says Bolton. Our suggestion is a little less stringent: scrape together as much cash as possible to pay for an automobile, and borrow as little as you can to fill in the gap between what you have and the sticker price.

Bad Debt

Now it's time to get tough. Want a surefire way to beat the money you'd make in the stock market return over time? Want a *guaranteed* annual return of 9, 12, even 15 percent on your money? Then heed these six magic words: *Pay down your credit card debt.*

We heard you snort. Admittedly, a full-out attack on a pile of plastic cards seems a bit Puritan in this era. Most Americans have a stack of obligations—students loans, car notes, home equity loans, property taxes. There are needs that can't seem to wait ranging from an air conditioner to new clothes for the kids when they return to school.

So you cut yourself a little slack. Those credit cards? Well, maybe you were intending to get around to them sooner rather than later. They're not that much, anyway, you might reason, perhaps 9 percent or 12 percent, if you're lucky. Certainly nothing as high as 20 percent.

So, surely it's possible to run a wee balance and still get your finances in order. Or even to get into the stock market now, and still pay credit card debt.

Wrong. Credit card debt is a sure way to sap any funds you might have for investing. Remember, the stock market averages a 10 percent or so annual return over time. That's to say for one year, the market could be up that amount or more, yes. It also implies that you might be invested and make less.

Credit card interest, on the other hand is fixed. It's a sure 15, 16, or 17 percent annually in some cases. So, if you divert money away from your credit card bill to invest, you're actually setting up a losing wager. Think of

CONSOLIDATION? BEWARE LOAN OFFICERS BEARING WHAT LOOK LIKE GIFTS

It seems as if it lightens your burden. It can appear like a godsend, a way to clump your debts in one tidy package. It can cut the amount of money you have to scrape together to pay off creditors. All the same, a consolidation loan can often turn out to be a short-term cure that becomes a long-term poison.

Here's the catch. A lender can often make a consolidation loan seem like a sweetheart deal by lowering the amount of money you pay each month. The problem is, that lower payment might free up a bit of cash now, but it does nothing to carve away at the amount you owe. In fact, bankers love to offer up lower minimum payments in various packages. The reason: They keep you paying off your debt over longer and longer periods, and all the while you'll pay interest on the amount you continue to owe. That's how the consolidation loan that looked like a bargain can actually inflate the amount you pay over time to an astronomical sum. Ironically, over time you are likely to pay one creditor a fortune more than you would have doled out to two or more credit cards, banks, or other lenders.

That's not to say that consolidation never works. In some instances, it can truly be an aid. But to determine whether a consolidation loan is a smart move, you need to find out one crucial fact: how much interest you're expected to pay over time.

Be especially careful with home equity consolidation loans. Why? First off, home equity loans are secured by your house. Miss out on a few payments and suddenly the bank has your castle. "You can't lose your house if you default on a couple of credit cards," says Margo Sanders of the National Consumer Law Center, a nonprofit organization that monitors the banking industry. "The minute you sign a home equity loan, however, you've put up collateral—in this case your home—which bankers can seize if things go wrong." Another caveat before you sign a note: Make sure you are aware of all the fees. Consolidation loans can carry a bevy of hidden costs, fees, and unfair loan terms, all of which can make what looks like a good deal go bad in a hurry.

it another way: the money you put on a credit card bill with a 13 percent interest rate is in actuality bringing you a 13 percent annual return. The stock market, meanwhile, isn't so trustworthy. You could luck out and make more than 15 percent on the money you invest that year. It's more likely, though, that you won't. Look back at data for the S&P 500 and you'll see that you

---

WEB SIGHTINGS
CALCULATORS

All this talk about debt and interest rates can seem terribly abstract without working through a few scenarios with your own numbers. Once you get down to a little data crunching of your own, you'll be glad to know that there's a place on the Internet like Financenter.

Financenter offers up a host of calculators—screens in which you can plug in the interest rate you pay and the money you owe—and walk through strategies you might want to try out. The great thing about calculators on the Web is that you can tinker with subtle changes in your budget or payment schedule and see how alterations you have in mind will affect your cash flow—all before taking a step.

---

stand a one-in-two chance that the market will exceed a 15 percent gain. That's okay, but the chances that a mutual fund or stock that you choose will match or outperform that figure are considerably slimmer. And, when you calculate what you've made or lost at the end of the day, you will have passed up a sure 15 percent gain by paying down credit card debt for something less than a sure bet.

What about making minimum payments to open up a little cash to put to work? It's indeed possible to skirt the issue by making minimum payments month after month. Over time, though, you won't make any headway. As an example, suppose you put $50 worth of groceries each week for a year on a credit card with an 18 percent rate. Make the minimum monthly payment, and you'll spend a little over 12 years paying off your bill. And, for a kicker, you'll pay $2,600 for your groceries and an additional $2,525 in interest.

Can Debt and Investing Mix? Yes, If You First Think Small

Now that you've faced some sobering truths, it's time to step back and take a deep breath. To get started investing and to factor in your debt, consider the advice from the American Bankers Association (ABA), a trade organization, for gauging how much you spend on credit obligations. The ABA recommends that what you owe on credit cards, car notes, student loans, and other monthly expenses shouldn't exceed 10 percent to 15 percent of your take-home pay. Your total monthly expenses—your rent or mortgage on top of those responsibilities—shouldn't top 35 percent to 40 percent of your gross monthly income.

If your debt burden exceeds those guidelines or you want to free up more cash to invest, you'd probably be better off spending extra money you have at the end of the month to whittle down the balances you owe. Of course, pay at least the minimum due on each loan or credit card. But, in addition, financial planners suggest that you choose one or more obligations to attack with more money. As a rule of thumb, the professionals suggest that you always target the debt with the highest interest rate. And an obvious way to carve a big debt down to size is to pay 50 percent, 75 percent, 100 percent or more above the minimum due each month. Once you've shrunk your debts, you'll have more money for investing than you previously thought. Otherwise, investing might actually sap your ability to get out of debt.

But what if you're a long way from paying down your debt? Should you write off saving forever?

Well, on that point, we'll cut you just a little slack. Los Angeles financial planner Percy Bolton says that saving is a good habit regardless of where you stand or how much you owe. The trick, however, is figuring a sum to save small enough to allow you to whittle down the heavy-duty credit card bills you may have stacked up over the years. Bolton advises readers to choose a small amount to set aside, just to get into the habit—perhaps $25 a month.

WEB SIGHTINGS
INTEREST RATES ONLINE

You could be hunting around for a cheaper credit card rate or looking into a mortgage. You might want to scout around to compare your bank's interest on a savings account with another institution's 6-month CD yield. Whether you're looking in Cucamonga or Kalamazoo, you'll likely find a quote on RateNet (www.rate.net).

RateNet lets you review a host of bank services and quotes on savings accounts and loans. It will help you scan across rates offered on credit cards, certificates of deposit, auto loans, mortgages, and even savings accounts. In fact, RateNet boasts that it carries quotes from 11,000 institutions and 175 markets or cities and towns across the country. Additionally, you can look for the highest yields and the lowest credit card rates around. Another excellent site loaded with rates for bricks and mortar and virtual banks is bankrate.com (www.bankrate.com). The bankrate.com site offers up much of the same information and even includes financial calculators to help you plug in all your numbers to see, plan, and even reshape your future.

STEP 2: A SAFETY NET

Trimming your debt qualifies as Step 1. Next, it's advisable to get fitted for a financial life preserver.

Call it a safety fund or a cushion. Whatever name you choose, you need to set aside a stash of cash that will be there should the unexpected arise or should things take a turn for the worse.

The reasoning behind a safety fund goes beyond the old truism, "Save your pennies for a rainy day." More often than not, investing or putting your money away for a long period to help it grow can conflict with sudden changes in your life. If your roof caves in, the only store of cash seems to be your 401(k). The minute you need root canal work that your dental plan just doesn't cover, it seems that your stocks are fat and ready for cashing in.

There's a major flaw, though. You're interrupting a sound investment plan. Moreover, the money you put into investments like stocks or bonds can't be retrieved instantly. You'll also have to ante up a considerable sum of money just to fish out your savings. Suppose that you dip your hands into an IRA account to take out $5,000. In some instances, you'll have to pay a 10 percent tax penalty or $500 in addition to paying regular income taxes on that same sum.

To make matters worse, you might even lose a substantial portion of your investment and any gains you might have made. Stocks, bonds, and other investments have a notorious way of fluctuating in value. So, it's clear that a safety fund is crucial if you want to invest and pay bills, balance checkbooks, and try to make ends meet. It's even more essential if you're a light sleeper, the sort of person who is haunted by scary headlines of layoffs, cutbacks, or even the seasonal fluctuations of your income. Maybe you're hearing rumors of a takeover and changes on the way. Perhaps you're paid on commission, and sales (of cars, homes, air conditioners) rise and fall, making budgeting a nightmarish exercise.

One way or the other, you'll want to stow away funds in case something goes wrong. How much? A year's worth of grocery bills? Two months' rent? Car payments for a month or so?

Deborah Breedlove, a financial planner for American Express in Columbia, North Carolina, advises a cash reserve equal to 3 to 6 months' salary. The choice of salary over expenses is simple. Over time, you're bound to have trimmed, tailored, and hacked your expenses down to match your paycheck. By salting away an amount equal to your take-home pay, you're guaranteeing no major disruption in your lifestyle while you scramble to fix what has gone wrong should that mean finding a new job, fixing the car, or recovering from an injury or illness.

Breedlove says there's a good reason to shoot for at least a 3-month minimum. "After an accident, you'll often have to wait 90 days before you receive a disability payout, and while sick leave might cover some of your needs, chances are it will come up short during an extended period," she notes. When should you angle for 6 months' worth of take-home pay? Well, if you're a jittery, nervous type, you'll probably gravitate to that amount automatically. You will want to have the maximum security possible. If you're paid from sales commissions or have a seasonal job like construction, you should put away at least 6 months' salary as well. That's because a year can have both ups and downs—harvests when the money seems to be tumbling down from the sky and droughts when things get tight.

Where to Put It Away

Let's face it. A lot of us probably wouldn't mind keeping a wad of cash in the mattress. We'd know just where our money was at all times, and how to get to it in a fix. Buried in the bed, it would be warm and safe from the rumblings of the outside world. And if somehow it would be possible to get interest for it, Sealy would surely be a financial institution on the order of Citigroup, Chase Manhattan, or Bank of America.

Quit dreaming. The "mattress" account of lore isn't practical, but it has some features that make a lot of sense for a safety account.

First off, the great thing about stashing your money between the box springs is that it would be in a readily accessible form: cash. In a pinch, you'd only need dip down under the sheets to get the funds you needed.

You want just that kind of instant "spendability," for your emergency fund. In finance, bankers call that same property *liquidity,* meaning it's easy to quickly transform your savings into something that pays the bills. Aside from offering up an ATM, the next best thing in the banking business is a check. You fill it out, sign it, tear it from a booklet, and suddenly you're paying for a tow truck.

You also should receive something in return for parking your money in an institution's vault for an extended period—interest. That's not an easy thing to find in any great quantity in the twenty-first century. In years gone by, you could stash your money in a savings account at your local bank branch. The friendly bank officers shook your hand, and suddenly you were earning money on your money. Checking—believe it or not—was free.

If you've opened a bank account anytime recently, you know all too well that those days are gone. Checking accounts drain away so much in fees it's easy to imagine your account disappearing in a matter of months. Savings accounts, meanwhile, dole out microscopic amounts of interest—2 percent or so, if you're lucky. If you opt for the corner bank's higher-interest accounts like certificates of deposit or money market accounts, you can get a percentage point or two more in interest a year, but you'll also tie your money up for 3 months, 6 months, or even years. Tap in before the account matures, and you'll get hit with stiff penalties.

The money market mutual fund, however, is an alternative that combines liquidity with a respectable amount of interest. It acts somewhat like a combination of a mutual fund, a checking account, and a money market account. Most importantly, you'll make more money on your savings than you would get from an account at the local bank. Money market mutual funds tend to pay several more percentage points' interest than any savings or checking account and will protect whatever principal you invest. Not only that, but you'll gain quick access to your cash. Often you can make withdrawals by check so you can draw on your emergency fund in a hurry, if need be. Finally, a money market fund, like mutual funds, holds a portfolio of short-term interest bearing notes or bondlike investments. That way, a professional investor or portfolio manager can pool your money with other folks' savings and seek out the highest return possible for your account.

Chapters 7 and 8 are devoted to mutual funds of all sorts. But, since money market funds are a key element in an investment plan, the following section describes their specific characteristics and uses.

MONEY MARKET FUNDS

Don't lump money market mutual funds all together in the same safe-deposit box. Many varieties are available, each specializing in its own investment mix and each with its own advantages.

We'll first tell you about a few things money market funds have in common. As with most mutual funds (see Chapter 8), they represent a pooling of investors' money. Whatever cash shareholders put into the mutual fund is in turn invested, most often in short-term note and debt obligations that are much like bonds or IOUs, holdings that mature in a little time, and generally are issued by the federal, state, or municipal governments. Sometimes though money market funds gravitate toward corporate debt obligations as well, but usually of the shortest duration.

Another characteristic that money market mutual funds share is accessibility. As we've mentioned, money market funds often allow you to tap your account by check or even a debit card, at no charge. (Provisions from one fund to the next may differ slightly, so review the privileges a fund grants you before you invest.) There are limits to keep in mind, however. Some money markets don't like you to write a lot of checks; clearing checks and keeping up with transactions is expensive for banks, and mutual funds aren't keen to rack up those kinds of costs either, so to discourage you from paying the hair stylist or the dry cleaner with money in your money market fund, most fund companies put a limit on the checks you can write. They require a minimum amount for checks—most keep it at $500, although some post the mark at $100.

Another aspect of money market mutual funds might seem quirky if you know anything about mutual funds in general. Shares you purchase cost $1 each. If you originally invest $3,000 in a money market fund, you'll be allotted 3,000 shares. Yet, whereas the price of a share of a stock or bond mutual fund fluctuates in price according to the worth of the fund's portfolio of investments, each of your money market fund's shares will still be worth $1 no matter how long you hold them. As an investor, you will earn money on your account by collecting dividends paid out by the mutual fund company. And just how much a money market fund pays in dividends or interest rises and falls as rates go up and down.

You can be sure of one thing, though. Your money market fund is going to beat your bank savings or checking account by a few percentage points. If you're looking to find out why, it has to do with just how your bank and the mutual fund company make money. Your bank pays only as much interest as it thinks it must, whether rates go up or down. The rest of the money earned from short-term notes goes to line the pinstriped pockets of the bank's board of directors. As pointed out in Chapter 8, a mutual fund makes its money by taking a set percentage of your invested money in fees. Simple math alone makes it clear why paying you the most interest possible would be in the fund's best interest: 5 percent in interest on $1,000 generates $50 in interest and $1,050 in principal for the assessment of the fund's fee; 6 percent, meanwhile, makes for $1,060 in principal against which the fund's fee will be calculated, guaranteeing that your mutual fund's management will be able to reap more fee income.

The interest paid by the short-term investments that money market funds hold changes daily. That sends the interest paid by money markets sliding upward and back down over time, but nearly always above what the bank is willing to pay. To check up on the yield or interest paid by money market mutual funds, look in publications such as *Barron's.*

If any one reservation keeps people from flocking to money market funds in droves, though, it's that their balances aren't protected by the federal government. Although bank accounts are insured by the Federal Deposit Insurance Corporation (FDIC), a branch of the government that promises to safeguard up to $100,000 of your savings, money market funds aren't covered by the same agency. Instead, the Securities and Exchange Commission (SEC) regulates the money market fund industry and the companies that run the funds. It keeps close tabs on money market funds' operations and is there to remind them of their responsibilities to investors.

If you're still concerned, you should be reassured by the fact that no one has yet lost a penny in a money market account. On those rare occasions in the past when a money market fund might have had an investment go awry, the fund's parent company quickly stepped in to shore up the fund and "hold the buck" (made sure that the fund's share price never dipped below $1).

Your Options

There are a few things you should consider when choosing a money market fund. First off, you need to determine what kind of money market best suits your needs. You can choose between three categories: general-purpose money funds, government-only funds, and tax-free funds.

General-Purpose Funds

It's no contest. Of all the money market funds out there, general-purpose funds pay the most interest. They can afford to fork over higher yields because the investments they choose—spanning the spectrum of short-term instruments from Treasury notes backed by the U.S. government to short-term agreements with corporations to certificates of deposit offered by banks and savings and loans—bring in a relatively high rate of return. In some cases, individual investors could go out and put their money into the very same securities and reel in the same return. They probably wouldn't make as much, though. General-purpose funds enjoy an advantage in the market because of their size. By combining your savings with other investors' cash, money market funds have enough deposits at their disposal to wield considerable leverage and get the best returns possible.

The dividends general-purpose funds pay are taxable, much like the interest on your bank account. Each January, the fund company that runs your money market will mail a statement listing how much you received in dividends. You report that figure on both your federal and state tax returns.

Government-Only Funds

Investors who are edgy about money market funds may want to look for government-only or direct-obligations-only funds, as they are sometimes called. You'll give up a bit in yield that you might receive in a general-purpose fund, but gain a virtually risk-free investment. That's because direct-obligation funds invest solely in debt issued by the U.S. government, widely deemed to be the world's most trustworthy, top-notch, risk-free debtor.

Government-only funds tap Uncle Sam's credit in several ways. They will put your money to work in U.S. Treasury bills, as well as obligations issued by federal agencies such as Ginnie Mae (the Government National Mortgage Association). Agency debt is one of the safest investments there is, another reason why government-only funds are the soundest money markets around.

There's another plus. The dividend yield of U.S. government-only funds may be tax-free in the state where you live. Currently, 39 states levy no taxes on government-only funds so ask the mutual fund company if their fund's yield is taxable or tax-free in your state. If your government-only fund turns out to be tax-free where you live, you'll have a pleasant surprise: its tax equivalent yield will be greater than the stated interest the fund pays.

WEB SIGHTINGS
MONEY MARKET MUTUAL FUNDS

If you're looking for information on money market mutual funds or a bit more guidance on choosing one, consult iMoneyNet, Inc., which monitors the industry. iMoneyNet's Web site (www.imoneynet.com) is a storehouse of data, and has in-depth guides to help investors like yourself choose a fund. You'll find a lengthy piece on how to select a fund and what to look for, the week's top-yielding funds in different categories, and as if that wasn't enough, you'll see a listing of all the money market funds iMoneyNet follows, complete with their current yield data. It's more information than most of us would ever need, but nevertheless a great starting (and ending) point for making a choice.

In other words, by taking into account the tax savings your fund offers, its effective dividend payout will be equivalent to the higher yield of a taxable fund. To find out just how much yield you're getting, you'll need to calculate a tax-free dividend's taxable equivalent yield. That math's not hard: take your tax-free money fund's yield and divide it by 1 minus your state tax bracket (see taxable equivalent yield table in Chapter 8).

As an example, say you live in California where the maximum state tax is 11 percent. If you fell in the 11 percent bracket and invested in a direct-obligation fund with a 5 percent yield, your fund's tax-equivalent yield would be 5 divided by 1 minus .11, or .89, or 5.62 percent, practically two-thirds of a point more in interest.

No matter what advantage you gain in state taxes on government-only funds, you'll still owe Uncle Sam tax on the money you earn in dividends. That is, unless you invest in tax-free money market funds.

Tax-Free Funds

Government-only money markets save you money on state taxes. Tax-free funds take that theme a step further, by getting you past federal taxes as well.

Tax-free funds get to bypass the IRS and state revenue collectors by investing in short-term notes issued by municipalities and states or bonds issued by nonprofit institutions and universities. Since that kind of debt isn't subject to federal taxes, the dividends it generates aren't taxable either, once they are passed on to your account.

The stated yield of a tax-free money market is even less than general-purpose or direct-obligation-only money markets but the tax savings it offers more than makes up for the difference. Once you figure out the taxable equivalent yield, as in the case of direct-obligations, you'll find that the higher your federal tax bracket the better you do with tax-frees.

The calculation involved is exactly the same as the one used to find the taxable-equivalent yield for direct-obligation funds except that you'll substitute your federal tax bracket for the state bracket. Again, it goes like this: tax-free yield divided by 1 minus your federal tax bracket.

Say you're in the 31 percent tax bracket and looking over a tax-free money market with a yield of 3.7 percent. To find out how your tax savings would beef up your yield compared with that offered by a taxable fund, you would take 3.7 and divide it by 1 minus .31, or .69. The result, 5.36 percent, certainly makes the tax-free money market look a lot better than before.

Take note how tax-frees make more and more sense the higher your tax bracket. If you're in the 28 percent bracket, your taxable equivalent yield for the above example is 5.14 percent; in the 31 percent bracket, it's 5.36 percent; in the 36 percent bracket, it's 5.78 percent. That's an important consideration because by investing in tax-free funds you're giving up yield.

If you're looking to skip over federal and state taxes, state-specific tax-free money markets are available for residents of Arizona, California, Connecticut, Florida, Massachusetts, Maryland, Michigan, Minnesota, New Jersey, New York, North Carolina, Ohio, Pennsylvania, Virginia, and Texas. Individuals pocket the dividend income from state-specific funds without owing a penny in federal, state, or even local taxes, provided they invest in a state tax-free fund tailored to their home state.

Expenses

Once you've sorted out what type of money market fund works best for you, you can use a few measures to whittle down the 1,414 money market funds out there to find one that best fits your needs.

A crucial consideration is just how much you're paying the fund company to put your money to work. Mutual fund companies make money from your savings by charging fees extracted directly from your account, as discussed in Chapter 7. For brevity's sake, it is enough to say here that fees add up over time and should be one of the primary things you review. And while finding a manager or company with low fees is of the highest importance when you're shopping stock or bond funds, it's even more pivotal for money markets. That's because from fund to fund, the difference in dividend yields more often than not comes down to a difference in expenses.

The best measure of fees is a simple number called an expense ratio, a figure calculated by dividing a fund's assets by its expenses. Money market funds typically charge less than 1 percent in fees—the average is around 0.6 percent, according to iMoneyNet. If you search for a fund with a ratio of 0.6 percent or less, you'll be handing over even less of your money to the mutual fund company.

Convenience

So far, we've separated your money market emergency fund from any thought of investing altogether. This is to be a safety fund, after all, a place where you can stash away savings in case the worst comes your way. There is, however, one way you can combine both safety and investing. A good many of the big mutual fund companies and brokerages run their own money market mutual funds, and do a good job at it, too. Additionally, they'll allow you to make transfers in and out of your money market fund account into other mutual funds that they operate. In the case of brokerages like Charles Schwab, you can withdraw money from your money market mutual fund and use it to buy stocks.

The link between money market fund and investment or mutual fund accounts becomes convenient when you start investing and have to keep up with paperwork such as annual statements and transaction slips. Having one company handle several investment functions means less paper to chase down when you sell shares or have to pay taxes.

If the convenience of one-stop investing appeals to you, look at a few of the larger mutual fund or discount brokerage firms out there (see Figure 1.1). Another bonus: the large companies enjoy economies of scale. They have many, many investors each helping to pay the fund's expenses. As a result, the big fund companies tend to charge lower expense ratios than their peers.

The Price of Admission

You can see two big differences between bank accounts and money market funds the minute you scan a mutual fund's prospectus. A bank savings

Figure 1.1   One-Stop Shopping—Money Market
Funds from the Big Players

The following big mutual fund companies and brokerage firms offer money market mutual funds that you can use as a springboard into other investments.

FIRM	TOLL-FREE PHONE CONTACT
Fidelity	800-544-8888
Vanguard	800-662-7447
TIAA-CREF	800-223-1200
Janus	800-525-8983
American Century	800-345-2021
Franklin Templeton	800-342-5236
Schwab	800-435-4000
Dreyfus	800-782-6620

account doesn't always require that you keep a minimum. There are no limits for your initial investment, either.

Money market funds, however, charge a price of admission, and often a steep one at that. According to iMoneyNet, a minimum initial investment often comes to $2,000 or more. If that sounds like a titanic sum right now, keep your spirits up: There are money market funds that take less.

Numerology

You need to look over several numbers when comparing money market mutual funds, figures you're likely to see in the pages of a financial publication such as *Barron's* or online at iMoneyNet's Web site. Here are some areas you should check.

Seven-Day Average Yield (Very Important)

You wouldn't plop your money into a bank account without knowing how much interest you would receive. Well, the same holds true for money market funds. Because money markets invest in very short-term notes, their interest rate is bound to fluctuate up and down during the year. That doesn't help investors understand what's in store. So, to provide some clue as to how much a fund is yielding, or how much of a dividend investors can expect on their money, funds put out a figure called a seven-day average yield.

BEGINNERS' LUCK

If you're starting from scratch, you'll be happy to know that you can get into a few good money market mutual funds for an initial investment under $500. For a low-minimum fund with a thrifty expense ratio, iMoneyNet's data points to the TIAA-CREF's Money Market Fund, which outranked the competition with a low expense ratio of .25 percent and required an initial investment of just $250 as of this writing.

The American Association on Retired Persons (AARP) offers another low-minimum fund. The AARP High Quality Money Fund and AARP High Quality Tax-Free Money Fund (800-225-2470) are operated by the investment firm Scudder and require a $500 minimum initial investment. Despite its name and affiliation, there's no age limit to get in on the AARP funds. Both funds, however, carry rather high expense ratios—0.93 percent for the Money Fund, as of the end of 1999, and 0.82 percent for the Tax-Free fund.

It's calculated by taking the interest or dividend yield a fund would provide any given week and multiplying it by 52 to suggest how much you'd make on your safety fund if things remained static. Numbers like this never do remain in one place, but at least you'll have a sense of how a fund you're considering stacks up to its peers.

Expense Ratio (Very Important)

You might want to look over more than funds yields. For one, as just pointed out, money market fund yields go up and down constantly. Besides that, all funds put their money to work in very short-term investments. Since they all draw from the same pool, there won't be much variation from yield to yield.

It is advisable to turn to another figure when shopping funds: the expense ratio. For mutual funds, an expense ratio is calculated by taking the fund's expenses—salaries, operation of office equipment, provision of 800-numbers to investors, and so on—and dividing that figure by the total assets of the fund, the money all investors have put in.

There's a wide difference in expense ratios, however. The average is about .6 percent, a tiny sum, although some funds will charge as much as 1 percent, and others as little as .2 percent.

Weighing percentages that small against one another might seem like shaving molecules. Think of it this way, though. An expense ratio represents how much money the fund company takes out of *your* savings to keep the shop open. The higher the expense ratio, the more money is being siphoned off, and probably the less efficient your fund is at running things. The lower the ratio, the more the fund company is providing in the form of returns to you, the investor.

Account Minimums (Important)

A lot of people use their money market fund as a sort of zippy checking account. They can draw on their savings by check, and yet get a goodly amount of interest for keeping their money with the fund.

There's a major limitation, however. Money market mutual fund companies like to draw up rules. And most of the regulations have to do with account minimums.

First, you'll have to scrape together a minimum initial investment in most cases to get started. Then, fund companies often require a minimum balance in fundholders' accounts. Dip below that figure and you could well incur a penalty. Often, however, a fund company will notify you when your balance gets low, and will give you a bit of time to increase the amount in your account.

Finally, many fund companies require a minimum amount for checks to avoid the expense of processing and clearing checks for small sums of money.

To find out what's in store, be sure to read the money fund prospectus before investing. Keep in mind your lifestyle and needs.

STEP 3: A FILE CABINET

Now that you have your extra store of cash for emergencies tucked safely away in a money market fund, it is time to get organized. Start with a file cabinet. We don't mean to sound like your first grade teacher, but we have to mention it sooner rather than later: get organized. Once you start investing, be ready to keep good records. Set up some sort of an orderly filing system that will help you put your fingers on transaction slips and statements quickly.

That might seem all too obvious. Still, as serious investors will be all too happy to warn you, when you need investment papers—the important ones with dates and numbers on them—they just can't seem to be found.

It's certainly no laughing matter at tax time. You'll find that Uncle Sam's interest in your portfolio is keen indeed. The Internal Revenue Service is looking to see when you bought shares, and at what price. If you've made regular investments monthly in a mutual fund, a good thing, you'll find that often enough you have to scrape up any sort of proof of how much money you put away, on what dates, and at what share price. For proof, look over Schedule D for a 1040 tax form (see Figure 1.2). There, in black and white, are slots for the dates you bought and sold shares; the number of shares you bought and the number you sold; the cost of purchase and the sales price; and the amount of money you made or lost. In short, everything that you'd expect to find on transaction receipts.

The solution is extremely simple: Keep all documentation for every transaction. That way, you won't need to round up the bloodhounds at the last possible second to sniff about for lost paperwork.

STEP 4: THE PERSONAL COMPUTER

No Computer? That Does Not Compute

It's the dawn of the twenty-first century. The personal computer (PC) has been a fixture in the American den, living room, or home office for 10 years or more. The Internet is no longer the great information superhighway of the future, it's Main Street. And since 1997, the average selling price of a PC has been cut in half to almost $800.

If you're seriously thinking about investing and you haven't yet taken the step into the brave new world of desktops and the Web, the best advice for you is to hurry up.

Yes, if you're a staunch Luddite, you can invest day and night and not own a PC. Wall Street started long before anyone had a electrical socket to plug one in. Brokers, analysts, traders, and the like had been making fortunes and losing them in stocks for years before Microsoft Word and America

Figure 1.2 Paper Trail

Before you jump into investing, get a place to keep your records in order. Why? Well, look over this Schedule D tax form investors have to fill out after trading stock, and you'll see the kinds of data, numbers, dates, and other things you must have at your fingertips. Count on having to supply the original prices you paid for investments as well as how much you sold them for. You'll also need to know the dates when you first bought shares and when you finally sold them.

SCHEDULE D (Form 1040) Department of the Treasury Internal Revenue Service (99)	Capital Gains and Losses ▶ Attach to Form 1040. ▶ See Instructions for Schedule D (Form 1040). ▶ Use Schedule D-1 for more space to list transactions for lines 1 and 8.	OMB No. 1545-0074 1999 Attachment Sequence No. 12

Name(s) shown on Form 1040   Your social security number

Part I Short-Term Capital Gains and Losses—Assets Held One Year or Less

(a) Description of property (Example: 100 sh. XYZ Co.)	(b) Date acquired (Mo., day, yr.)	(c) Date sold (Mo., day, yr.)	(d) Sales price (see page D-5)	(e) Cost or other basis (see page D-5)	(f) GAIN or (LOSS) Subtract (e) from (d)
1					

2 Enter your short-term totals, if any, from Schedule D-1, line 2 . . . . **2**

3 Total short-term sales price amounts. Add column (d) of lines 1 and 2 . . . . **3**

4 Short-term gain from Form 6252 and short-term gain or (loss) from Forms 4684, 6781, and 8824 . . . . **4**

5 Net short-term gain or (loss) from partnerships, S corporations, estates, and trusts from Schedule(s) K-1 . . . . **5**

6 Short-term capital loss carryover. Enter the amount, if any, from line 8 of your 1998 Capital Loss Carryover Worksheet . . . . . **6** (   )

7 Net short-term capital gain or (loss). Combine lines 1 through 6 in column (f) ▶ **7**

Part II Long-Term Capital Gains and Losses—Assets Held More Than One Year

(a) Description of property (Example: 100 sh. XYZ Co.)	(b) Date acquired (Mo., day, yr.)	(c) Date sold (Mo., day, yr.)	(d) Sales price (see page D-5)	(e) Cost or other basis (see page D-5)	(f) GAIN or (LOSS) Subtract (e) from (d)	(g) 28% RATE GAIN or (LOSS) *(see instr. below)
8						

9 Enter your long-term totals, if any, from Schedule D-1, line 9 . . . . **9**

10 Total long-term sales price amounts. Add column (d) of lines 8 and 9 . . . . **10**

11 Gain from Form 4797, Part I; long-term gain from Forms 2439 and 6252; and long-term gain or (loss) from Forms 4684, 6781, and 8824 . . . . **11**

12 Net long-term gain or (loss) from partnerships, S corporations, estates, and trusts from Schedule(s) K-1 . . . . **12**

13 Capital gain distributions. See page D-1 . . . . . **13**

14 Long-term capital loss carryover. Enter in both columns (f) and (g) the amount, if any, from line 13 of your 1998 Capital Loss Carryover Worksheet . . . . . **14** (   ) (   )

15 Combine lines 8 through 14 in column (g) **15**

16 Net long-term capital gain or (loss). Combine lines 8 through 14 in column (f) ▶ **16**
Next: Go to Part III on the back.

* 28% Rate Gain or Loss includes all "collectibles gains and losses" (as defined on page D-5) and up to 50% of the eligible gain on qualified small business stock (see page D-4).

For Paperwork Reduction Act Notice, see Form 1040 instructions. Cat. No. 11338H Schedule D (Form 1040) 1999

721

(continued)

Figure 1.2 (continued)

Schedule D (Form 1040) 1999

Page **2**

Part III   Summary of Parts I and II

17 Combine lines 7 and 16. If a loss, go to line 18. If a gain, enter the gain on Form 1040, line 13   **17**

   Next: Complete Form 1040 through line 39. Then, go to **Part IV** to figure your tax if:

   ● Both lines 16 and 17 are gains, **and**

   ● Form 1040, line 39, is more than zero

18 If line 17 is a loss, enter here and as a (loss) on Form 1040, line 13, the **smaller** of these losses:

   ● The loss on line 17, **or**

   ● ($3,000) or, if married filing separately, ($1,500)   **18** ( )

   Next: Skip **Part IV** below. Instead, complete Form 1040 through line 37. Then, complete the **Capital Loss Carryover Worksheet** on page D-6 if:

   ● The loss on line 17 exceeds the loss on line 18, **or**

   ● Form 1040, line 37, is a loss.

Part IV   Tax Computation Using Maximum Capital Gains Rates

19 Enter your taxable income from Form 1040, line 39   **19**

20 Enter the **smaller** of line 16 or line 17 of Schedule D   **20**

21 If you are filing Form 4952, enter the amount from Form 4952, line 4e   **21**

22 Subtract line 21 from line 20. If zero or less, enter -0-   **22**

23 Combine lines 7 and 15. If zero or less, enter -0-   **23**

24 Enter the **smaller** of line 15 or line 23, but not less than zero   **24**

25 Enter your unrecaptured section 1250 gain, if any, from line 16 of the worksheet on page D-7   **25**

26 Add lines 24 and 25   **26**

27 Subtract line 26 from line 22. If zero or less, enter -0-   **27**

28 Subtract line 27 from line 19. If zero or less, enter -0-   **28**

29 Enter the **smaller** of

   ● The amount on line 19, **or**

   ● $25,750 if single; $43,050 if married filing jointly or qualifying widow(er); $21,525 if married filing separately; or $34,550 if head of household   **29**

30 Enter the **smaller** of line 28 or line 29   **30**

31 Subtract line 22 from line 19. If zero or less, enter -0-   **31**

32 Enter the **larger** of line 30 or line 31   ▶ **32**

33 Figure the tax on the amount on line 32. Use the Tax Table or Tax Rate Schedules, whichever applies   **33**

   Note. If line 29 is less than line 28, go to line 38.

34 Enter the amount from line 29   **34**

35 Enter the amount from line 28   **35**

36 Subtract line 35 from line 34. If zero or less, enter -0-   ▶ **36**

37 Multiply line 36 by 10% (.10)   **37**

   Note. If line 27 is more than zero **and** equal to line 36, go to line 52.

38 Enter the **smaller** of line 19 or line 27   **38**

39 Enter the amount from line 36   **39**

40 Subtract line 39 from line 38   ▶ **40**

41 Multiply line 40 by 20% (.20)   **41**

   Note. If line 25 is zero or blank, skip lines 42 through 47 and read the note above line 48

42 Enter the **smaller** of line 22 or line 25   **42**

43 Add lines 22 and 32   **43**

44 Enter the amount from line 19   **44**

45 Subtract line 44 from line 43. If zero or less, enter -0-   **45**

46 Subtract line 45 from line 42. If zero or less, enter -0-   ▶ **46**

47 Multiply line 46 by 25% (.25)   **47**

   Note. If line 24 is zero or blank, go to line 52.

48 Enter the amount from line 19   **48**

49 Add lines 32, 36, 40, and 46   **49**

50 Subtract line 49 from line 48   **50**

51 Multiply line 50 by 28% (.28)   **51**

52 Add lines 33, 37, 41, 47, and 51   **52**

53 Figure the tax on the amount on line 19. Use the Tax Table or Tax Rate Schedules, whichever applies   **53**

54 **Tax on all taxable income (including capital gains).** Enter the **smaller** of line 52 or line 53 here and on Form 1040, line 40   **54**

Schedule D (Form 1040) 1999

722

22

Online were even a twinkle on a computer monitor. The point is, however, that a PC makes investing much simpler for individual investors like yourself. And, whether you're just starting out or an ace, you probably realize that every bit of help, every edge counts for a lot.

Today, hundreds of software packages and Web sites are around for new investors as well as mountains of statistical matter for seasoned pros—this book includes many. There's plenty of data, plenty of insight, copious amounts of expertise, and advice everyone can use when making decisions to buy or sell. Passing up that kind of help when you're shaping up your finances or shuffling a portfolio is not just a shame, it's foolish.

A PC? That's a item priced under $1,000 as of this writing, and likely to get cheaper with each passing month. Anyway you look at it, it's money well spent when you start investing. What's more, a home computer has thousands of applications for your business or your children's education. So, if you are postponing your entry into the twenty-first century, wait no more. Break down and get a computer.

The Electronic Checkbook

Relatively routine tasks such as budgeting and balancing a checkbook are part of the drudgery of setting up a financial plan. If done properly, they can even help you set aside enough money for savings and investments. At the same time, they're time-consuming chores, busy work that can break a pencil point, and cause a cramp in your writing forearm. Thanks to financial

---

WEB SIGHTINGS
BUYING A COMPUTER ONLINE

If you need a little prodding before you pony up for a computer of your own, log on to a friend's PC, or go to the public library, where you will find free access to the Internet, as well as someone to help you. Visit the Web site Gomez Advisors (www.gomezadvisors.com), where you'll find a ranking of practically every computer sales outlet known to humankind and located on the World Wide Web. Gomez Advisors is a Lincoln, Massachusetts, firm that tracks almost any type of e-commerce imaginable. Gomez also collects consumers' reviews and has devised a rating system based on its surveys. The site offers up ratings of companies according to your profile—if you're a first-time computer buyer, there's a ranking with a recommendation of the retailers that will probably cater best to your needs.

WEB SIGHTINGS
ONLINE INVESTMENT HELP

A lot of space in this book is devoted to the Internet and the myriad spots throughout Cyberspace where individual investors can collect information about mutual funds, investing plans, and even . . . stocks.

You can pull plenty of help off the Internet, as well. Cyberspace is full of financial tools, data, and tutorials that will help you do everything from whittle down debt to research stocks and bonds. Better yet, as you'll discover by checking the following sites, a mountain range of information is available gratis online:

- The Web site associated with *Black Enterprise* magazine (www .blackenterprise.com) provides financial calculators for everything from mortgages to tuition. The Black Enterprise site also provides quotes on stocks, tracks stock performance from day to day, and help you home in on financial news affecting the markets and your finances.
- Another good place to start looking is a search engine, the Web's version of the now obsolete card catalog at your local library. By plugging in a brief description or key words related to what you're looking for, you can send a search engine far and wide to gather up sites for you to visit and use. Some of the most popular are Altavista (www.altavista.com), Yahoo! (www.yahoo.com), Lycos (www.lycos.com), or HotBot (www.hotbot.com). You might also check personal finance sites offered up by your Internet access provider—even if you aren't a subscriber! America Online (www.quicken.aol.com), MSN (www.moneycentral.msn.com), and others serve up a wide array of articles and access to plenty of information, be it mortgage rates, stock quotes, or articles covering recent investment trends.
- Then there are the big financial Web hubs, where you'll find links to many home pages and Web sites. Two hubs that are devoted exclusively to investing are Dailystocks (www.daily-stocks.com) and Investorama (www.investorama.com). Both have links to the sites already mentioned and too many more to fit into these pages.
- The Motley Fool site (www.fool.com) is a place on the Web where you can learn about personal finance and investing, look up

WEB SIGHTINGS (CONTINUED)

stock quotes, keep up with daily news on the financial markets, and even mix it up with fellow investors in a chat room.

- For the latest on the markets and company news, check Bloomberg (www.bloomberg.com), run by the financial news service.

- Take some time out to visit Web sites of the big investment firms—Fidelity (www.fidelity.com), Vanguard (www.vanguard.com), TIAA-CREF (www.tiaa-cref.com), Merrill Lynch (www.merrill-lynch.com), T. Rowe Price (www.troweprice.com), or Salomon Smith Barney (www.salomonsmithbarney.com). Sure, each will carry promotions for the company that's paying the bills. All the same, there's a lot of useful guidance on each, *for free.* That includes stock quotes, personal finance calculators, investment guides, and research.

- Don't overlook Morningstar (www.morningstar.com), the Chicago firm that keeps close tabs on the mutual fund industry. Morningstar's pages include charts and data on mutual funds and stocks. The Morningstar site has articles and guides on virtually every nuance of investing. It's well worth a visit.

- The Web isn't limited to commerce. Many organizations have sites in Cyberspace that bring investors a wealth of ideas, help, and tools. The Investment Company Institute or ICI (www.ici.org) and Mutual Fund Education Alliance (www.mfea.com) or MFEA are two groups linked to the mutual industry that have assembled impressive Web sites. ICI's spot serves up excellent instructions on how to find and choose a mutual fund. MFEA's Web site lets you plug in data to a screen to dig up a mutual fund practically custom-tailored to your needs. On the American Association of Individual Investors site, special calculators can help you hash out practically any investing or personal finance conundrum—all available and ready to download on your computer. On the site for the American Association of Retired Persons (www.aarp.org) you can sit down for a discussion on retirement planning.

WEB SIGHTINGS
ONLINE BANKING

You shop bestsellers at Amazon.com. You've surfed the Web for airline tickets, or a new car. So what's keeping you from opening up an online banking account? Virtual banking certainly isn't such a novel thing. We all use ATMs to tap our checking accounts, and probably go months—maybe even years—without talking one-on-one with a bank teller. What's more, cyberbanking is convenient—you can eyeball your balances anytime, day or night, in your pajamas or Sunday finest. You can check records or transfer funds, and the fees you pay can sometimes be less than for a checking account.

Presently, most banks offer you the ability to check account balances, transfer funds, and arrange electronic bill payments. Others allow you to download account information, trade stocks or mutual funds, and even look at images of their checks and deposit slips.

Your bank may call it PC banking or online financial management. Some will require you to install special software on your computer, although the trend these days is to have customers use the bank's site on the Internet. Whatever the name, and no matter what the setup may be, once you decide to bank on the Web, you'll have more than a few choices to make. For one, you'll have to settle on a bank. Quite a few traditional stand-in-line banks such as First Union, Citibank, and BankOne have opened branches on the Internet for business, as have fledgling e-banks such as Net.B@nk and Wingspanbank.com. For ratings and a detailed comparison of what's out there, check in with Gomez Advisors (www.gomezadvisors.com), a firm that examines and rates consumer net services. There, you'll find feedback on Internet banks filed by readers and experts alike. You will also find banks ranked by performance in several categories including convenience and resources, and overall cost. To compare online rates for everything from checking to certificates of deposit and credit cards, check with bankrate.com (www.bankrate.com) which offers up lists of Internet banks and their current offerings.

software like Quicken or Microsoft Money, though, some of the tedium becomes a snap. You plug in a few numbers and the heavy calculations are done. If you're in a mood to draw up extensive plans, a Quicken can help you jostle figures back and forth. You can project your future, adjust assumptions, crunch numbers and, most important of all, make plans. If you're into charts, graphs, and tables, some of the better programs allow you to convert your numbers into something more vivid.

If you think budgeting is a pain, then owning stocks, bonds, and mutual funds and keeping up with their ups, downs, your purchase price, and whatever profit you stand to make so far is going to seem downright overwhelming. Again, a PC can come to your rescue. Financial software like Quicken allows you to plug in data on your stocks and mutual funds while tracking their gains over time. Online, you'll find a host of sites that explain the market. Other Web sites cull financial stats on stocks and companies by the bushel load. Still others provide information on the market and its direction.

Then, come January 1 of each year, you can opt to put a little money into tax programs, many of which can link to a budget and checkbook program like Quicken to make filing a lot easier than it normally would be. Come tax time, you can purchase a moderately priced software package like TurboTax or Tax Cut to make preparations for April 15 a little less hectic. These days, you can even file your taxes online if you choose.

The benefits don't end there. Quicken and Microsoft both offer up Web sites with plenty of financial numbers and data on the financial markets. At the same time, you'll be glad to know that most financial software packages make it a snap to import data from your budget to a tax package.

Cyberspace sites now help you determine how much house you can afford and allow you to shop for mortgages nationwide as well. One to check is sponsored by Quicken, the well-known financial software, at the address: www.mortgage.quicken.com. There, you can determine how large a loan you might prequalify for and even submit applications to participating mortgage lenders. And if you're considering refinancing or even Federal Housing Authority programs, the site has user-friendly instructions that walk you through. The crowning touch is an option to check current mortgage rates in your state.

BACK TO SCHOOL

Now that you're done with the prep work, it's time to tackle some of the thinking behind the financial markets. In Chapter 2, you will learn how investments work, how they relate to things that are going on in the world around us, and how professionals rely on some important basics to get the most out of the money they manage.

2

LEARNING THE MARKETS

This chapter covers the basics of investing including not only the ins and outs of stocks, bonds, and mutual funds, but also an overview of the economy and the role the government, big business, and even investors like yourself play in the financial markets. That way, you'll fully understand what's happening to your money and how investing can truly benefit you and your family.

This crash course in investment basics provides a rundown of rudiments that you can use for ready reference as you make your first steps out onto Wall Street. You will learn how the three primary asset classes—stocks, bonds, and cash—fit together in a portfolio and why they're used the way they are. You'll also be able to measure the performance of your investments and review many of the choices the pros make on a regular basis. Balancing your portfolio with a mix of high-, low-, and medium-risk opportunities is crucial to building a successful financial future. Most importantly, the information here gives you the know-how to make the best decisions with your savings.

On the face of it, the markets seem to be swirling, murky, and uncharted waters. Tides rise and fall, fortunes are made and are lost. Dangers—icebergs, sharks, and typhoons—lurk about ready to wreck your investment boat and send your savings to the bottom of the sea.

Once you grasp the basics, though, things suddenly seem to make more sense. Think of it this way: Most people have little if any knowledge of the intricacies of meteorology. A cumulus cloud soars by one day, a cirrus formation whips through the skies the next, and few viewers notice the difference. At the same time, though, people have a pretty good idea of just how warm 50 degrees Fahrenheit is and what to wear when the temperature is 90 degrees with a humidity index of 70 percent. They might even have an inkling of what a drop in barometric pressure means, or what global warming might do to the world's climate.

The fundamentals of the markets and investing in this chapter can give you the same working acquaintance with investing that you have with the weather outside. You will start to see the links between the economy, corporations, interest rates, and investing in general. Just as Al Roker's forecast helps you decide how to dress for the day, a rudimentary understanding of the stock market and interest rates, added to a smattering of Econ 101, will go a long way in helping you invest wisely. You'll find that stocks often follow the course of our national economy. When the economy grows, people, businesses, and the government seem to bring in more money. When companies make money, they become more valuable. It stands to reason, then, that shares will appreciate as well. Share prices also move when interest rates rise and fall. Not only that, but stocks also react to a host of political changes.

THE TOOLS

In some ways, solving the mystery of investing couldn't be simpler. What are the bricks and mortar, rivets and girders that portfolio managers, financial planners, and individual investors use to build wealth, protect it, and seize new opportunities? They all break down to three basic building blocks. The pros often call them asset classes. You know them as stocks, bonds, and cash (see Figure 2.1).

Each member of that trio has a different and well-defined function. Still, you need to make all three work together to enhance your chances of converting your savings into wealth.

Investment professionals will tell you that *stocks* are for growth. *Bonds* help protect your stock market gains while still earning a return. And finally *cash* has a dual role: It's held for emergencies, and to help you jump on timely investments as they pop up.

Figure 2.1   The Building Blocks to an Investment Portfolio—Three Asset Classes

Stocks	Company shares will provide most of the growth for your investment portfolio over time. Stocks help turn steady savings into wealth over time.
Bonds	Bonds have a steadying influence on your holdings. Bonds can maintain your principal as well as provide a predictable income on your investment, much like a bank account.
Cash	Cash has two functions. First, it's great for emergencies. Second, it can help you take advantage of great investment opportunities when they come up.

Stocks

Stocks are the workhorse of your investment portfolio. Company shares provide the gains you'll need to realize retirement dreams or help your kids through college.

Stocks have established a track record of consistent, long-term appreciation in the past. They have handily outpaced inflation, and delivered investors a return of just over 11 percent on average for large company shares, and 13 percent for small company shares. Here's another way of thinking about it: That average return will double your money in between 6 and 7 years, something that becomes important when you consider costly responsibilities like retirement, college tuition, or even a new home.

Stocks, nevertheless, can be volatile investments. Page through history and you'll see. Since 1926, the market has risen 30 percent or more in 18 years, as measured by the S&P 500. There have been famines to accompany the feasts, however. In 8 years, the market has fallen 10 percent or more.

You can take your stake in stocks a couple of ways. You can buy shares of a company, for example. That's a decision that can bring you substantial gains if the company you choose is doing well and if Wall Street's favor helps its stock rise in price. It's a risky decision if the company stumbles, or if its fortunes change for the worse.

A second way to invest in stocks is through mutual funds. Your money is pooled with the savings of other investors. In turn, that collection of cash is put to work in a collection of investments, the mutual fund's portfolio. The advantage of mutual funds is that you'll own a part of a large group of investments, and thus be protected if any one holding heads south. The drawback? The success of any individual stocks within the portfolio will be muted.

Bonds

Bonds steady a portfolio. They're an anchor that pays investors dividends—stable, regular income. As of this writing, the 30-year Treasury, a bond issued by the U.S. government that's commonly used as a measure for the group, was paying annual interest of between 6.5 and 7 percent.

All the while, bonds protect your principal, provided you cash them in at maturity, when a bond's life has come to an end, and investors are due to receive their original investment. That becomes important when the stock market goes through ups and downs. Stock values may slide over time; hold a bond for its duration, and you'll have protected your investment.

Those are the benefits. At the same time, you've muffled some of the bang you'd get from stocks on the rise. Long-term U.S. Treasury bonds, investments issued by the government that many professionals use as an indicator of the bond market, have averaged an annual return of 5.3 percent since 1926 according to the Securities Industry Association or SIA, a trade group that represents the brokerage business. That's just below half the yearly return that large company stocks have averaged over the same period.

Cash

The cash portion of your portfolio is a cushion, the kind of protection investors like yourself need just in case something comes up. Cash, too, can be your hunting stash, money you'll use to seize opportunities in the stock market, or savings you want to keep out of a turbulent market until things calm down a little bit. It's important, however, to distinguish cash on hand for investing from your emergency fund (see Chapter 1).

Cash in your stock portfolio is money beyond the 3- to 6-months' salary you've set aside in your safety fund. Instead, it's a sum you've earmarked for the stock market, but haven't yet put to work. You might find that you want to accumulate a certain sum before looking for new investments. You could choose to set aside $200 monthly just so you can build up an amount for a technology stock that has been tearing through the market. Maybe you've looked into a new mutual fund that you'd like to get into but that requires an initial investment of $3,000. Collecting cash over time for shopping funds, as you might opt to call it, will help you pounce on those opportunities and others. And while you're stockpiling, don't forget that you ought to get the highest return possible for your cash.

No matter how long you're salting away your cash, there's incentive to put your money, beyond emergency savings, to work. Over the long haul, you'll probably earn less on your cash than you would in stocks or bonds. iMoneyNet, the Westborough, Massachusetts, firm that tracks money market mutual funds reports that, on average, your cash would have earned approximately 4.98 percent annually during the 1990s. Longer term, to gauge how the same type of investment has fared, you might look at the 90-day Treasury bill (T-bill), a holding that money market mutual often invest in to provide their shareholders with yield. According to Vanguard Investments, the 90-day T-bill has averaged an annual total return of 3.92 percent between the years 1926 and 1999.

Spreading the Wealth Around

What is the secret mix that yields that greatest results over time? That question keeps professionals such as money managers and financial planners busy for much of the workday. Their assigned task—concocting financial recipes or blends of stocks, bonds, and cash—has an imposing name:

asset allocation. In laypeople's terms, nonetheless, asset allocation is a relatively simple task with a goal that is easy to understand. It calls for a blueprint by which you can divvy up your portfolio between stocks, bonds, and cash to snare the highest possible return with the lowest risk. That way your money is growing as much as it can, while allowing you to rest comfortably at night.

What makes asset allocation complicated is that no two investors are alike. Some are daredevils and don't mind taking risks to help boost the returns on their money. Others are more staid and are willing to sacrifice a few points of extra gains to have their money stashed away safe and sound.

There's also time to consider. Funds that you don't need for a long while—say until retirement 30 years in the future—can be invested a lot more aggressively over time than a pile of money you might need in a year or two. The reason: As much as stocks can hiccup and change in value over time, the longer an investment has to grow, the smoother its results tend to be. Statistics always approach long-term averages the longer the time period you take into account.

Short-term goals—say 3 to 5 years—call for conservative plans incorporating more bonds and fewer stocks. The reason: Stocks, for all their impressive historical returns sometimes slip.

Finally, before you sign off on any given mix of stocks, bonds, or mutual funds, think about your peace of mind. Whatever your asset allocation, you should be able to rest easy. If leaning more heavily on bonds lowers your stress, by all means do so.

Diversification

Asset allocation qualifies as one way to shift around the money in your investment accounts to bolster returns and lower risk. In a sense, it's a way to diversify your portfolio. It's not the only one, though.

Here's an example that drives the concept of diversification home. Three stocks—Compaq Computers, Monsanto, and Waste Management—in 1998 and 1999 carried the highest recommendation of a good number of Wall Street analysts. If you had followed the financial press at all during that 2-year period, you might have been tempted to buy shares of at least one, if not all three of those companies.

Well, the outlook for Compaq, Monsanto, and Waste Management changed. And by the summer of 1999, July 31, to be exact, all three had stumbled. Looking back a year, Compaq was down 26 percent on troubles in the PC market; European farmers and consumers were having no part of Monsanto's genetically altered seeds, which dragged the stock down 44 percent; and Waste Management found it difficult to keep up with Wall Street's outlook for the company and went on to slide 54 percent.

Put together in a portfolio, the group would have made a good amount of money disappear during a year when the stock market, as measured by the S&P 500, piled on a 20.21 percent gain. In fact, the cumulative 41 percent drop by the three combined would have taken a $3,000 portfolio down to $1,760 in value; an investment of the same amount in the stock market would have turned the same $3,000 into $3,606.

Believe it or not, though, there are mutual funds that invested in all three, yet still returned investors a healthy amount during the very same year. According to Morningstar, the Chicago mutual fund ratings company, 10 mutual funds held all three companies during the year and still faired better than the S&P 500 over the same time span. The Fidelity Growth Company Fund, the Growth Fund of America, Fidelity Magellan, the Vanguard Tax-Managed Capital Appreciation Fund, and the TIAA-CREF Growth Equity Fund all managed to produce total returns between 23.8 percent and 34.64 percent over the same 12-month period.

The reason funds that invested in three troubled stocks could still keep on singing in the downpour is simple. They each held a portfolio of shares large enough to *block out* any blow from individual stocks. The moral is that dividing your money among several investments may cost you the fantastic gains of any one but will certainly protect your assets should anything go awry. You'll be pleasantly pleased to find out that diversification significantly cuts the risk that you'll lose money on any one investment.

Several Degrees of Diversification

As an investment concept, diversification comes in several hues. It can be as simple as adding some Cisco Systems shares to the Intel stock in your brokerage account. From a simple move like that, there are many ways to go even further in varying your portfolio, each more sophisticated than the next (see Figure 2.2).

In addition to asset allocation, there's diversification within one asset class (a term professionals use to mean one type of investment such as bonds or stocks). There are stocks of small, growing companies. There are blue chips—shares of well-established industry leaders like Ford, AT&T, and IBM. And for a bit of international exposure, you might buy into the stock of an overseas power like Nokia or DaimlerChrysler.

Built-in Diversification

Diversifying your portfolio requires some calculations and regular checkups. You'll want to determine just what amount of risk you're willing to take on (Chapter 9 covers asset allocation in detail). You'll want to figure out what

Figure 2.2 Diversification

There are several ways to build a diversified portfolio.

Investing in Several Asset Classes
Mixing stocks, bonds, mutual funds, and cash is the easiest way to diversify a portfolio across asset classes.

Investing in a Variety of Mutual Funds, Stocks, or Bonds
Thanks to the wide variety of mutual funds, stocks, and bonds available to investors, it's easy to diversify within asset classes. For example, if you owned an aggressive, high-risk, potentially high-return mutual fund, you might opt for a stake in a lower-risk, more conservative fund to give your holdings some balance.

Investing Abroad
There's a world full of investment opportunities. Overseas stocks, funds, and bonds offer investors a way to add variety to a portfolio and provide a window onto new opportunities, as well as a way to counter periods when the U.S. financial markets may be weak.

mix of stocks and bonds seems too risky, what strikes you as too stodgy, and what combination is just right.

Mutual funds can provide the kind of variety that will stretch your portfolio, beef up gains, and at the same time lower the overall level of risk of your investments. A mutual fund's portfolio generally spans anywhere from a dozen to hundreds of investments all linked together. Should a company's management miscalculate the impact of a flood on its bottom line, its share price will fall. And any and all mutual funds that own a stake in the same corporation will take a hit, however small. The padding provided by the fund's other holdings, however, will absorb much of the shock, and you'll probably not suffer a major setback.

RISK AND REWARD (RETURN)

Investment professionals kick around another couple of words when they're talking about setting up portfolios and choosing stocks, bonds, or mutual funds: risk and reward.

The balance between risk and reward is straightforward. As simple as it sounds, however, it affects every single investment decision you'll ever make. Risk implies a gamble. You're putting up something, in this case your money. There's the chance that in time you'll get back more than you originally put in. And then, there's the chance that you'll lose some or all of your stake (see Figure 2.3).

Some investments are very risky. Some aren't. Take the Standard & Poor's 500. The 500 is a portfolio of 500 stocks chosen by the investment research firm Standard & Poor's (S&P) to gauge how the market has performed.

Figure 2.3   Risk and Return

You might picture risk and return as . . .

High-Risk Investment
The potential for bigger returns
in the financial markets.

Plus
The potential for bigger drops
when things go wrong.

Low-Risk Investment
Lesser returns likely on your
investment.

Plus
Protection for wild swings up or
down in the value of your
investment.

Happy Medium
The type of returns you desire.

Plus
An amount of risk you can live
with.

Since 1946, there have been years when the stock market and the S&P 500 have
hit new peaks. There have also been years when investors felt as if they
were marching through Death Valley, and even hitting sinkholes. The highest
yearly gain during that period, for the investors lucky enough to be in the
market, was a whopping 53 percent. But all wasn't ice cream and cake for investors; there have been years most stockholders would rather forget altogether, such as 1974 when the market as measured by the S&P 500 fell 26
percent—the worst showing since the 1930s.

That kind of volatility illustrates the risk shareholders take on: During
any given year, investors might see their portfolio increase in value, or decrease. Nevertheless, stocks have an ironclad long-term record of providing
very favorable gains. According to Vanguard Investments, the S&P 500 has
averaged a total return of 11.32 percent a year since 1926, a healthy amount
that most investors would be pleased to attain. That's the reward you get for
taking on the risk of investing in stocks.

Make no mistake. The stock market can be a roller-coaster ride. Still,
these averages certainly make it look like an excellent place to park your
money—for the long term. And, over extended periods, the market's historical

averages have a magical way of smoothing things out and patching over rough stretches.

As you examine the record of the S&P 500 over time, the secret to keeping risk to a minimum becomes clear: It's patience. Stick it out, and chances are your money will benefit from the same economic upswings that helped share prices weather 26 percent drops, or the great October crashes of 1929, 1987, or 1989.

Risk isn't uniform across the breadth of the financial markets. It varies from investment to investment. Stock prices can go up and down quite a bit. Bonds, by comparison, are less risky. In fact, if you hold a bond until it matures, you almost certainly will get your money back along with a decent return for your savings. And cash, held in a money market fund or a savings account, is just as safe.

Risk also varies from stock to stock. An Internet company that has yet to show profits may see its shares zoom past earth's orbit. It's nevertheless a volatile investment, with considerable risk. Tomorrow, the next day, or sometime later this year, its stock price could plummet back to earth. Then again, the company could have a business plan as ingenious as any hatched by John D. Rockefeller. If it does, you win, and win big. If not, you lose, and probably could see a good share of your investment disappear.

A large, well-known company with well-respected management—say General Electric—meanwhile, is a less risky stock. That's because over the years, the company has earned a reputation for growing profits at a high rate. It raises dividends for shareholders.

The trick to successful investing is to balance the two—risk and reward. First ask yourself how much of a loss could you live with. Could you walk away from 10 percent of your savings? 30 percent? Half? The entire amount, even?

Once you've answered that question, you'll have a better idea how much risk you can stand. Then, when you shop for investments, you'll find it easier to pick a mix of stocks, bonds, and cash that fits your profile as an investor.

DOLLAR-COST AVERAGING

List a few examples where an awkward mouthful of words can make a simple concept seem unwieldy, ugly, or overly complex. The term *dollar-cost averaging* belongs in that category.

Dollar-cost averaging makes sense; it just sounds bad. Essentially, it means that if you invest steadily over time, you can forget about the market going up or down or whether the investments you buy are expensive or cheap at the time. Over the weeks, the months, the years, the cost of the stocks, mutual funds, or bonds will average out to help you lock in a sizable gain on your

money. And by keeping up a regular flow going into the market, into investments, you'll be able to take advantages of periods when the market goes
down, or, in other words, when investments are cheaper than they otherwise
would be.

Here's a scenario as an example. Shares of Acme Bean Sprout Company
might be $25 in March, $50 in July, and $45 in September, reflecting the nor-
mal ebb and flow of almost every stock in the market over time. Next suppose that you had $1,000 in February, $1,000 in June, and $1,000 in August to
invest, and decided to pick up some Acme shares each time. In March, you
can buy 40 shares. In July, you purchase 20, and in September you can get 22
shares, with $10 left over. Your average cost for your position in Acme? That
would be $36.59 a share, or 3,000 (the money you spent) divided by 82 (the
number of shares you now have).

Proponents of dollar-cost averaging (that phrase does rattle around)
would point this out: You've saved money. If you had bought your 82 shares
in September you'd have spent $3,690 instead of $3,000. If you had bought

Figure 2.4   Dollar-Cost Averaging

"Dollar-cost averaging" is a relatively simple concept. What it amounts to is this:
Make regular investments over time—whether a fund or stock is high or low—
and the purchase price you pay rounds out. It's especially effective if you're
investing in something that's increasing in value over time. Buy a little bit in regular installments, and your average price actually works out to be less over time.

Take AT&T, for example (assume that purchases were made at the close of each
month listed here).

DATE	NUMBER OF SHARES	PRICE	TOTAL PAID
January 1997	10	$39.38	$ 393.80
February 1997	10	39.88	398.80
March 1997	10	35.25	352.50
April 1997	10	33.50	335.00
May 1997	10	36.75	367.50
June 1997	10	35.06	350.60
July 1997	10	36.81	368.10
August 1997	10	39.00	390.00
September 1997	10	44.25	442.50
October 1997	10	48.88	488.80
November 1997	10	55.88	558.80
December 1997	10	61.31	613.10
Total	120		$5,059.50

Average cost: $42.16 per share

If you had waited until December 31, you would have bought 120 shares at $61.31
per share for a total of $7,357.20.

the same stock in July, you'd have shelled out $4,100. Sure, if you'd have had the money in March you would have paid only $2,050, but that's assuming a lot. For one you would have needed to scrape up all the money at that particular point. Instead, by investing regularly without focusing too much on the level of the market, you'd have saved a sizable sum merely by setting aside a set amount at regular intervals (see Figure 2.4).

TIMING THE MARKETS

They throw billions of dollars into researching stocks and bonds. They have legions of analysts, experts, and number crunchers whose sole aim is to identify when the market is going up or down.

The funny thing, though, is that the mighty brokerage firms on Wall Street simply don't know for sure when the market is headed up or down and what is the best time to invest because, nobody—repeat, nobody—can time the market. No one, from the Psychic Friends Network to the soothsayer flipping over tarot cards at the booth down the street, can predict what's in the future.

If you think about the stock market, the impossibility of the task becomes obvious. There are almost 10,000 stocks trading up and down daily. An infinite number of factors steer stocks up or down and make bonds look great one day but lousy the next. Then, there are institutional investing firms with billions of dollars at their disposal. They alone can make or break a stock if they decide they like a company's prospects or suddenly turn cold to a corporation's management. Don't forget foreign investors, some of whom have billions, even trillions at their fingertips. Their quest for high-value investments might make markets like the New York Stock Exchange or Nasdaq here at home seem like El Dorado this month and like a dry gulch a matter of weeks later. Individual investors factor in as well. Their individual accounts may seem small, but small-time investors number in the millions, each with his or her own particular take on economic events and how changes affect the stocks, bonds, and mutual funds they own.

In short, there are simply too many variables at play to safely handicap the market or its direction at any given moment in time. And, if the professionals with their deep pockets and manpower can't time the market, why should you attempt it?

Count taxes as another reason to refrain from timing. Trading in and out of the market can help rack up capital gains taxes, the amount you owe Uncle Sam on profits you make on your investments. If you hold an investment a year or less, that amount could go as high as 31 percent, 36 percent, or even 39.6 percent, depending on your tax bracket. You're giving up almost a third or even more of your gains, all because of your impatience. If you hold on for more than a year, the IRS is a little less greedy. It still takes a sizable chunk of your money, nonetheless, a maximum 20 percent, again contingent on your tax bracket. And, the more often you trade and make money, the more money you owe, as discussed later in this chapter.

Tinkering can also cost you a lot in gains, too. For evidence, we ask that you look no further than stock market performance statistics compiled by the brokerage firm Sanford C. Bernstein & Co. using returns generated by investing in the Standard & Poor's 500 index between 1965 and 1999. Bernstein statisticians found that while the average monthly return over the 420 months between 1965 and 1999 was about 1.0 percent, it was by no means even. Instead the stock market tended to make big leaps in bursts. Over that 35-year pan, during the best 60 months, or about 14 percent of the time, the S&P 500 averaged a 7.5 percent monthly return. Over the remaining 86 percent of the time period examined, the S&P 500 managed only a 0.1 percent average monthly loss. In other words, jumping into the market and out would only serve to increase the likelihood that you miss out on a growth spurt.

Another set of Bernstein calculations is equally telling. In this case, statisticians examined what might happen to someone holding a portfolio of S&P 500 stocks should they follow one of three strategies, either sticking with the market during ups and downs, exiting when the market went down and staying out of stocks until the market logged a decent year, and third exiting the market when it was judged to be too high and staying on the sidelines until stocks had a down year. Again, the evidence shows that a steady, patient approach came out ahead. Those who stuck with the market were rewarded with an average annual return of 12.4 percent between 1965 and 1999, enough to turn a $10,000 investment to $500,000. Leaving the market behind when it was deemed to be too high generated an 11.6 percent average annual return, or enough to turn that $10,000 investment into $380,000. And finally, running away from a declining market and staying away until an up year put up an 11.0 percent average annual return that would have grown the $10,000 sum into $320,000, a full 36 percent less than investors who stuck with the market would have reaped.

COMPOUNDING

Call compounding the snowball effect. We've all seen cartoons or spoofs of a ski resort. Near the top of a mountain, a tiny snowball starts winding its way downward. All along its path to lower altitudes, it gathers more and more snow, growing larger and larger. At last, it's as large as an entire wall of the lodge. Compounding might not make your savings large enough to engulf a resort, but it will certainly help snowball your funds over time. If you leave your money invested in an account and plow back into investments any returns or dividends you earn, as the years pass, you'll start to notice the money you've stowed away grow to a surprising sum.

As an example, let's say you invested $1,000 in a money market fund that yearly yielded 6 percent interest on average. Patient investor that you no doubt are, you leave the money in the fund and make sure that all interest accrued is turned back into the account to earn its own interest in turn. At the end of 12 years' time, you will have cracked the $2,000 mark, with some $2,012 in the account. Now, for comparison's sake, suppose you skimmed from the account the $60 interest you earned every year. Twelve years later, you'd have earned $1,720, not bad work for leaving your principal alone, but almost $400, or 15 percent, less than you would have made by compounding during the same period.

INFLATION

Picture the slow spread of rust over a brand-new paint job. Imagine a million-dollar waterfront property sliding ever so gradually toward the sea as the hillside below it erodes. Now you're starting to sense what inflation can do to the best of investment portfolios both large and small.

Inflation is the steady rise of prices over time. It creeps up on consumers and investors like ivy up a wall. In part, it has taken what was a $1,900 Volkswagen beetle in 1974, and slapped a $20,000 price tag on it by 1999. By and large, you have the same model automobile, only its sticker price is considerably larger. And inflation will just as quietly, almost imperceptibly eat away at the money you put away if you're not careful.

In recent years, inflation has moved along on tiptoe. Over the past 15 years, the Consumer Price Index (CPI), the government's statistic used to track inflation has risen an average 3 percent a year. In 1997 and 1998, the CPI didn't crack 2 percent; in 1990 the highest in 10 years, it hit just over 6 percent. In years like 1974, 1979, and 1980 it rose to 12 percent and 13 percent annually, a rate that, to use a real-life example, would have meant that whatever cost a dollar one year would require you to dig up a buck and 12 or 13 cents the next. But over the long term, inflation has averaged about 3 percent a year.

That relatively tame 3 percent might tempt you to write off inflation and its effects on your money altogether. Don't. All the while, inflation is still there diminishing the sum you put away for retirement or a new home. To ignore it is to dismiss a pack of termites busily gnawing at your house's foundation.

The fact is, whenever you invest, save, or stash your money away in some form, you're taking it out of circulation, mothballing it. When you bring your money out of hiding, the floor, or level of prices, will most probably have risen. You'll need more money next year to buy what $100 could pick up today. Inflation of 3 percent means you'll need $103 a year from now to buy what that $100 banknote would purchase today. In 10 years' time, you'll need $138, and after 25 years you can expect to shell out $215 for the same items.

All of which is to say that if your money isn't earning at least 3 percent a year, on average, you're losing purchasing power. Say your bank account is only paying 2 percent annually, and inflation is still running at the same 3 percent clip. The $100 you put away now will come out a dollar short in a year; you'll need a spare $12 a decade from now; you'll need to hit someone up for a full $45 in 25 years (see Figure 2.5).

Your investments not only have to keep stride with inflation, they have to beat rising prices as well. One way to keep abreast of inflation's toll on your portfolio is to think of your real rate of return over time, the percentage you're making from your savings and investments, minus the long-term inflation rate of 3 percent. If your stock portfolio averages 15 percent a year, in real terms, counting how much inflation is taking away, the rate is 12 percent annually. If your money market mutual fund is paying 6 percent, you'll actually be making 3 percent a year, factoring in inflation.

That's not to say that inflation ravages the entire economy or that it is a sign that things are falling out of control. A modest level of inflation can actually be a sign that the economy is doing well. It might indicate that factories and businesses are running at full tilt and have to hire workers. Employers might find that to lure new employees they must raise wages. In turn, they'll raise prices to cover the increased outlay on salaries. More money in workers' pockets, meanwhile, will work its way back into the economy by way of more television sets, automobiles, and clothing bought. Figure 2.6 shows the rate of inflation from 1989 through 1999.

An inflationary period can also be good for those companies that can raise their prices. Often corporations in competitive industries find they

Figure 2.5   Inflation

Inflation gnaws away at your savings over time. The result: Your money has less purchasing power.

Need an incentive to start investing? How about inflation? Here's what inflation can do to $1,000 over time. Each column shows how much you can expect $1,000 to purchase over a specific period at different inflation rates.

INFLATION RATE	PURCHASING POWER OF $1,000				
	5 YEARS	10 YEARS	15 YEARS	20 YEARS	30 YEARS
2%	$904	$817	$739	$668	$545
3%	859	737	633	544	401
5%	774	599	463	358	215
7%	696	484	337	234	113
10%	590	349	206	122	42

Figure 2.6 The Consumer Price Index

Here's how inflation has done over the past 15 years, according to the Consumer Price Index. The percentage price increases show that while inflation has looked pretty tame, it's still enough to be a consideration when you're investing.

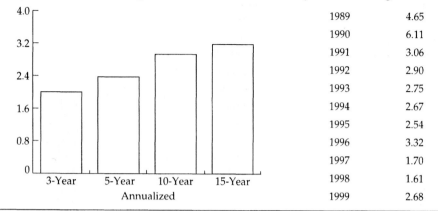

1989	4.65
1990	6.11
1991	3.06
1992	2.90
1993	2.75
1994	2.67
1995	2.54
1996	3.32
1997	1.70
1998	1.61
1999	2.68

Source: The Vanguard Group.

must keep a lid on costs and prices to keep up with their rivals. Inflation eases that pressure somewhat and allows firms to mark up prices.

All the same, if you've followed the moves of the Federal Reserve, the government's central bank, you know that Washington would surely like to keep a lid on inflation. There are a few reasons for that. For one, the government does a lot of its borrowing through the bond market. It issues IOUs and pays back investors at a fixed rate of return. When inflation is high, the yields (interest) on U.S. Treasury bills, bonds, and notes have to rise to attract investors. Then again, times of high inflation can stall an economy. Money is tight because lenders have to raise rates to get a decent return on their money. As a result, fledgling businesses can't get the lifeline of credit they need to get off the ground and running.

To help stem inflation, the Federal Reserve, the U.S. government's central bank, often tightens money by raising the rates it charges banks that borrow money from it. In turn, banks have to turn around and raise the interest charged on all sorts of loans to consumers and businesses. Higher rates persuade a good many borrowers to think twice before signing promissory notes.

If you're the sort of person who likes stats, look to the Consumer Price Index (CPI) for a definitive measure of inflation. The CPI, which is sometimes called the cost-of-living index as well, is compiled monthly by the U.S. Bureau of Labor Statistics and takes into account the costs of electricity, food, shelter, and transportation. You've probably already heard of the CPI if you collect a pension or if your salary is tied into it. When the CPI rises, the money you receive goes up, too, in an attempt to keep up with inflation.

It is not necessary for you, as an investor, to obsess on inflation. It's going to be there, sometimes moving up at a faster rate than other times. Still, you'd be wise to at least keep the phenomenon of inflation in the rearview mirror, understanding that price increases will ultimately affect whatever you do with your money.

THE BIG PICTURE

What makes the stock market go up and down? Why is it good to have a stake in bonds? How do interest rates affect the market and why?

All of those are very good questions. The next few pages, provide a crash course in the stock and bond markets.

Economy-Sized

It is an understatement to say that the stock market and the economy are linked. The economy, that amalgam of businesses, government activity, consumers, and the like has and will always have a profound effect on the market. Investors, after all, like companies that are making money. In fact, they prefer companies that make more and more money every year.

So let's say the economy is growing. Reports are that the gross domestic product (GDP) is rising. Production is inching up and consumers are doing well, benefiting by getting more work, or receiving higher pay for their labors. People are spending money, and companies are making a good income.

That rise in income, even after figuring in salaries and expenses for advertising and production, helps spike up the profit most companies bring in—their earnings, as profits are often called on Wall Street. Higher earnings, in turn, enable companies to grow and take advantage of good times and consumer spending by reaching out to buy more factories, equipment, or other companies. When the economy is growing, that kind of expansion enables companies to make even more money.

Companies have several ways at their disposal to raise capital, or the money they need to operate and even grow. They can rely solely on profits, a prudent method, but one that might limit expansion. They can borrow from banks, often tapping lines of credit they have established with big financial institutions. Or, they can turn to the financial markets. That way, they can make deals with investors, getting a healthy infusion of capital in exchange for something. If a company issues stocks, it's swapping a chunk of the company, or equity, in exchange for investors' capital. If a company issues bonds, then it's drawing up a loan agreement with investors in exchange for capital.

Stocks, or shares as they're called, represent ownership of a piece of a corporation. And owners are entitled to a few privileges. For one, they might get a piece of a company's profits called a dividend (see Chapter 4). Also, when company profits rise, shares rise in value as well because a company that makes more is worth more, is more highly valued. It's only logical, then, that portions of that same company, or shares also are worth more.

Washington Gets Involved

The federal government plays a major role in the economy and all the wheeling and dealing of financial markets, for that matter. You can't have the famous Chicago Bulls' lineup without Michael Jordan and Scottie Pippen; you can't have a U.S. economy without the federal government.

Never underplay the government's role: It has a lot of money at its disposal. In 1999, it took in revenues from taxes and other sources on the order of $1.722 trillion. That same year, it spent an impressive $1.653 trillion.

Those exchanges of money involve many activities. The government collects taxes from corporations and individuals. It hands over a treasure in funds to corporations it has contracted with to provide things like battleships, paper clips, or computer training. It doles out heaps to people who receive some sort of aid from Washington. And to help pay for the U.S. budget, Washington also does a good deal of borrowing. By floating Treasury bonds, bills, and notes, Uncle Sam scrapes together the money to keep Air Force planes flying, subsidies going strong, and the government humming right along. Believe it when you hear that there's no debtor quite like the U.S. government: U.S. Treasury bonds, and even those of agencies like Fannie Mae, or Freddie Mac have a reputation for being the soundest investments around. Professionals are assured that Washington isn't packing it up and leaving town any time soon. Not only that, but the U.S. government hasn't once defaulted on its debt in over 210 years of existence.

The government also helps set monetary policy, a fancy way of saying that it tries to lift and lower interest rates—and quite successfully, we might add. When the Federal Reserve Bank raises rates, or tightens the money supply, it charges banks for short-term loans. Interest rates, in turn, rise. Loans that businesses or consumers take out are more costly; their interest rate is higher. And, as a result, the economy slows. Look for the Fed to tighten or raise rates whenever inflation appears to be simmering up to a boil.

Then, there are times when the Fed eases or lowers rates charged to banks. As a result, interest rates far and wide in the economy drop and lenders charge less interest, meaning more businesses and consumers will likely borrow money for expenditures. In that way, lower rates help spur growth in the economy.

Very Interest-ing

Interest rates have their own effect on the financial markets. The majority of investors like sure, steady returns whenever they can get them. A good number of them are especially fond of Treasury bonds and their rock-solid reputation in the financial markets. Or, perhaps, they're equally enamored of creditworthy bond issues, which guarantee a set return at a set level. Whatever the motivation, as soon as interest rates rise, and bonds are set to pay a higher yield, stock prices fall. That's a signal that a flock of investors have abandoned prospecting in the stock market. They've moved to bonds.

When interest rates climb, more and more investors see an opportunity and seize it. To their way of thinking, the government or other bond issuers has offered up a surefire way to lock up a good rate of return. They'll keep some of their money working away at the stock market, but they'll also be sure to snatch up a guaranteed or close-to-guaranteed return. Sure, they love the stock market's overall gains, but when given half a chance to secure a dependable return on at least part of their money, they jump at it.

That's why the stock market often stalls when interest rates climb. What's happening is a migration of sorts. Bond fans are moving some of their money out of stocks and into bonds. That causes a decrease in demand for stocks. And, as everyone knows from Economics 101, lower demand can often start to drag prices down (see Figure 2.7).

The year 1994 is as close to a textbook example of this phenomenon. On six occasions during the year, the Federal Reserve moved to help lift interest rates higher. The 30-year Treasury bond opened the year yielding 6.23 percent, and closed December 31 at 7.86 percent. Sure enough, that sapped the stock market. In fact, the S&P 500 could muster no better than a 1.32 percent gain for the year.

For a view of the opposite—the Fed helping to bring interest rates down and fueling a rally in the stock market—look no further than 1991. Ten times during the year, the Federal Reserve took action to lower its lending rates. The 30-year Treasury bond, which started the year yielding 8.20 percent, ended 1991 with a 7.51 percent interest rate. Investors, meanwhile charged into the stock market in droves, helping to drive the S&P 500 to a 30.48 percent gain for the year.

Figure 2.7   Interest Rates and the Market

When interest rates swing upward . . .	Many investors head for bonds and the stock market often flags.
When interest rates drop . . .	Many investors seek higher returns in stocks and abandon bonds.

Taxes—When Paper Becomes Real

There's a funny thing about investments you ought to know. It's that a loss isn't always a loss and a gain isn't always a gain.

Here's what we mean by that. Say a mutual fund you own runs off a 30 percent gain in a year. Your account with the mutual fund firm is 30 percent larger than it was a year ago. But that doesn't mean you have $300 extra dollars in your pocket for every $1,000 you've invested. No. At least not yet.

To realize that $300 gain—to hold it, hug it, spend it, or reinvest it—you have to cash in your mutual fund investment. At that point, you'll turn what's called a "paper gain" into a "capital gain." That paper gain, after all, is nothing more than a number until it's put into real dollars and cents.

Alas, the capital gain is also a sum you have to pay taxes on. Your brokerage firm or mutual fund company reports capital gains to Uncle Sam yearly. Then it's your duty to pay taxes on the money you've made, just like any other income. Washington divides capital gains into two categories. There are short-term gains for stocks, mutual funds, and bonds that you've held for a year or less. The IRS targets those gains at your overall tax rate—15, 28, 31, 36, or 39.6 percent (see Figure 2.8). Hold off converting paper gains to capital gains for a year or more, and the IRS takes a little less; in most cases no more than 20 percent.

What about losses? Washington takes a little bit of pity on your part if your investments backtrack. That mercy takes the form of an offsetting write-off. That means the IRS will take your capital gains any one year, and let you subtract capital losses from that total, all in the name of lowering your tax burden. Paper losses, meanwhile, are treated just like paper gains—they're imaginary until you cart off and sell the security in the market.

If there's anything to learn from capital gains it is that long-term investing gives you an opportunity to realize a larger return on your investments. Here's a scenario to make that clear. You invest $1,000 in Zoom Zoom Inc., a maker of rocket accelerators, and pay a rock-bottom commission of $10 to buy the shares, although it would be just as easy to spend two to three times more. Over the next year, Zoom Zoom does just that; it runs off to a 50 percent gain making your investment worth $1,500, the original $1,000 you invested plus a

Figure 2.8   Federal Tax Brackets for 1999 (Top Limits Listed)

PERCENT	SINGLE	MARRIED FILING SEPARATELY	MARRIED FILING JOINTLY	HEAD OF HOUSEHOLD
15	$27,750	$21,525	$43,050	$34,550
28	62,450	52,025	104,050	89,150
31	130,250	79,275	158,550	144,400
36	283,150	141,575	283,150	283,150
39.6	over 283,150	over 141,575	over 283,150	over 283,150

paper gain of $500. Then you sell the shares turning that $500 paper gain into a real-live capital gain, the kind the IRS loves to nibble at, and you subtract the brokerage commissions of $20. When Uncle Sam finishes with you that year, your tax bill on the transaction will be $134.40, 28 percent of the $480 you made on the transaction. You'll be left with $1,345.60, meaning your 50 percent gain will have slacked off somewhat to 34.56 percent, impressive but a good deal less than before.

Let's say that instead of selling Zoom Zoom, you hold on another 5 years. Zoom Zoom slows down to a strut; it makes only 10 percent a year, a bit closer to the stock market's historical averages. You end up with $2,415.77, meaning you've made a capital gain of $1,415.77 or 141.6 percent. Again, you'll pay a commission of $10 to sell off your shares, and will owe the IRS 28 percent on $1,395.77, your gains minus commissions. Uncle Sam will take his share—$398.82—and you'll be left with $996.95, all for being patient.

SAFEKEEPING

After you gather up your investments—your portfolio—of stocks, bonds, or mutual funds, you need a place for safekeeping in accounts you might hold or choose to open up with investment firms, brokerages, or banks. The wide variety of investment accounts can be divided into two categories: taxable accounts and tax-deferred accounts.

As the name implies, taxable accounts are slapped with government taxes. If it's any easier, think of taxable accounts as a sort of personal stash— money you're saving for special, relatively simple projects such as the down payment for a new home or the purchase of a new convertible or station wagon. They're ordinary accounts with a discount broker or mutual fund. Within the account, you'll divvy up your savings among investments that include stocks, bonds, and even cash, typically held in a money market fund set up by the financial company that manages your account.

Whatever money you make over time in capital gains when you buy and sell investments, or in dividends or interest, is assessed taxes that are payable to the government each year. Typically, your brokerage firm or mutual fund company will send you the 1099 forms you need to keep up with what you owe (see Figure 2.9). In any case, keep close tabs on whatever trading activity you do.

If you've been at your job for a couple of years, you might already know about tax-deferred accounts. They tend to be special savings programs for major long-term goals such as retirement or college tuition. Tax-deferred accounts get special treatment from the government. The IRS and state collectors promise to hold off on taxes you might otherwise pay on your savings. You need only hand over taxes once you tap money from

Figure 2.9   Form 1099

Mutual fund companies, brokerages, and stock programs all will supply you with Form 1099 after the year ends. On it, you'll find the money you made from your investments and the sums that need to be reported to the IRS when you file your taxes.

1999 FORM 1099-B

THEVanguardGROUP

Proceeds From Broker and Barter Exchange Transactions

P.O. Box 2600 · Valley Forge, PA 19482-2600

PAGE 25 OF 25

Vanguard Shareholder
Anytown USA

Recipient's Taxpayer Identification Number

999-99-9999

> This is important tax information and is being furnished to the Internal Revenue Service. If you are required to file a return, a negligence penalty or other sanction may be imposed on you if this income is taxable and the IRS determines that it has not been reported.
> DEPARTMENT OF THE TREASURY - INTERNAL REVENUE SERVICE

Fund Name		Fund's Fed. I.D. No.	Box 1b: CUSIP No.	Recipient's Account No.			
Box 1a: Trade Date	Box 5: Description		Share Price	Shares		Box 2: Gross Proceeds	Box 4: Federal Income Tax Withheld
INSTITUTIONAL INDEX FUND	23-2601141		922040100	9999999999			
09/24/1998	CHECK REDEMPTION		46.86		2.134	100.00	0.00

FORM 1099-B
OMB NO. 1545-0715

Copy B for Recipient

(Keep for your records.)

Source: The Vanguard Group.

your account. Meanwhile, your nest egg or savings is allowed to compound over time, accumulating all the more because no taxes are paid until later.

Tax-deferred accounts come in several varieties. There are 401(k) or 403(b) accounts, sponsored by your employer. Often the company has made arrangements with a big investment firm to offer you a retirement account such as a 401(k); at a nonprofit organization, it will be a 403(b) account. As a perk, your employer will make contributions to your 401(k) and often will allow you to make investments to the fund as well. Then, under provisions of the plan your bosses have set up, you can choose from an array of investments (often a list of a half-dozen or more mutual funds), individually or in tandem, where you can put your money to work. Over time, you can shift your money around within your 401(k) to take advantage of changes in the financial markets. Caution: In some cases, you're allowed to tap your 401(k) tax-free, but most often you'll be assessed a double whammy for any money you take out prior to the age of 59½. For one, Washington will hit you with a 10 percent penalty on the money you withdraw. Second, you'll owe taxes on whatever you remove prior to retirement.

A second sort of tax-deferred retirement account is the trusty IRA or individual retirement account. You can establish IRAs with a host of different financial institutions—banks, brokerage firms, mutual fund companies. Better yet, you can bag a small tax deduction for IRA contributions—up to $2,000 for individuals or $4,000 for couples. IRA accounts also offer up a good deal of variety. Within your IRA, you might choose to invest in stocks, bonds, or mutual funds. And, as is the case with the 401(k), whatever capital gains, dividends, or distributions you happen to pile up over time, you owe no taxes until you start making withdrawals. That said, you'll still get assessed the same penalties for withdrawals you make before reaching 59½, unless you've invested in a Roth IRA, a special exception that allows you to dip into your savings without penalty.

The federal government has also been hard at work creating new ways for you to salt away funds for your children's college years. The education IRA is an account much like its retirement-plan cousins except that it's earmarked for your son or daughter's future. Funds set aside in an education IRA account get the same benefits of tax-deferred compounding, too, with taxes due only when you tap the account. You can open an education IRA with a variety of financial firms or mutual fund companies.

THE RULE OF 72

Can't find the calculator the very minute you're trying to figure out how quickly your money is growing? There's a way to run a rough calculation off the top of your head.

The pros—financial planners and money managers—call it the "rule of 72." Choose an average annual total return figure—what percentage gain you expect to get for your money under a certain investment plan. Next, divide that figure into 72. Your result: the approximate number of years it should take your money to double at that rate.

As an example, choose 12 percent, roughly the average yearly gain for the stock market as measured by the S&P 500 index over time. Using the rule of 72 as an indicator, your savings should double every 6 years, provided you manage an average 12 percent return during that period. Do the math, and you'll find that a 12 percent gain each of 6 years in a row will garner a 97.4 percent gain, a hair's breadth shy of doubling your money. Try, instead 10 percent. The rule of 72 says your money should double in 7.2 years. Multiply it out, and you'll find that your investment will gain 94.8 percent during the seven years. That's close enough for a good estimate.

BENCHMARKS

Shopping is shopping, whether you're looking to plunk down $20,000 on a new car, $1,000 on a designer suit, or $2,000 into a mutual fund.

There's just one catch. From showroom to showroom, you have a pretty good idea what you've seen and how one sedan stacks up against the next. You've sat in the seats, taken your test drive, turned on the air, peeked in the glove compartment. You've probably even checked into maintenance records as listed by a consumer magazine or reference book. The suit? You've tugged at the seams. You might run your hands over the material again and again. You sift through the racks, check the labels, and then make the rounds at several department stores to compare prices.

Stocks, bonds, and mutual funds are a different matter. You gauge them by stacking numbers against numbers almost exclusively—how much money they've made investors stated in percentages. Nevertheless, shopping for financial holdings is just as important, if not more so, than kicking the tires of a half-dozen SUVs. It's your future and a good deal of savings we're talking about, after all.

One way to see if an investment you're considering measures up is to look at historic averages. Stocks, as represented by the S&P 500, have increased returns an average 11 percent a year since 1926. A stock mutual fund or equity fund looks good if its return to investors has regularly exceeded 12 percent. It's so-so if it averages 10 percent to 12 percent annually. It's a dud if it's short of 9 percent a year.

Long-term averages, however, aren't always fail-safe. The reason: Markets can go through long stretches when they leave the historic mean in the dust or just don't measure up. Take the stock market over the past few years. If you've been following the financial press, you've probably seen story after story on how market pundits have been baffled by the relentless climb in share prices. Between 1995 and 1999, the market by some measures rose an average 28.54 percent a year. It goes without saying that a fund that merely keeps up with historic averages—17 points less—isn't going to look too impressive. It shouldn't. After all, a mutual fund manager is, in all likelihood, charging you fees to invest your money for higher returns than an index fund, which would mirror the benchmark.

For a better vantage point on market performance, you need to learn a little about indexes, the benchmarks professionals use daily for measuring investments. Indexes are essentially baskets of stocks or bonds, that help show how a segment of the financial markets has done.

If you've even peeped at anything written on the stock market, or cast an ear toward the television set during the financial news, you've no doubt heard of the Dow Jones Industrials. The Dow, as it's commonly called, is a benchmark made up of 30 stocks, large companies that represent the creme de la creme of corporate America (see Figure 2.10). Its roster is chosen by a

Figure 2.10 Members of the Dow Jones Industrial Average for 2000

These 30 companies make up the most widely quoted stock market index around.

Alcoa	Intel
American Express	International Business Machines
AT&T	International Paper
Boeing	Johnson & Johnson
Caterpillar	McDonald's
Citigroup	Merck
Coca-Cola	Microsoft
Du Pont	Minnesota Mining & Manufacturing
Eastman Kodak	J.P. Morgan
Exxon	Philip Morris
General Electric	Procter & Gamble
General Motors	SBC Communications
Hewlett-Packard	United Technologies
Home Depot	Wal-Mart
Honeywell Intl.	Walt Disney

Source: Dow Jones Indexes.

special editorial board assembled by the financial publishing company Dow Jones. Dow stocks tend to be "blue chips," the big, reliable corporations that have virtually conquered their industries and have a record for turning in sizable profits and rewarding investors with solid returns on their money. That reputation often makes Dow stocks an attractive choice for investors ranging from big pension plans to mutual funds, from overseas aristocracy to the night manager at the filling station down the street (see Figure 2.11).

The problem is, that just 30 stocks, even spread across a variety of industries doesn't cover much territory if you're talking about a market made up of 9,000 or more stocks. For a broader view, keep tabs on at least one of the other indexes that track a bigger cross-section of companies, especially large company stocks or large cap stocks, as they're called in the business. The term *cap* refers to capitalization, a measure of a company's size calculated by taking the number of shares it has out and multiplying that figure by its stock price. As of this writing, large cap stocks were generally classified as those with $5 billion or more in stock market value. Large cap stocks are thus the shares of some of the biggest companies around, midcaps tend to be slightly smaller corporations, and small caps are often young companies just getting rolling.

Among the broader indexes, the Standard & Poor's 500, usually abbreviated to the S&P 500, is one of the most respected and most widely used measures of large cap shares (see Figure 2.12). As you can no doubt guess from the name, the S&P 500 was devised by Standard & Poor's, a stock and bond research firm based in New York. And, as the name implies, the S&P 500 is

Figure 2.11   The Dow Jones Industrial Average

Widely considered the Cadillac of stock market indexes, the Dow Jones Industrials chart the peaks and valleys of 30 top companies providing investors with a barometer of how the biggest corporations are faring in the market.

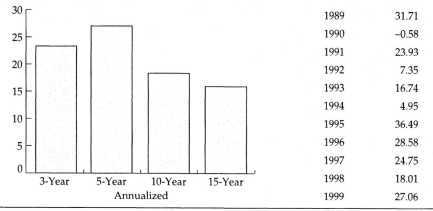

Year	Value
1989	31.71
1990	−0.58
1991	23.93
1992	7.35
1993	16.74
1994	4.95
1995	36.49
1996	28.58
1997	24.75
1998	18.01
1999	27.06

Source: Dow Jones Indexes.

composed of 500 of the largest companies around. That sort of breadth makes the index a better gauge of the climbs and falls of the stock market.

While the S&P 500 provides a good reading on large companies, many small- and mid-sized companies fall through the 500's net. Those company shares are important, too, because they represent huge segments of the U.S. economy. Their ranks are filled with up and coming companies, start-ups that are just beginning to flex muscle in the economy and innovative outfits

Figure 2.12   Standard & Poor's 500

As a comprehensive overview of the market's biggest stocks, the Standard & Poor's 500 is the index of choice to gauge how shares of companies across the United States' economic spectrum are faring.

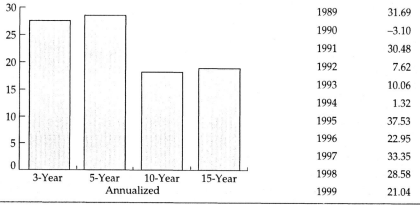

Year	Value
1989	31.69
1990	−3.10
1991	30.48
1992	7.62
1993	10.06
1994	1.32
1995	37.53
1996	22.95
1997	33.35
1998	28.58
1999	21.04

Source: The Vanguard Group.

Figure 2.13   Standard & Poor's Midcap 400

For a benchmark that follows medium-sized companies look to the S&P Midcap 400.

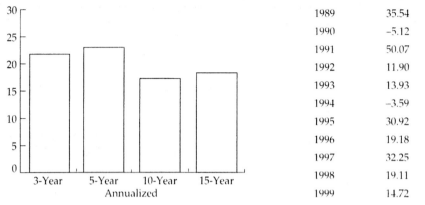

Year	Value
1989	35.54
1990	–5.12
1991	50.07
1992	11.90
1993	13.93
1994	–3.59
1995	30.92
1996	19.18
1997	32.25
1998	19.11
1999	14.72

Source: Morningstar.

that will soon rock the business world. They're also a useful gauge of how new businesses are faring under certain economic conditions.

Another widely quoted Standard & Poor's index is the Midcap 400. It covers medium-sized companies, those with a market cap of $200 million to $5 billion (see Figure 2.13).

Of late, the Nasdaq Composite has been a benchmark in the headlines. It follows the performance of over 5,000 stocks listed on the Nasdaq (National Association of Securities Dealers Automated Quotations) system (see Figure 2.14). The Nasdaq Composite is often used to monitor the performance of

Figure 2.14   The Nasdaq Composite

A benchmark that tracks over 5,000 stocks, the Composite is a good way to monitor the ups and downs of stocks of companies in hot new sectors such as technology and biotechnology.

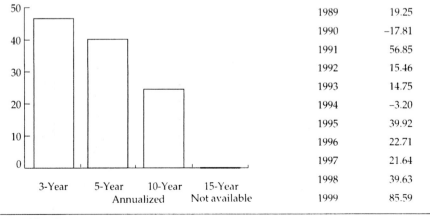

Year	Value
1989	19.25
1990	–17.81
1991	56.85
1992	15.46
1993	14.75
1994	–3.20
1995	39.92
1996	22.71
1997	21.64
1998	39.63
1999	85.59

Source: Morningstar.

Figure 2.15 The Wilshire 5000

For a comprehensive index that includes the largest companies down to small new-comers, check the Wilshire 5000, which tracks over 6,800 companies on the New York, American and Nasdaq exchanges.

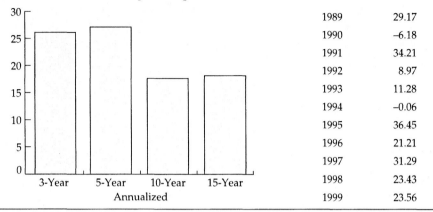

Year	Value
1989	29.17
1990	–6.18
1991	34.21
1992	8.97
1993	11.28
1994	–0.06
1995	36.45
1996	21.21
1997	31.29
1998	23.43
1999	23.56

Source: Wilshire Associates.

technology shares, especially since the exchange is home to big names in cutting-edge industries such as Intel, Amgen, Dell, and Cisco.

Some indexes are tailored to give investors a wider view of just what's going on with companies large and small. One such measure, the Wilshire 5000, covers every stock listed on the New York Stock Exchange and the American Stock Exchange, as well as stats for Nasdaq shares, too (see Figure 2.15).

Say you wanted to isolate small company stocks. For a measurement on how the up-and-comers are doing, turn to the Russell 2000, an index of small

Figure 2.16 Russell 2000

Perhaps the most widely used benchmark for small company stocks is the Russell 2000. It tracks a group of companies whose market capitalization falls between $222 million and $1.4 billion as of 1999.

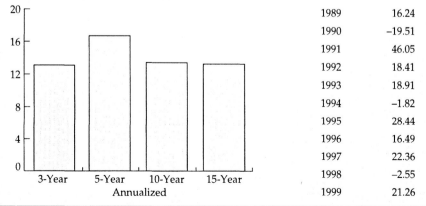

Year	Value
1989	16.24
1990	–19.51
1991	46.05
1992	18.41
1993	18.91
1994	–1.82
1995	28.44
1996	16.49
1997	22.36
1998	–2.55
1999	21.26

Source: Frank Russell Company.

company stocks (small caps). Don't think Russell 2000 stocks are microscopic or fly-by-night outfits. The average market cap for Russell 2000 companies is just over $500 million; the largest in the group has a capitalization of $1.3 billion (see Figure 2.16).

Let's not forget the world beyond our borders. Overseas investing's a hot topic (as explained later in this chapter). Although the S&P includes many domestic and international companies, the world at large is beyond its reach. To cover that vast territory, the Morgan Stanley Capital International has developed the MSCI EAFE, a widely quoted international index com-

Figure 2.17   MSCI EAFE and MSCI Emerging Markets Indexes

For an idea of how overseas markets are doing, check two indexes, the MSCI EAFE, which includes companies in Europe, Asia and Australia, and the MSCI Emerging Markets, which follows firms in developing nations.

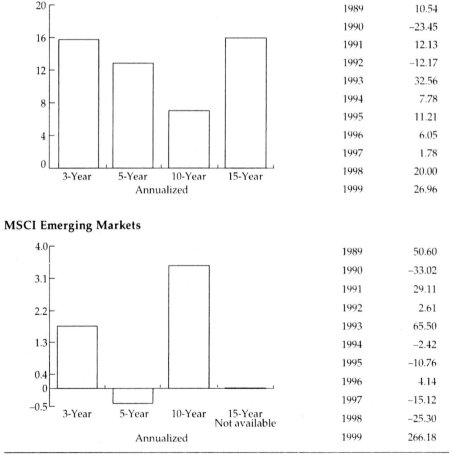

MSCI EAFE

1989	10.54
1990	−23.45
1991	12.13
1992	−12.17
1993	32.56
1994	7.78
1995	11.21
1996	6.05
1997	1.78
1998	20.00
1999	26.96

MSCI Emerging Markets

1989	50.60
1990	−33.02
1991	29.11
1992	2.61
1993	65.50
1994	−2.42
1995	−10.76
1996	4.14
1997	−15.12
1998	−25.30
1999	266.18

Source: Morningstar.

piled by the Wall Street investment bank Morgan Stanley Dean Witter. The letters E-A-F-E stand for Europe, Australia, and the Far East—regions the index covers. Morgan Stanley's index looks at the stocks of about 1,000 companies in 20 countries (see Figure 2.17).

The EAFE, has its limits, though. It's focused on industrial nations that have steadier stock market performance and established economies. Many nations, however, are nurturing new markets, enjoying explosive growth, and rewarding investors with some great, albeit volatile, returns. Morgan Stanley tracks those markets, too, under a different package: Its MSCI Emerging Markets index, which tracks over 800 companies in 25 countries (Figure 2.17).

Figure 2.18   S&P Barra Indexes

The S&P Barra indexes divide up the stocks in the S&P 500 benchmark to help investors better understand how certain groups of stocks are faring in the current market in terms of value and growth.

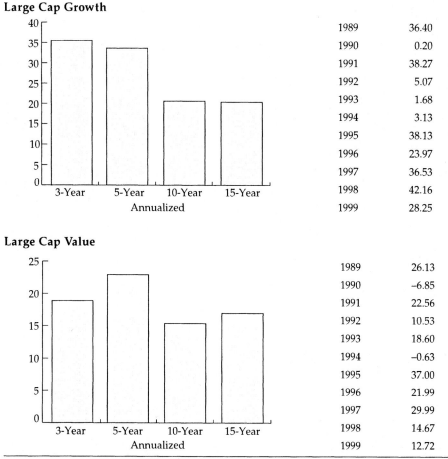

Large Cap Growth

Year	Value
1989	36.40
1990	0.20
1991	38.27
1992	5.07
1993	1.68
1994	3.13
1995	38.13
1996	23.97
1997	36.53
1998	42.16
1999	28.25

Large Cap Value

Year	Value
1989	26.13
1990	−6.85
1991	22.56
1992	10.53
1993	18.60
1994	−0.63
1995	37.00
1996	21.99
1997	29.99
1998	14.67
1999	12.72

Source: Barra, Inc.

Figure 2.19   Lehman Brothers Aggregate Bond

The Lehman Brothers Aggregate Bond Index monitors returns from the bond market. It covers a variety of bonds—government, agency, corporate—and then calculates an average annual total return to gauge how investors would have fared in the market as a whole.

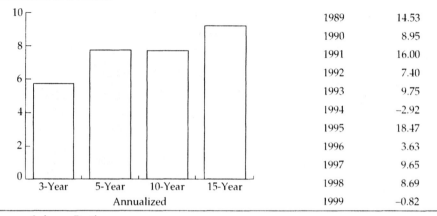

Year	Return
1989	14.53
1990	8.95
1991	16.00
1992	7.40
1993	9.75
1994	-2.92
1995	18.47
1996	3.63
1997	9.65
1998	8.69
1999	-0.82

Source: Lehman Brothers.

Indexes don't just carve up the world of stocks according to countries or size. Some look into investment styles as well. The S&P Barra Growth index does just that for what Wall Street calls growth stocks—shares of companies that are increasing earnings at a rapid rate. The S&P Barra Value index, meanwhile, examines value stocks. In stock market parlance, value refers to shares of companies that might seem under appreciated or cheap in comparison to the market at large (see Figure 2.18).

Track the bond market, read up on fixed-income investments, as they're called, and you'll run across a few specialized indexes that monitor this part of the investment world. To gauge yields, or the amount of interest bonds are paying investors, most professionals turn to the 30-year Treasury bond, or long bond, an investment put out by the U.S. government. Then, to follow overall returns on bonds, the pros check the Lehman Brothers Aggregate Index, a benchmark compiled by the brokerage firm of the same name. The Lehman Aggregate covers a lot of territory including company bonds and government bonds (see Figure 2.19).

OVERSEAS INVESTING

Forgive the pun, but why in the world would you want to invest abroad when the U.S. market has posted nonstop gains the past few years? By keeping your money at home, you would have pocketed some pretty impressive gains. A decision to stash your savings in a mutual fund tracking the S&P 500, for instance, would have been an excellent choice. You would have seen it climb 38,

---

WEB SIGHTINGS
BENCHMARKS, WHERE TO LOOK, WHAT TO LOOK FOR

So many indexes slice and repackage the financial markets in myriad ways that it becomes overwhelming. It is best if you stick to just a few for the time being. Your first choice probably should be the S&P 500, the yardstick against which most money managers are measured. The Dow gets a lot of press, too, so it's a good idea to keep abreast of its ups and downs.

You'll find listings for most indexes in the newspaper, particularly the financial press. Publications such as *Barron's,* the *Wall Street Journal,* and *Investors' Business Daily* publish comprehensive lists of the benchmarks mentioned here as well as many more. On the Web, you might check a couple of sources as well. Bloomberg (www.bloomberg.com) is a financial news wire packed with late-breaking stories, stats, and analysis. All-inclusive sites such as Dailystocks (www.dailystocks.com) or Investorama (www.investorama.com) have links to the companies that crank out the numbers for major benchmarks and for sites that track the indexes.

23, 33, and 29 percent in the years 1995 through 1998, a streak of good fortune that would have taken a $1,000 on a climb of 191 percent to $2,912.

What else makes it difficult to put up a convincing case for investing overseas? How about the fact that during the late 1990s downright glum economic headlines were in the news from lands both near and far. Almost daily, another financial mishap seemed to be occurring in some new spot around the world. Russia teetered on the brink of chaos; Southeast Asian economies slumped into a crisis, throwing governments in that region into jeopardy. One minute, Brazil seemed to have righted its finances; not long after, though, a drastic currency devaluation tripped the South American nation up once again.

That might make global investing seem like a hard sell, but bear in mind long-term patterns. Don't be fooled by a sizzling half-decade in the U.S. stock market—the world abroad is a great place for your money to be.

More than ever, you should consider spreading some of your money across the border, and even across oceans. For one, it makes sense from an economic standpoint. Thanks to an era of far-reaching trade agreements, our nation's economic well-being is now inextricably tied to events in places from Timbuktu to Thailand. Global markets are intertwined, and becoming more and more interdependent.

At the same time, all that economic activity abroad has spurred growth in stock markets overseas. U.S. stock markets now make up around half the total capitalization (the value of stocks) of worldwide stock markets. Overlook stocks overseas and you're leaving yourself out of a lot of the action.

And despite well-publicized trouble in markets around the world, some exciting economic developments are going on. In 1999, a number of European countries adopted a common currency, the Euro, in the hope of spurring economic growth on the continent. In countries like India and China, businesses are sprouting up quickly. Democracies in Latin American nations like Argentina and Brazil are keeping tighter rein on their currencies, trimming government budgets, and giving the private sector plenty of room to grow. Even nations in Africa—Botswana and South Africa, for example—are starting to clean house and set their economies on an upward trajectory.

Be aware that there are some great companies overseas, corporations whose products you depend on day in and day out. Nokia, the leading maker of cellular phone handsets, calls the Scandinavian country of Finland home. Shares in Nokia have made a good investment in the past few years. Thanks to the wireless communications craze, Nokia's stock has appreciated an amazing 1255 percent in the years between 1996 and 2000.

Then, you might think about SmithKline Beecham, a British company that ranks among the biggest drug manufacturers in the world. The local pharmacy is stocked to the rafters with SmithKline wares including Contac, Tums, Geritol, and Nicorette. Just as important to investors, however, is that the company stock has zoomed some 97 percent in the 3-year period ending at the start of 1999.

International investing makes sense for several reasons. Start with cold, hard figures. Investing professionals will tell you that things that go up have an uncanny way of either (a) slowing down or (b) falling. So, if the U.S. market has raced off to gains, it won't keep rising forever. There will be periods when the New York Stock Exchange and Nasdaq will inevitably slow, slip, or take a breather. Meanwhile, investments that have tumbled have a way of getting back up and turning around. Applied to international investing that means some of the fast-growing emerging markets that stumbled in the late 1990s, will probably bounce back, sooner rather than later. And often enough, when the United States sputters, there are markets in the world that might be doing quite well at the same time.

Indeed, many of the same overseas markets that faltered during the latter 1990s, had started to show increased vigor by 1999. South Korean stocks finished the year up an astonishing 110.63 percent. Mexico's market rose 91 percent, while Hong Kong, Indonesia, Japan, and South Africa all climbed 65 percent or more during the year.

Not every year will be like the last 12 months of the twentieth century. What you can safely conclude is that there will probably be markets that outdo U.S. stocks any given year. Even between 1994 and 1999, when the U.S.

stock market performed exceedingly well, there were numerous world markets that did better still. In 1994, when the U.S. stock market finished the year off almost 3 percent, the world outside of the United States, as measured by the MSCI EAFE index, finished the year up almost 2 percent. That same year, the Japanese stock market rose 16 percent as did the market in Sweden; Finland closed the year up 43 percent.

The next year, 1995, saw the U.S. stock market bounce back with a 36 percent gain. Even then, Switzerland finished the year up 37 percent. In 1996, the U.S. market rose 19 percent, but trailed Portugal, Spain, Malaysia, Hong Kong, Sweden, and Canada.

Long-term figures support global investing. For evidence, examine calculations by Morgan Stanley's MSCI division for the world stock markets, looking 10 years back from 1994, a decade that includes off years like 1991 and 1994 and market crashes in 1987 and 1991. During the 10-year period, the world's markets as pegged by a MSCI index rose on average 12.39 percent yearly, compared with 10.4 percent for the United States; the Morgan Stanley EAFE index, which includes Asia, Australia, and a number of European nations climbed 15.34 percent a year during that same time.

GETTING A LITTLE HELP FROM YOUR FRIENDS?

You're buried in numbers. Investment brochures are piled high on your desk, and you have a stack of newspapers and magazines with headlines that scream the latest and greatest mutual fund picks. You're confused, lonely, and suddenly struck with a feeling of inadequacy. Sometimes a cold, cruel world of investing seems to lurk outside your window.

Does it make sense to get help? Well, that's a question most every investor faces. One of the first decisions you must make is whether to have a broker handle most of your investing, knowing you'll incur some sizable fees. Or should you do much of it yourself, perhaps with an online broker handling some of your trades? This saves money but you forgo the hand-holding and advice a broker would offer. The pros and cons of this debate are covered in Chapter 11.

If you hate to go it alone, there's another avenue you might consider: investment groups. Several organizations are out there to help you cope with everything from understanding investing to finding a broker. Some are free. Some charge a fee. Figure 2.20 lists some prominent organizations.

The Coalition of Black Investors (COBI) was founded by Duane Davis, a stockbroker for over 15 years, who felt it was time to set up a group to address African Americans and their particular investment needs. COBI, run by Davis and his wife Carol, is a busy group. In 1999, it hosted six conferences in cities across the country to teach beginners what investing is all about. Members receive a quarterly newsletter that spells out ways you can

Figure 2.20   Investment Groups

NAME	SERVICES OFFERED	TELEPHONE NUMBER	WEB SITE
Coalition of Black Investors (COBI)	Basics on investing Contact with other African Americans Investors' Seminars	336-922-6240	www.cobinvest.com
Association of Individual Investors (AAII)	Basics on investing Seminars	800-428-2244	www.aaii.com
National Association of Investors Corp. (NAIC)	Basics on investing Tips on investment clubs	877-275-6242	www.better-investing.org.

get into the stock market or put your money to work, along with stock and mutual fund picks readers might find of interest.

Davis's dream is to have COBI act as a clearinghouse of information to help black investors. "The most important thing is to educate African Americans [about] the importance of saving and investing," he says. "COBI's job is to form a network so the wealth of individuals can actually be banded together. . . . That way African Americans as a group can flex more financial muscle and wield more influence. If we can harness two million black investors saving $25 or $100 a month, you're talking about millions of dollars a month, billions of dollars a year."

COBI charges a membership fee of $10 for individuals or $10 for investment clubs plus a $5 fee for each member. In exchange, you'll get the group's newsletter, a list of African American brokers and brokerage firms, a quarterly newsletter, a guide to starting an investment club, and other educational material. The group also organizes investment symposiums around the country. You can write to COBI at P.O. Box 30553, Winston-Salem, N.C., 27130-0553.

Another investment group worth investigating is the American Association of Individual Investors (AAII). The AAII offers up a Web site full of investment guidance and tips for beginners. For a $49 annual membership fee, you'll receive guides from the organization including a mutual fund booklet and a publication on tax strategies. The AAII lets members in on its seminar series as well as Standard & Poor's and Morningstar investment reports on its online site.

An organization that also offers up information about investing is the National Association of Investors Corp. (NAIC). Based in Madison Heights, Michigan, the NAIC has been something of the investment clubs' club, and has helped launch a wave of investment clubs, including the famed "Beardstown Ladies." Whether you're in a club or on your own, the NAIC offers up information sheets, a monthly magazine on investing, and a guide for investment clubs. Membership is $39 a year for individuals. Clubs can enroll for $40 annually plus $14 a member in dues.

On to Stocks

It's time to push forward for a look into the investment that makes pulses rise and excites everyone from grandmothers to teens: stocks. In the following chapter, you'll learn what they are, what makes them tick, and more importantly what makes them work well for you.

3

STOCK BASICS

How to Track Company Shares, the Exchanges, Bull and Bear Markets, Global Investing, and More

Forget bonds, money markets, or CDs. These days, when people talk about investing, they mean stocks. Mind you, much of this book is focused on explaining why it's smart to balance a portfolio with those other items—bonds, money market funds, and so on. All the same, over time, owning company shares has been *the* way to make money. Think of it this way: Today, owning stock is practically as important as drawing a salary.

You may be able to run from the stock market, but we're willing to bet that you'll find it quite hard to hide. To escape any news of the S&P 500, you'd have to retreat to the deepest recesses of the Amazon jungle. There are a lot of hermits who track the Dow Jones Industrial average on their PCs. Your neighbors are keen on stocks like AOL Time Warner, Cisco Systems, or Amgen. The manager at the supermarket down the street thinks he knows a couple technology stocks ready to go into orbit. Whether you check the morning paper, turn on a 24-hour cable news station, or chat current affairs with co-workers at the office, you'll probably get a face full of the latest on the stock market. Almost anyone you pass on the street will have a sense of whether stocks in general are up or down. Little wonder, then, that over $20 trillion worth of stock changed hands daily last year on the New York and Nasdaq exchanges, according to 1999 average volume figures compiled by the Securities Industry Association.

It's no mystery why the stock market is so captivating. Stocks are simply one of the best investments around. Their total return on average far exceeds

Figure 3.1   Stocks Are for You If . . .

- You need to grow the money you've saved for long-term goals.
- You are willing to do a bit of number crunching and research to find companies with the best possible prospects.
- You can buy an investment and stick with it for between 2 and 5 years.
- You're a patient person who can ride out the ups and downs of the market.
- You've got a good anchor in mutual funds and are looking for more pep in your portfolio.

that of bonds or cash. And, perhaps most importantly, stocks have the financial power to trounce inflation, the sneaky, quiet rise of prices that eats away at your savings over time. It's a snap to accomplish all that and more if you're generating average annual returns of 10 percent or greater (see Figure 3.1).

For proof of the power of stocks, just witness what the equity market has done in recent years. To say that over the past two decades, the broad market

---

REALITY CHECK

Anita Davis-Townsend figures it's time to work her way into the stock market. Dr. Davis, an OB-GYN who lives in Houston, got into investing two years ago, after contacting a local financial planner, Cheryl Creuzot. Davis had a lot of things to sort out. She was joining a multi-specialty group practice and had to figure out a retirement program. Her husband Talbert Townsend was about to head back to school to finish up an engineering degree. And her son, Cameron, now 18 months old, was on the way at the time.

Creuzot steered Davis-Townsend into a few mutual funds as a base, taught her the basics of investing and told her to hold off on buying individual stocks for a little bit. Meantime, Davis-Townsend and her husband started reading up. They have friends invested in technology companies like Qualcomm and Dell, who've done quite well. Whenever she goes in to perform surgery, the television in the doctors' lounge is tuned into CNBC, and Davis-Townsend gets a dose of financial news throughout the workday. Finally, her husband has taken to hunting through the papers for companies that might make good investments. "He reads the *Houston Chronicle* daily . . . he looks for stock ideas, reads up on mergers, and sees how some companies are growing and changing," says Davis-Townsend. She adds, "I'd say we'd like to buy a stock soon, just to get the experience, and now that we've studied up and have a pretty good foundation, I feel good about it."

has enjoyed a phenomenal run might be mincing words. Looking back (as of 12/31/99) over the past 15 years, the S&P 500 index reaped a healthy 18.92 percent in average annual returns, almost twice stock's historical yearly gain of 10 percent or so. In raw numbers, if you had bought a $1,000 piece of the Standard & Poor's 500, say in a Vanguard fund tracking the index back in 1984, you'd have an investment worth $15,998.47 at the end of 1999.

TWO WAYS STOCKS MAKE MONEY

Stocks offer investors two ways to grow the money they earmark for retirement or college tuition or the down payments for new homes. First, they rack up capital gains, the appreciation share prices make over time as determined by the stock market. If a company shows that it not only can make a healthy profit but also can increase the amount of money it makes year after year, investors will bid its share price ever upward. If you own that same company's shares, you'll likely see the stock go up in value. It also means you could sell your stock later at a profit, a capital gain.

Second, shareholders also may receive a bonus of sorts, too, called a dividend. Stock investors get dividends when companies opt to carve out a certain portion of profits to share with shareholders. It's a sum that tends to come regularly every quarter, and is preannounced (see Figure 3.2).

Stocks can disappoint investors as well. If Acme Gravel Corporation seems to be barely treading water or its profits are falling, investors will often abandon its shares. Its stock price will fall, and shareholders will suffer losses if they sell their stakes in the company. And, when stocks fall, they can do so swiftly and with little warning.

Investors in Oxford Health Plans know just how fast that kind of reversal can happen. The company had reported several years of solid results to the investing public; between January 1, 1993, and September 30, 1997, Oxford rose 960 percent. No sooner had reports of earnings problems hit the

Figure 3.2 How Stocks Make Money

Capital Gains
The old-fashioned way stocks benefit investors is by increasing in value over time. Patient investors will find that their company shares will rise in price over the years. When shareholders finally cash out and sell their stock, they'll realize capital gains, a profit on their original investment.

Dividends
Dividends can make a stock market investment seem much like a bank account. They are regular payments companies make to shareholders, usually quarterly. They're a perk you're likely to see offered up by solid, well–established companies that generate dependable profits. That said, don't expect much in the way of dividends these days; corporate generosity hasn't been very high of late.

newsstand in 1997, than Oxford shares took a dive, falling 62 percent in one day alone. By the end of 1998, the company stock had shed almost 80 percent of its value. That's proof enough that stocks are riskier investments than bonds or savings accounts. They're great for long-term gains, but are volatile as well. They sometimes hit rough times.

So, it's of the utmost importance to choose stocks well. There's no getting around doing some old-fashioned homework to get a sense of what kind of company you're buying into. Don't forget, too, it's best to approach the stock market with patience. The market offers some great opportunities, but only if you're willing to stick with your investments.

In all the talk about money and risk, it's easy to overlook a primary feature of stocks: ownership of a piece of corporate America. Buy a stock, slip it into your investment portfolio, and you've just pocketed a portion of the economy, a piece of Big Business, USA. You're in line to benefit directly from the health of nation's industries and share in the expansion of key sectors—technology, healthcare, consumer goods, to name a few. Think of it this way: in your armchair, reading the newspaper or staring at the evening news, you're just an observer. As a shareholder, you're a participant, and one whose expertise is bound to grow over time. Once you become a shareholder, or partial owner of a company, you'll be asked to vote on some key issues, not day-to-day business activities, but weighty matters, nonetheless. One day, it might be just who will get to sit on the company's board of directors. Another time you may be asked to vote on a takeover offer a company has received from an outside firm.

Think of it. Your portfolio is a way to cast your vote on other issues. Should you decide to buy stock, you should purchase shares in companies that are not only profitable, but whose products and practices you know and believe in. Your backing is a form of popular approval, a thumbs-up to the chief executive that the new gadgets rolling off the assembly line look great or that the promotion of an African American to the company's highest ranks is an encouraging sign to you. Shareholding can be your means to stand up and be counted, to whisper in the ear of the bosses and clue them into what's on your mind.

WHAT IT'S ALL ABOUT

Welcome to your piece of the executive suite.

Buying stock after all, makes you the partial owner of a publicly traded company, one of the nearly 9,000 corporations whose shares are exchanged on the New York Stock Exchange, the Nasdaq, or the American Stock Exchange.

From all outward appearances, owning stock is a most modest take on the average CEO's perks. There's no plush furniture to speak of; no reserved parking space for your Mercedes Benz nor a chauffeur to whisk you to and from the helipad. You won't get a secretary to clean up your correspondence. And by the way, forget about playing on the office intercom, too.

Despite the lack of flash, you're in line for some worthwhile benefits. First of all, you join many other shareholders in ownership of a vital corporation that manufactures goods or provides key services; that hires workers, buys equipment, and fans out across the globe in search of new markets; and—you hope—that knows how to turn a profit. The list of shareholders may include pension funds, money managers, mutual fund gurus, movie stars, and athletes, a host of groups and individuals who are looking to tap into a company's growth while saving for the future.

There's more, starting with a slice of your company's profits, or earnings, a label Wall Street likes. Shareholders get to benefit from a well-run company and its flow of profits in several ways. First, companies with a history of strong earnings are likely to turn around and share a chunk of their intake with investors in the form of a dividend. Profits also help your stock investment to increase in value over time. Many stock market investors gauge the worth of a stock by the value of its parent company's earnings. Companies that bring in more money and retain a larger share of their sales have more funds for expansion. They can conquer new markets. They can hire more workers. They can increase dividends. They can take over other corporations and increase earnings as well. They can *grow*.

Most of the time when there's an increase in the profits that a company pulls in, you'll see its stock price climb. That increase, called capital appreciation, is the second—and arguably the most beneficial way—a stock makes money for shareholders.

There's potential downside, too. Don't be fooled—stocks don't always appreciate in value. Sometimes they slump or, individual companies fall behind the times. They lose ground to the competition or their products fall out of favor with consumers. Whatever the reason, that kind of sea change is bound to affect their profits, and soon enough the company's share price as well. Read the financial pages of your local paper, or leaf through the *Wall Street Journal* or *Barron's* to find accounts of companies that slip and whose shares slide.

How do you fight that? There are a couple of ways. For one, thoroughly investigate any stock you're about to buy. Read up on the company that has caught your interest. Request a prospectus, and check out the management. Look at key stats listed in the Numerology section of Chapter 4. Compare the figures with the broad market and with the company's rivals in the same industry as well.

Another tactic: When you buy a stock, prepare to hold it for 5 years or more. Even great companies with the savviest of managements and the most innovative of products see poor results at some time or another. Most of them find a way to bounce back. Should you sell a firm's stock on a whim,

THE EXCHANGES

What exactly is the stock market? What are the exchanges? Is there any difference between the New York Stock Exchange and the Nasdaq? Should you care?

Whether you're into investing or a casual observer of the ups and downs of the economy, you hear a lot about this mysterious thing called a market. The fact is, there is no one market. There are exchanges, where stocks are traded in much the same way old works of art are traded at an auction. There are people who come to market ready to buy. There are those who are participating because they want to sell a commodity—in this case shares.

The market is simply a large clearinghouse where shares trade hands. An exchange is just another take on that same meeting place for buyers and seller, a spot where orders for shares are sorted out and filled. The largest is the New York Stock Exchange (NYSE), often called the Big Board, if only because the companies it lists are often large corporate movers and shares. The other well-known exchange is the American Stock Exchange or Amex. There are regional exchanges as well in cities such as Chicago, Philadelphia, Boston, and Cincinnati. Overseas, there are exchanges in most nations, including France (located in Paris), the United Kingdom (London), and Germany (Frankfurt).

You might have heard the Nasdaq often called "over-the-counter market" or OTC, a name professionals use for the exact same exchange. The Nasdaq is no different from the NYSE, except that it is a computer network run by the National Association of Securities Dealers where brokers can match orders to buy and sell shares.

What does it all mean to you? Well, in all honesty, not particularly much. When you trade in shares you'll very likely rely on a broker to arrange your order and buy or sell your shares. That process is the same whether you go through a discount outfit such as Jack White or a full-service brokerage such as Salomon Smith Barney. Your broker will deal with dealers who work at the exchanges or field large orders and match buyers with sellers.

And, for the individual investor, there's not much difference between the NYSE, Amex, and Nasdaq, either. Your focus, after all, should be on the company you choose to invest in, which will determine how much you make on your money. Figure 3.3 provides data about the principal exchanges.

Figure 3.3   The Principal Stock Exchanges

There are three main stock exchanges in the United States. Here's how many companies have been listed on each over time.

Exchange	1980	1985	1990	1995	1999
New York Stock Exchange (NYSE)	1,570	1,541	1,774	2,675	3,025
Nasdaq	2,894	4,136	4,132	5,122	4,829
American Stock Exchange (AMEX)	892	782	859	791	769

Source: The Securities Industry Association.

on one bad turn in fortune, you lose out on the chance to realize any gain during a rebound.

Or, finally, you can leave stock-picking to a professional money manager and invest in a mutual fund that has a stake in company shares. While mutual funds are discussed in Chapters 7 and 8, even as a mutual fund investor you'll want to know the nuances of the stock market so you can better appreciate what's happening to your fund investment.

The trick of investing in stocks is essentially this: Look to take advantage of a company's great track record, but at the same time, try to contain risks as much as possible. Painstaking research will help. And so will patience.

WHAT'S IN IT FOR THEM

Why in the world would a company hand over a piece of its ownership to the cold, insensitive world outside its headquarters? Money.

Offering shares to the public bags a company a lot in funds. In 1999, 545 companies raised $69.2 billion in initial public offerings, according to *IPO Reporter*, a weekly publication that tracks how many stocks are brought to market. Those proceeds can be earmarked for any number of projects or tasks. Perhaps the chief of information technology for Acme Corporation says she'd like to upgrade computer systems. Maybe the sales force needs new cellular telephones. Perhaps a new factory could put out the company's wares cheaper and quicker. Whatever the need, selling shares to the public can fund it.

That kind of reasoning has brought a number of big-name companies to the market of late. Shares of United Parcel Service or UPS started trading on the New York Stock Exchange in late 1999. Goldman Sachs made its way onto the Big Board during the same year.

One reason corporate management loves selling shares to the public is that there's no interest to pay. When it sells shares, a company receives the cash with little in the way of formal obligations. There is no money that needs to be paid back to creditors and no interest payments to make as is the case when a corporation issues bonds or borrows from the bank. Once the shares are on the open market, the top brass is free to take the money and do as it pleases.

Corporate management doesn't get a free ride after finishing the stock offering, however. Shareholders get to vote on crucial issues affecting the company and its operations. If management decides to issue more stock or if another corporation makes an offer to take over, shareholders will receive ballots to vote yes or no on the issue. Shareholders are told of the bid and will often get to vote for or against the merger in question.

Shareholders have expectations, too. As owners, they want their cake, a goodly amount of icing, and the right to eat it a la mode, too. First and foremost, they look for their stock to appreciate in value and generate a sizable return. They'd like a dividend, if at all possible, thank-you.

Should they own large numbers of shares or if many band together behind one issue, shareholders often can make things uncomfortable for the corporate management. Big institutional investors like mutual funds, or pensions like the California Public Employees' Retirement System (Calpers) can be some of the peskiest backseat drivers around because they often own thousands, sometimes millions of shares, and hold a lot of sway. At times, they'll question the chief executive officer and all her cohorts— publicly. They try to unite shareholders large and small behind their causes. They may even get a company to take steps to sell itself off to a suitor or to lop off unprofitable units—all in the name of increasing the value of its stock.

That's why CEOs and high-ranking company officials often stress "shareholder value" in the pages of the financial press. What they mean is this: "We hear you dear investor, and we intend to make enough money to help this stock go up, or we'll figure a way to boost your returns."

Paying the Middle Man

Also keep in mind that other folks benefit from your choice to become a shareholder, too. Unless you buy—or sell—shares directly from a company itself (explained later in Chapter 4), you'll have to pay an intermediary, a middleman, to take your money and purchase shares on the stock market. The dealer is your broker. The price you pay is called a commission.

While the task at hand is essentially the same transaction after transaction, the commission, or cut, you pay a broker varies from firm to firm. For discount outfits on the Internet, like E*TRADE or Ameritrade, you can pay between $10 and $15 for a purchase or sale of shares—sometimes less. If you

SIGN LANGUAGE—SYMBOLS

The stock market has its own special way of identifying companies—a tag, usually three or four letters long—that analysts, brokers, and other professionals use to refer to a company. That abbreviation or nickname for a stock is called a ticker, ticker symbol, or sometimes just a symbol. Tickers originated in the days when brokers and institutional investors followed a ticker tape spewing from a telegraph machine and needed an easy way to identify companies without spelling out long names. There was only a little bit of room on the ticker tape, and there were a lot of companies to identify. Tickers have since stuck and often come in handy when talking to a broker or looking a stock up online.

Symbols vary in length, according to the exchange where a stock trades. New York Stock Exchange companies have one-, two-, or three-letter symbols (e.g., C is Citigroup, GE is General Electric, PEP is Pepsi). American Stock Exchange firms have either two- or three-letter symbols. On the Nasdaq, stocks carry four, and sometimes five-letter symbols (e.g., INTC stands for Intel). Figure 3.4 lists some well-known symbols.

use a firm such as Charles Schwab & Co. you might pay $29.95 for the same deal. And, at a full-service broker, that same order to buy or sell shares will cost more, possibly as much as $60 all told.

Brokers are discussed in a later chapter. For now, however, here are a couple suggestions. First, always figure a broker's commission into your initial investment and your sale of shares. After all, it's money coming out of

Figure 3.4 Symbolism

Ticker symbols for some popular stocks.

COMPANY	TICKER	EXCHANGE
General Electric	GE	New York Stock Exchange
Coca-Cola	COK	New York Stock Exchange
Intel	INTC	Nasdaq
General Motors	GM	New York Stock Exchange
Cisco Systems	CSCO	Nasdaq
SBC Corp.	SBC	New York Stock Exchange
Dell Computer	DELL	Nasdaq
Foodarama Supermarkets	FSM	AMEX
Greenbriar	GBR	AMEX

BULL MARKET, BEAR MARKET, CRASH, OR CORRECTION?

The phrases "bull market" and "bear market" are often used to describe the market and the overall mood of investors. A bull market is a time when stocks are rising in value. Bulls are investors, market players, who feel the market—or a particular stock—is going to keep climbing on that same upward trajectory. A bear market, meanwhile, is a period when stock prices slide. A bear feels the market is headed downward. How far do share prices have to drop to constitute a bear market? There's no standard decrease, but, by and large, a 15 percent fall, as measured by the Dow Jones Industrial Average or the S&P 500 qualifies for a bear market. Bear markets tend to show up every five years or so.

Bears in the wild come in several species, some with claws that are sharper than others. Bear markets, too, come in a few varieties, some more ferocious than others. The scariest bear market around is a crash. During a crash, share prices drop drastically during a day, maybe two, of trading. The last crash the stock market suffered was in October 1987, when share prices fell 22 percent. The only other true crash occurred in October 1929, on the eve of the Great Depression.

Another less ornery sort of bear is a correction. It knocks the wind out of stocks, usually a good 10 percent of their share price at least. The nice thing about a correction? Well, even though a correction tends to hit the market every two years, its impact on stocks is less than a crash or bear market (see Figure 3.5 to review definitions).

Figure 3.5 Bulls, Bears, Crashes, Corrections

The pros use the following terms for stock market activity.

WHAT IT'S CALLED	WHAT IT MEANS
Bull Market	The prices of many stocks or stock benchmarks like the S&P 500 are increasing in value.
Bear Market	Share prices for many companies and the value of market benchmarks are falling; experts say a 15% decrease in the value of the Dow Jones Industrial Average or the S&P 500 constitutes a bear market.
Correction	Share prices for many companies and the value of market benchmarks are falling; experts say a 10% decrease in the value of the Dow Jones Industrial Average of the S&P 500 signals a correction.
Crash	The scariest fall of all, a market crash, occurs when stocks shed 20% or more of their value in one day. The last big market crash took place in October 1987.

your gains and off on its way to line the pockets of others. The need to pay commissions should serve as a motivation not only to avoid trading over and over (which would run up your commission bill) but also to wait until you have a sizable chunk of cash. One rule of thumb: Buy enough stock to keep your commission to 1 percent or less of the total sale. For example, the transaction cost of a $2,500 stock purchase shouldn't be more than $25. If your broker charges more—say $40—then, you should wait until you can buy $4,000 worth of the shares of whatever company has caught your fancy.

THE INVISIBLE CERTIFICATE

Once you purchase shares, don't expect your stock certificate to come in the mail. Don't starting looking for a cozy place around the house to hide proof of purchase once you've bought stock.

Sure, we all remember seeing stock certificates—most probably in old movies. Widows would clutch them tightly when a villain came over to foreclose the mortgage. Or, once they had dynamited the bank safe, robbers would snatch them out of safe-deposit boxes.

Certificates have quite a history, and in the past, they were beautifully decorated documents. They've also headed the way of the dinosaur. In this era, stock ownership, stock purchases, and sales are recorded electronically and monitored in accounts you might set up with your brokerage or in some cases with the company whose shares you own.

If you're nostalgic, get ready to pay the price for your piece of the past. Some brokerage firms charge a fee to issue you a certificate. But who knows . . . these days the value of the old-time certificates has risen and they have become collectors' items.

AMERICAN DEPOSITORY RECEIPTS

You don't need a passport to buy shares of an overseas company like Toyota, or Sony. If you're wondering just what's the ticket abroad, you'll find it in three letters: ADR, or American depository receipt. Don't let the acronym scare you. An ADR operates much like an ordinary stock with each ADR representing a set number of shares in a foreign company held in an overseas stock market. An ADR for Toyota, for example, represents shares of the company's stock in Japan. A sponsor bank—Bank of New York and Citibank are the two largest in the business—buys and holds the shares, negotiates fees with foreign brokers, and goes so far as to make sure a daily price quote in dollars appears in the newspaper.

With interest in overseas investing booming, the ADR market mushroomed from $40.6 billion in 1988 to $563 billion in 1998 according to the

Bank of New York. The number of corporations available to tap into has grown as well. From Brazil's primary telephone company Telebras to British Petroleum, from pharmaceutical giant Glaxo Wellcome to cellular equipment maker Nokia, the choices are broad enough to cover just about every industry imaginable. There are many nations represented in the ranks of ADRs as well including companies in Ghana, the Philippines, Argentina, and South Africa (see Figure 3.6).

That's not to say there aren't factors to consider prior to jumping into the global investing fray. One thing to check is whether the ADR is sponsored or unsponsored. Sponsored issues must conform to many U.S. reporting requirements, ensuring that investors receive regular documentation such as annual reports and the like covering the company's results and operations. Another factor investors should consider is the nation where the company operates. A foreign company's results often are tied to its local currency. A strong home economy can often diminish local currency risks, that is, the effect exchange rates have on the company's profits. Should that local money's value shrink relative to the U.S. dollar, investors might be in for a rough ride. The stability of the local government and economy are other things to ponder, especially the possibility of political upheaval or nationalization of key industries.

If that seems like a lot of precautions to take, you might want to think about investing in an overseas mutual fund (one that focuses entirely on companies outside the 50 states). Another option: a global mutual fund (one that mixes investments in U.S. companies with stakes in foreign corporations). Besides monitoring the world's markets and country-by-country outlooks, mutual funds give you a measure of diversity spread over foreign shares.

Figure 3.6   ADRs

Here is a list of some of the overseas companies whose ADRs trade on these shores. Some you may recognize; others may be unfamiliar.

COMPANY	HOME NATION	INDUSTRY
Ashanti Goldfields	Ghana	Gold
BP Amoco	United Kingdom	Oil
Canon	Japan	Photography, electronics
Caribbean Cement	Jamaica	Construction
DaimlerChrysler	Germany	Autos
LVMH Moet-Hennessy Louis Vuitton	France	Fashion
Royal Dutch Petroleum	Netherlands	Oil
Mitsubishi	Japan	Autos
Nokia	Finland	Mobile phone
Reuters	United Kingdom	Media
Sony	Japan	Electronics
Telebras	Brazil	Telecommunications
Vodafone Airtouch	United Kingdom	Telecommunications
Volkswagen	Germany	Autos

WEB SIGHTINGS
AMERICAN DEPOSITORY RECEIPTS

The investment bank J.P. Morgan runs a Web site (www.adr.com) that keeps a close eye on ADRs. It lists ADRs, stock prices, and data, and provides plentiful background information on overseas companies that trade on the U.S. market.

ARMCHAIR TRAVELER?

One way of getting around the question of overseas investing is by putting your money in big multinational corporations. That's what Bill Roach, an African American money manager and President of the Atlanta investment firm Globalt does. "Eighty percent of the world's goods and services are sold outside of the United States," notes Roach, "and when you consider that 19 of every 20 consumers lives abroad, you want to be in companies that have a strategy to tap into growth overseas."

Roach swears by global trade as an engine for domestic companies to increase earnings to such a degree that he won't invest in a stock unless 20 percent of a company's revenues come from beyond U.S. borders. Where does Roach find the stats? Easy. He reads through company annual reports and 10-K filings, sources discussed further in Chapter 4. He looks a company up and down to make sure it's on the right track and that overseas sales meet his target.

A good example is Cisco Systems, says Roach. As of 2000, the maker of computer network equipment and gear used for hooking up PCs to the Internet made 28 percent of its sales overseas, 24 percent coming from Europe and the balance from Asia and Latin America. The list of corporations that meet the 20 percent overseas sales mark is a long one, full of household names such as Citigroup and American Express. "We're certainly buying into the big, pretty companies, like Proctor & Gamble, Intel, Nike, and Microsoft," he says. "That way, we've found a way to play global economic growth through some familiar companies at home."

WHAT'S UP NEXT

Now that you've seen how the stock market works, it's time to sharpen a pencil, turn on your PC, and jump in. In Chapter 4 you will learn how to choose stocks. The information includes the numbers and sources professional money managers use as well as trade secrets money managers refer to again and again.

4

HOW TO PICK THE BEST STOCKS

So you now know how stocks work, and some of the ins and outs of owning company shares. And yet, you still freeze up at the slightest mention of calling a broker or buying shares of a company online.

One guess why? You don't know what to choose.

Too many choices at hand have a funny way of spoiling a good thing, and the stock market is no exception. Just open up the financial pages of the daily newspaper one day, and glance at column after column of stock-yields, 52-week highs and lows, and more. You'll quickly realize how difficult it is to find the information that matters. You can, however, narrow your focus to make a level-headed investment choice if you learn which "experts" to trust and know the criteria that the professionals use to trim the market down to size.

NARROWING CHOICES DOWN

To make the best possible decision on which stocks to own, you'll need to do some research. You'll want to check out the company's main focus—the products it makes and markets it serves. You'll want to know how much a company makes and how its financial results—earnings and sales, for example—have done over time. You'll want to read up on the folks who run operations at headquarters. You'll want the skinny on what competitors are doing and how well they've fared.

There are many places to look and plenty of information that's yours to have with little effort. You can find it in reference books and stock analyses put out by research firms like Standard & Poor's, Morningstar, or Value Line.

REALITY CHECK

He's a hedge fund manager in San Francisco. He manages $25 million and counting in assets for his own firm, Thomason Capital management, LLC. You wouldn't know it by looking at him, but William S. Thomason, 38, a former director of portfolio management for Parnassus, got his start in investing 20 years ago by putting $25 a month into the stock market.

It started the day Thomason, a teen growing up in Detroit in the late 1970s, asked his mother how stocks worked. He remembers that she went to the library, borrowed some books on the financial markets, and encouraged him to read up. Thomason began calling up companies to get prospectuses when he stumbled across DSPs—direct reinvestment plans set up to let investors buy shares without going through a broker. "I started with companies any teenager would know," he recalls. "First off, I put in $25 a month into Coca-Cola. I got my stock certificate in the mail, and I was on my way." Thomason moved on to other companies whose names he recognized and quickly had a burgeoning portfolio on his hands, with stakes in McDonald's, Wrigley's, Detroit Edison, and AT&T.

Even after he got a degree in electrical engineering and went into the high-finance world of money management, Thomason never left his direct purchase plans behind. In fact, he still owns Coke and has set up accounts with Lucent Technologies and other corporations. When he got married 4 years ago, he enrolled his wife in Intel's direct purchase program.

You'll be able to tap into data aplenty on Web sites such as Quicken.com or Investorama. And in many cases, it's provided by the companies themselves in public documents such as annual reports or 10-K filings.

HOW GOOD IDEAS MAKE FOR GREAT STOCKS

It all starts with a few good ideas. And that's the hard part.

Coming up with a list of 4, 6, even 10 companies to invest in may sound easy, but it's a lot easier said than done.

Many of the great investors of all time have turned to one starting point again and again: companies that make things you buy. Peter Lynch, the stock-picking guru who once made Fidelity Magellan into the largest, best-known mutual fund around and arguably is this nation's most famous former portfolio manager advises novices to think of products you use. Items that you think are good values, or ingenious in some way qualify. It might be your television set, the shoes on your feet, or something in your refrigerator or medicine cabinet. It might include the brands of juice you drink, the cough syrup you rely on, or the maker of your stereo system. The company that manufactures your car or even the shirts you like best can be good places to start, too. Whatever has caught your attention, chances are it has attracted other shoppers at the grocery store, department store, or on the Internet and they are helping to push that company's sales to the stars.

Once you've compiled a list of things that appeal to you, check the labels to find out the manufacturer or the parent company. At that point, you can surf the Net or check a Web site such as Dailystocks or Yahoo! to see whether the makers of your favorite brands have *publicly traded* stocks available to investors like yourself.

You might also choose companies that do business in your hometown. If you live in Seattle, you might want to look into Microsoft or Boeing, which both have headquarters in the Emerald City or nearby. St. Louisans might look into Monsanto or Anheuser-Busch. There's good reason to consider investing in hometown stocks. Being close to the company in question, you may be privy to the scuttlebutt wafting about in the factory, or at corporate headquarters. Think of all the conversations you have with neighbors and friends about their jobs. Although it seems like routine chitchat, many times you'll get a sense of just how well the business is doing.

By no means limit your ideas to the store, the furnishings around the house, or the companies in town. You should glean as much as you can from the financial press including newspapers like the *Wall Street Journal,* weeklies like *Barron's,* and monthlies like *Black Enterprise* or *Worth.* Because most financial and business publications pride themselves on their coverage of the stock market, they include interviews with all-star analysts or articles about the latest successes of hotshot portfolio managers. Television broadcasts including CNBC, *Wall Street Week,* and the *Nightly Business Report* provide a wealth of

Figure 4.1   How Great Stock Ideas Are Born

SOURCE	WHAT IT WORKS
What you buy, what you use, what you like	Products and services you like probably are winning over other customers as well.
What's close by	You're likely to get news about the hometown companies both good and bad through the local grapevine.
The financial press	Magazines, newspapers, telecasts, and interviews are all chock-full of investment ideas and recommendations, as well as some research.

tips on the market and companies on the rise. Those same sources are often brimming with news about company stocks that look particularly attractive or investment ideas well worth your time. And, good ideas often lead to good investments, once they've been properly researched. Figure 4.1 outlines likely sources for leads about stocks.

FACT-FINDING

The press is always a good launching point when you are hunting for facts about companies, and will often have culled information from a variety of sources. *Fortune, Forbes, BusinessWeek,* and others make a living picking the minds of company management. A text search in a local newspaper might also turn up articles and tidbits of information on corporations near and wide.

Check search engines on the Web. They sometimes provide you a good amount of investment data themselves. On the Yahoo! site, you can

---

WEB SIGHTINGS
STOCK RESEARCH MADE EASY

The Web contains treasures aplenty on companies large and small. These are some of the best:

- Dailystocks (www.dailystocks.com) has compiled a seemingly endless list of company references, industry sites, investments forums, and stats pages. You could easily click away for days and not exhaust half of the links Dailystocks provides investors.

- Investorama (www.investorama.com) is much like Dailystocks—a veritable clearinghouse of every sort of investing information and data you could possibly want. And like Dailystocks, Investorama is a springboard, a list of links to Web sites of every size and sort imaginable. You'll find a portal to Web sites on overseas investing, for instance, or direct stock purchase plans, too.

- Yahoo (www.yahoo.com), Altavista (www.altavista.com), Lycos (www.lycos.com), Excite (www.excite.com) all are search engines and offer a first line of attack. A search engine allows you to hunt far and wide through the Web for sites that have what you're looking for. All you need to do is supply a few key words (clues about the subject you're researching) that help the search engine locate places you might like to look at.

find earnings estimates provided by Zacks Investment Research, a company that interviews financial analysts on Wall Street and then calculates consensus figures for profit projections, revenue estimates, and even brokerage firm ratings.

Next, there are great sources at the company itself. Start with a home address on the Web. Many corporations now have Web pages that offer a smorgasbord of information. You'll find a rundown of company products, information on past and current results, and news releases that spell out everything from new product launches to reaction to a competitor's latest moves. And, perhaps most importantly, you'll find a company's annual report and Form 10-K (see Figure 4.2).

Whether you download them off the Web or call a company to get its annual report and 10-K, they're essential documents to have. Both outline a company's results over time. Everything from earnings per share to sales, from debt to a letter from the CEO discussing strategy and results are packaged together in a document you certainly should read.

What's the difference between an annual report and Form 10-K? Well, the annual is a glossier document. It's usually festooned with bright illustrations, fancy charts, and snazzy photography. So if pictures make or break a book for you, the annual will definitely be your favorite. Make an effort, nevertheless to get the 10-K and work your way through it. You'll immediately be able to tell that the corporate art department didn't have to work overtime on the 10-K. It's a meaty, thick text and can seem a bit dry. Get over it. The Securities and Exchange Commission (SEC) requires companies to file the 10-K, and it is packed full of warts and worries management doesn't put in the annual report. For openers, you find anywhere from a paragraph to a couple of pages on the risks a company faces, and on its competition in the industry. What's more, any section or subsection in an annual report is there for the reading in a 10-K, probably spelled out in greater detail. The annual report is the company's document. The 10-K, on the other hand, is primarily a government document. Often, a company will supply you with its 10-K. Otherwise it's available from the SEC in Washington, D.C., or online at Hoover's (www.hoovers.com), a library of information on companies traded in the stock market. Another source of company reports is Edgar Online, a site that offers SEC filings and company reports free at the Internet address (www.freeedgar.com).

You'll want to check sources outside the company, too. Stock market and industry analysts make a living studying companies and their prospects. This has always been a big business, but suddenly it has been booming, mushrooming during the past decade to help feed the need of investors big and small for information. The analysts do a lot, too. They provide investors with an intelligent interpretation of company and industrywide news. They gather up and glean a company's vital statistics—its P/E multiple, it's projected earnings growth, its price-to-book value. They'll even provide projects or

Figure 4.2 A Company's Annual Report and 10-K

Corporations are required to supply investors and the public with reports on their performance. The slicker version, the annual report is often prettier, printed on better paper, and full of colorful illustrations and charts. It's also somewhat condensed. A more thorough, yet blander, document is the 10-K, a filing required by the Securities and Exchange Commission. The document provides an in-depth look at the company.

The Colorful Annual

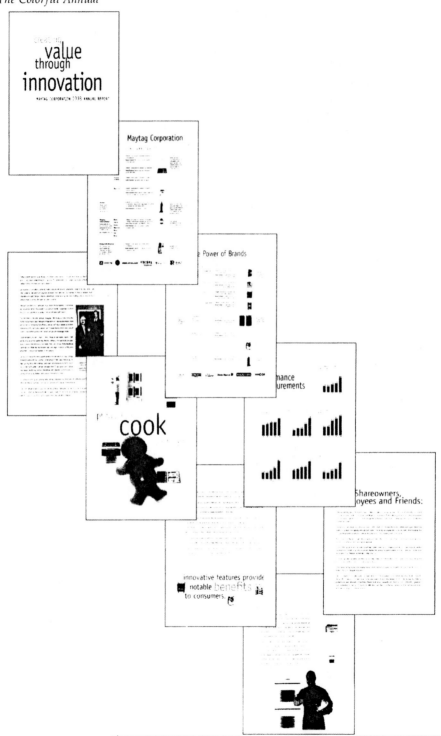

Figure 4.2 *(continued)*

The Staid 10-K

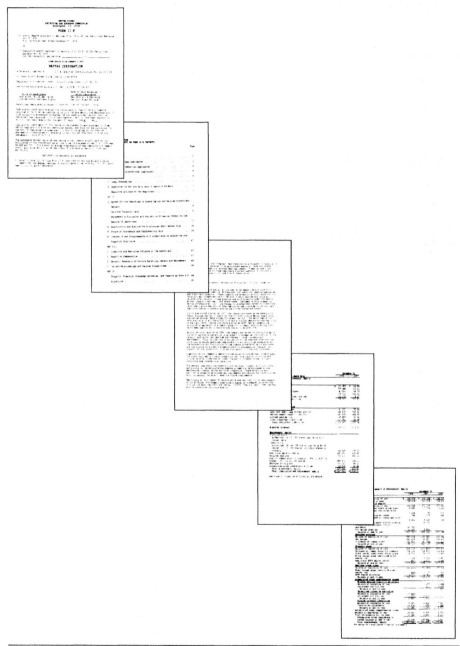

Source: Maytag Corporation 1998 Annual Report, Maytag Corporation 1998 10-K.

estimates for both a company's profits and share price not only this week but this year.

Not so long ago, that kind of data and analysis wasn't as readily available as it is now. If you had a brokerage account with a firm like Merrill Lynch, Salomon Smith Barney, or Paine Webber, your broker would get you access to reports put together by research analysts or equity analysts. You'd then have a document that included facts and figures, an explanation of trends and company news. Better yet, the whole thing would be packaged by an expert on the company and its industry, often someone with a business degree or special qualifications. Brokerage reports can still be some of the best info around; and these days, you don't always have to have a brokerage account to get them. If you have an online trading account, you can often receive them gratis.

THREE SHEETS TO THE WIND

The art might be a joy to behold. The chief executive's words might serve up inspiration aplenty. Still, the annual report you get from the company wouldn't be worth the glossy paper it's printed on without three little charts.

They are, in no specific order, the company's balance sheet, income statement, and cash flow statement. All three are full of numbers. They have accounting terms labeled in plain view. Management will also include a couple years' worth of figures so you can compare one column of numbers with another. And though they may look very much like the driest, most unappealing portion of an annual report, each qualifies as a "must read," pages you should hunt up as soon as you can.

Income Statement

Start reading the income statement from the bottom (see Figure 4.3). There, you'll find a company's earnings, a corporation's profits, or what professionals call the "bottom line." At the end of the income statement, there may be a breakout of earnings per share, a convenient measure of profits and how they relate to a company's share price. You'll also find out how much shareholders made in dividends paid by management.

Next stop, go to the top. At the very beginning of a company's income statement, you'll get an idea of what customers think of its products or services. On the very first line, a company will chart out its sales or revenue, that is what customers think about the products it produces and whether they like them more than they used to. An income statement will also give you an idea of how much it costs a company to get its wares to market. When sales go up and the cost of sales rises, too, you can bet that a company is

Figure 4.3   The Income Statement

This part of a company's annual report or 10-K breaks down profits, pure and simple. It shows how a company made money, how much money it made per share of its stock, and how much—if any—it paid in dividends.

Look for:

1. Sales	The money a company brought in by just taking care of business.
2. Expenses	What's being spent by management to keep the business going.
3. Net Income or Earning per Share	Profits in a form that is easy to understand and track.

CONSOLIDATED
STATEMENTS OF INCOME

In thousands except per share data	Year Ended December 31		
	1998	1997	1996
1. Net sales	$ 4,069,290	$ 3,407,911	$ 3,001,656
Cost of sales	2,887,663	2,471,623	2,180,213
Gross profit	1,181,627	936,288	821,443
2. Selling, general and administrative expenses	658,889	578,015	512,364
Restructuring charge			40,000
Operating income	522,738	358,273	269,079
Interest expense	(62,765)	(58,995)	(43,006)
Other - net	10,912	1,277	2,164
Income before income taxes, minority interest and extraordinary item	470,885	300,555	228,237
Income taxes	176,100	109,800	89,000
Income before minority interest and extraordinary item	294,785	190,755	139,237
Minority interest	(8,275)	(7,265)	(1,260)
Income before extraordinary item	286,510	183,490	137,977
Extraordinary item - loss on early retirement of debt	(5,900)	(3,200)	(1,548)
Net income	$ 280,610	$ 180,290	$ 136,429
Basic earnings (loss) per common share:			
Income before extraordinary item	$ 3.12	$ 1.90	$ 1.36
Extraordinary item - loss on early retirement of debt	(0.06)	(0.03)	(0.02)
Net income	3.05	1.87	1.34
Diluted earnings (loss) per common share:			
Income before extraordinary item	$ 3.05	$ 1.87	$ 1.35
Extraordinary item - loss on early retirement of debt	(0.06)	(0.03)	(0.02)
Net income	2.99	1.84	1.33

3.

See notes to consolidated financial statements

Source: Maytag Corporation.

enjoying something of a growth spurt, and is expanding to help get its popular goods out to eager buyers.

The numbers in an income statement under "Operating Expenses" show just how lean and efficient of an operation management runs. It's a good idea to examine those costs over time, and compare them to the growth of sales and earnings to get an idea of how a company is expanding to meet its costs.

Cash Flow Statement

The next chart on your annual report agenda, the cash flow statement, shows a numerical breakdown of how a company is bringing in money for its operations and just what it pays out to fuel its growth. You'll see how much money flows in the front door at headquarters in the form of earnings or profits. You'll also see details on how much a company doles out for financing—money borrowed by issuing bonds, or money paid out to shareholders. There will also be entries accounting for funds the company put toward plant, property, and equipment. That's a fancy way of saying how much the honchos funneled into factories, offices, cars, cellular phones, and the like to improve how

Figure 4.4   The Cash Flow Statement

A cash flow statement shows how a company is bringing money in and putting it to use. It indicates how companies raised funds in the stock or bond markets and then funneled it into new equipment or technology to help make even more money.

Look for:

1. Investments   Companies use a cash flow statement to show investors how they're putting money to use by purchasing new equipment or businesses.

2. Stocks or Bonds   A cash flow statement also tells you how much money a company has raised in the stock or bond markets.

Other – net		26,258	1,930	(1,456)
Net cash provided by operating activities		539,878	357,665	264,893
Investing activities				
Capital expenditures		(161,251)	(229,561)	(219,902)
Investment in securities			(10,015)	
Business acquisitions, net of cash acquired			(148,283)	(29,625)
Total investing activities		(161,251)	(387,859)	(249,527)
Financing activities				
Proceeds from issuance of notes payable		14,687	60,493	34,094
Repayment of notes payable		(20,880)	(3,142)	
Proceeds from issuance of long-term debt		102,922	133,015	26,536
Repayment of long-term debt		(75,743)	(124,123)	(20,500)
Debt repurchase premiums		(5,900)	(3,200)	(1,548)
Stock repurchases		(318,139)	(138,051)	(164,439)
Forward stock purchase amendment		(63,782)		
Stock options exercised and other common stock transactions		52,643	52,308	6,795
Dividends		(70,537)	(65,243)	(57,223)
Proceeds from sale of LLC member interest			100,000	
Investment by joint venture partner		6,900	18,975	8,625
Proceeds from interest rate swaps				38,038
Total financing activities		(377,829)	31,032	(129,622)
Effect of exchange rates on cash		(147)	(390)	585
Increase (decrease) in cash and cash equivalents		651	448	(113,671)
Cash and cash equivalents at beginning of year		27,991	27,543	141,214
Cash and cash equivalents at end of year	$	28,642	$ 27,991	$ 27,543

See notes to consolidated financial statements

4-1

Source: Maytag Corporation.

they get goods and services out to the public and boost earnings. A company that reels in more operating cash flow than it spits out in the form of costs is in better shape than an outfit that doesn't. It has "positive" cash flow, money that then shows up in the form of earnings (see Figure 4.4).

Balance Sheet

The last stop on your chart tour should be the balance sheet. Here you'll get an idea of what a company brings in and how much it owes. Balance sheet entries for current assets show how much cash a company keeps in its coffers, how much money it is due for the sale of goods, and how much of an inventory of salable items it has managed to store up. You'll also get a sense of the worth of the land and equipment management controls. On the liabilities or debt side, you'll see how much a company owes to creditors like banks or bonds holders. Take assets, subtract liabilities like debt, and you have equity, or the value in the hands of shareholders. A tip: If current assets are worth more than current liabilities by a wide margin, professionals get a sense that a company will be able to service its debt without having to issue more stock or more bonds (see Figure 4.5).

SUPER SLEUTHS

A handful of independent companies hash through numbers and rate stocks that you might want to check out. There is a good reason to call them *independent*. Often, the brokerage firms that put companies under the microscope and pore over number after number have two relationships with corporate management. Yes, they hunt up information on companies and scout about for industry news so they can make good judgments on stocks and their prospects. At the same time, however, their corporate banking units might turn to the most promising companies to line up deals to issue stock and bring bonds to market.

That possible conflict of interest can confuse things. In fact, the big brokerage houses have a reputation for being a little light in their pronouncements on stocks. The intent here is not to tar all of Wall Street with the same brush, but to point out how outside sources can provide both more information and a different viewpoint.

There are other advantages of looking over the surveys and data gathered up by firms such as Value Line, Standard & Poor's, and Morningstar. For starters, they are literally chock-full of news, numbers, and information. They'll let you know the big industry trends. They'll give you insight on how the economy affects a company you're interested in. They'll even rate a stock and estimate how a company's shares might fare in the market (see Figures 4.6, 4.7, and 4.8).

Figure 4.5 Balance Sheet

The balance sheet lets you see how much money a corporation has brought in, and how much it owes to creditors.

Look for:

1. Cash   Money on hand to pay down debt, purchase new equipment, or buy back shares.

2. Property and   Rock-solid assets often used to figure a company's price to book.
    Equipment

3. Debt   How much a company owes creditors.

CONSOLIDATED
BALANCE SHEETS

In thousands except share data	December 31 1998	1997
ASSETS		
Current assets		
1. Cash and cash equivalents	$ 28,642	$ 27,991
Accounts receivable, less allowance for doubtful accounts (1998 — $22,305; 1997 — $36,386)	472,979	473,741
Inventories	383,753	350,209
Deferred income taxes	39,014	46,073
Other current assets	44,474	36,703
Total current assets	968,862	934,717
Noncurrent assets		
Deferred income taxes	120,273	118,931
Prepaid pension cost	1,399	2,160
Intangible pension asset	62,811	33,819
Other intangibles, less allowance for amortization (1998 — $98,106; 1997 — $85,071)	424,312	433,595
Other noncurrent assets	44,412	49,660
Total noncurrent assets	653,207	638,165
Property, plant and equipment		
Land	19,317	19,597
Buildings and improvements	333,032	309,960
Machinery and equipment	1,499,872	1,427,276
Construction in progress	102,042	59,376
	1,954,263	1,816,209
Less accumulated depreciation	988,669	874,937
2. Total property, plant and equipment	965,594	941,272
Total assets	$ 2,587,663	$ 2,514,154

See notes to consolidated financial statements

36
MAYTAG CORPORATION

Figure 4.5 *(continued)*

In thousands except share data	December 31 1998	December 31 1997
LIABILITIES AND SHAREOWNERS' EQUITY		
Current liabilities		
Notes payable	$ 112,898	$ 112,843
Accounts payable	279,086	221,417
Compensation to employees	81,836	62,758
Accrued liabilities	176,701	161,344
Current portion of long-term debt	140,176	8,276
Total current liabilities	790,697	566,638
Noncurrent liabilities		
Deferred income taxes	21,191	23,666
Long-term debt, less current portion	446,505	549,524
Postretirement benefit liability	460,599	454,390
Accrued pension cost	69,660	31,308
Other noncurrent liabilities	117,392	99,096
Total noncurrent liabilities	1,115,347	1,157,984
Minority interest	174,055	173,723
Shareowners' equity		
Preferred stock:		
Authorized — 24,000,000 shares (par value $1.00)		
Issued — none		
Common stock:		
Authorized — 200,000,000 shares (par value $1.25)		
Issued — 117,150,593 shares, including shares in treasury	146,438	146,438
Additional paid-in capital	467,192	494,646
Retained earnings	760,115	542,118
Cost of common stock in treasury (1998 — 27,932,506 shares; 1997 — 22,465,256 shares)	(805,802)	(508,115)
Employee stock plans	(45,331)	(48,416)
Accumulated other comprehensive income	(15,048)	(10,862)
Total shareowners' equity	507,564	615,809
Total liabilities and shareowners' equity	$ 2,587,663	$ 2,514,154

3. Long-term debt, less current portion

See notes to consolidated financial statements

Source: Maytag Corporation.

91

Figure 4.6 Value Line

Value Line sheets provide information on a company's business, its profits, and its outlook. They're available at your local library, in brokerage firms' or financial planners' offices, and from Value Line itself at 800-634-3583.

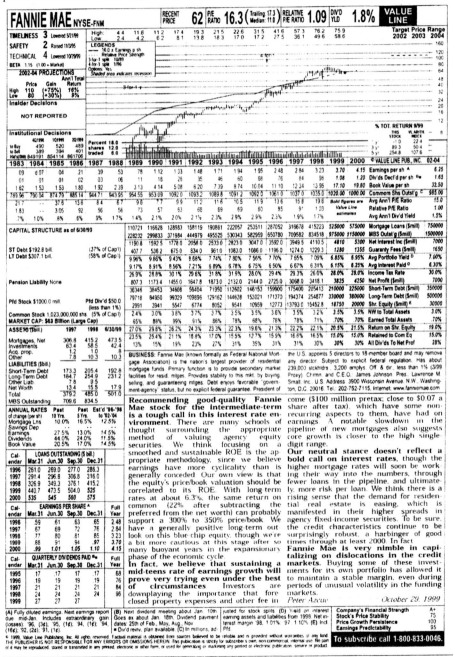

Source: Value Line.

Figure 4.7 Standard & Poor's

Standard & Poor's analysts pore over a company's operations to provide data on its business and its prospects. They provide a detailed breakdown of results over time. They're available either at your local library, at brokerage firms' or financial planners' offices, or from the company at 800-221-5277.

Lilly (Eli)

NYSE Symbol **LLY**

STOCK REPORTS

In S&P 500

13-MAY-00

Industry:
Health Care (Drugs - Major Pharmaceuticals)

Summary: This major worldwide maker of prescription drugs produces Prozac antidepressant, Zyprexa antipsychotic, diabetic care items, antibiotics, and animal health products.

S&P Opinion: Hold (★★★)	Recent Price Σ75¹§ Yield Σ 1.4%
	52 Wk Range Σ80¹§-54 12-Mo. P/E Σ 28.3

Quantitative Evaluations

Outlook
(1 Lowest–5 Highest)
Σ **2**

Fair Value
Σ**76¹§**

Risk
Σ **Average**

Earn./Div. Rank
Σ **A-**

Technical Eval.
Σ **Bullish**since 3/00

Rel. Strength Rank
(1 Lowest–99 Highest)
Σ **86**

Insider Activity
Σ **NA**

Earnings vs. Previous Year
▲=Up ▼=Down ▶=No Change

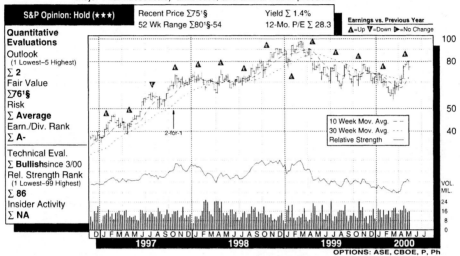

10 Week Mov. Avg. – –
30 Week Mov. Avg. · · ·
Relative Strength —

OPTIONS: ASE, CBOE, P, Ph

Overview - 08-MAR-00

Bolstered by growth in newer drugs, sales are expected to increase about 9% in 2000. Despite likely continued slippage in the company's principal Prozac antidepressant line, volume should be augmented by strong gains in Zyprexa (schizophrenia), ReoPro (antiplatelet agent), Gemzar (anticancer therapy), and Evista (osteoporosis). Zyprexa sales are expected to climb about 25%, aided by the drug's high efÆcacy proÆle and possible label expansion. ReoPro has emerged as a leading therapeutic agent to prevent adverse events following angioplasty procedures, while Gemzar should beneÆt from wider applications in oncology. A strong contribution is also seen from recently launched Actos treatment for type 2 diabetes. However, margins are likely to narrow somewhat, on the projected decline in Prozac sales.

Valuation - 08-MAR-00

The shares have been in a downtrend in recent months, mirroring weakness in the overall drug sector and investor concern over the Prozac patents, which begin to expire in February 2001. Prozac antidepressant, Lilly's principal product, accounted for 26% of 1999 sales from continuing operations, and an estimated 30% to 35% of proÆts. Prozac has been on the market for about 13 years, and sales have already begun to slip, under competitive pressure from newer antidepressants, most recently Forest Laboratories' Celexa. However, Lilly is working with Sepracor on an improved version of Prozac that could extend patent protection until 2015. LLY has also brought to market a number of other promising prescription drugs, such as ReoPro, Zyprexa, Gemzar, Evista and Actos, which should generate good double digit EPS growth for the foreseeable future. The shares, recently valued at a discount to the average drug group multiple, merit retention.

Key Stock Statistics

S&P EPS Est. 2000	2.63	Tang. Bk. Value/Share	4.49
P/E on S&P Est. 2000	28.7	Beta	0.72
S&P EPS Est. 2001	2.95	Shareholders	58,200
Dividend Rate/Share	1.04	Market cap. (B)	$ 82.3
Shs. outstg. (M)	1090.5	Inst. holdings	62%
Avg. daily vol. (M)	3.629		

Value of $10,000 invested 5 years ago: $ 49,742

Fiscal Year Ending Dec. 31

	2000	1999	1998	1997	1996	1995
Revenues (Million $)						
1Q	2.451	2,256	2,087	1,953	1,783	1,717
2Q	–	2,342	2,155	1,989	1,698	1,615
3Q	–	2,585	2,359	2,160	1,804	1,632
4Q	–	2,821	2,635	2,416	2,061	1,800
Yr.	–	10,003	9,237	8,518	7,347	6,764
Earnings Per Share ($)						
1Q	0.77	0.56	0.47	0.38	0.35	0.33
2Q	E0.60	0.52	0.44	-1.57	0.31	0.27
3Q	E0.70	0.67	0.46	0.40	0.37	0.27
4Q	E0.71	0.71	0.50	0.40	0.33	0.28
Yr.	E2.63	2.30	1.87	-0.35	1.36	1.13

Next earnings report expected: late July

Dividend Data (Dividends have been paid since 1885.)

Amount ($)	Date Decl.	Ex-Div. Date	Stock of Record	Payment Date
0.230	Jul. 19	Aug. 11	Aug. 13	Sep. 10 '99
0.230	Oct. 18	Nov. 10	Nov. 15	Dec. 10 '99
0.260	Dec. 20	Feb. 11	Feb. 15	Mar. 10 '00
0.260	Apr. 17	May. 11	May. 15	Jun. 09 '00

(continued)

Figure 4.7 *(continued)*

Eli Lilly and Company

Business Summary - 08-MAR-00

This leading maker of prescription drugs is well known for its popular Prozac antidepressant drug. It also produces a wide variety of other ethical drugs and animal health products. The company traces its history to Colonel Eli Lilly, a Union ofÆcer in the Civil War, who invented a process for coating pills with gelatin. Foreign operations accounted for 37% of sales in 1998. Lilly completed the divestiture of its medical device businesses in 1995.

Prozac, which accounted for 26% of sales from continuing operations in 1999, is Lilly's most important product. A selective serotonin reuptake inhibitor (SSRI), Prozac is also prescribed in many countries for bulimia and obsessive-compulsive disorder. About 13 years after its Ærst launch, Prozac remains the world's most widely prescribed antidepressant with about 20% of the U.S. market. Another growing central nervous system drug is Zyprexa, a new breakthrough treatment for schizophrenia (19% of 1999 sales).

Endocrine agents (14%) are another key business. Lilly was a pioneer in the early commercialization of animal-based insulin, as well as genetically engineered human insulin. Licensed from Genentech, recombinant insulin is sold as Humulin. Other endocrine products include Humatrope, a recombinant human growth hormone, and Humalog, a rapid-acting recombinant insulin.

Other drugs (34%) include anti-infectives such as Ceclor/cefaclor, Vancocin HCl, KeØex and Keftab, and Lorabid; Evista, a drug used in the prevention and treatment of osteoporosis in postmenopausal women; Gemzar, a treatment for lung cancer and pancreatic cancer; ReoPro, a drug used to prevent adverse effects from angioplasty procedures; Actos for type 2 diabetes; Axid, a medication that reduces excess stomach acid; Cynt for hypertension; Dobutrex for congestive heart failure; and Darvocet-N analgesic.

Animal health products (7%) include cattle feed additives, antibiotics and related items. In January 1999, the company sold its PCS Health Systems pharmacy beneÆt management services subsidiary to the Rite Aid retail drug store chain for $1.6 billion in cash.

Research and development expenditures totaled $1.8 billion in 1999, equal to about 18% of sales (representing one of the highest R&D to sales ratios in the drug industry). Clinical trials are underway studying new uses and formulations of existing Lilly drugs, as well as on entirely new compounds. Some of the trials are studying a new panic disorder indication and an extended dose formulation of Prozac; a bipolar indication for Zyprexa; breast cancer prevention for Evista; and stroke and acute coronary syndrome indications for ReoPro. Other compounds are being evaluated to treat sepsis, urinary incontinence and other ailments.

Per Share Data ($)

(Year Ended Dec. 31)	1999	1998	1997	1996	1995	1994	1993	1992	1991	1990
Tangible Bk. Val.	4.49	2.66	2.83	1.87	1.21	0.81	3.56	3.79	3.88	2.81
Cash Flow	2.70	2.31	0.11	1.89	1.64	1.40	0.76	1.01	1.38	1.17
Earnings	2.30	1.87	-0.35	1.39	1.15	1.02	0.42	0.70	1.13	0.97
Dividends	0.92	0.80	0.74	0.69	0.66	0.63	0.60	0.55	0.50	0.41
Payout Ratio	40%	43%	NM	49%	57%	61%	145%	78%	44%	42%
Prices - High	97¾	91¹/₄	70¹/₂	40¹/₄	28¹/₂	16⁵/₈	15¹/₂	22	21¹/₄	22⁵/₈
- Low	60¹/₂	57⁷/₈	35⁷/₈	24¹/₂	15¹/₂	11⁷/₈	10⁷/₈	14¹/₂	16⁷/₈	14³/₄
P/E Ratio - High	42	49	NM	29	25	16	37	31	19	23
- Low	26	31	NM	18	14	11	26	21	15	15

Income Statement Analysis (Million $)

	1999	1998	1997	1996	1995	1994	1993	1992	1991	1990
Revs.	10,003	9,237	8,518	7,347	6,764	5,712	6,452	6,167	5,726	5,192
Oper. Inc.	3,803	3,315	2,968	2,591	2,536	2,227	2,224	2,089	2,079	1,764
Depr.	440	490	510	544	554	432	398	368	311	224
Int. Exp.	242	181	234	325	324	129	97.0	109	88.9	93.8
Pretax Inc.	3,245	2,665	510	2,032	1,756	1,699	702	1,182	1,879	1,599
Eff. Tax Rate	22%	21%	175%	25%	26%	30%	30%	30%	30%	30%
Net Inc.	2,547	2,096	-384	1,524	1,307	1,185	491	828	1,315	1,127

Balance Sheet & Other Fin. Data (Million $)

	1999	1998	1997	1996	1995	1994	1993	1992	1991	1990
Cash	3,700	1,496	1,948	955	1,084	747	987	728	782	751
Curr. Assets	7,056	5,407	5,321	3,891	4,139	3,962	3,697	3,006	2,939	2,501
Total Assets	12,825	12,596	12,577	14,307	14,413	14,507	9,624	8,673	8,299	7,143
Curr. Liab.	3,935	4,607	4,192	4,222	4,967	5,670	2,928	2,399	2,272	2,818
LT Debt	2,812	2,186	2,326	2,517	2,593	2,126	835	582	396	277
Common Eqty.	5,013	4,430	4,645	6,100	5,433	5,356	4,569	4,892	4,966	3,467
Total Cap.	7,962	6,864	7,187	8,993	8,321	7,670	5,531	5,644	5,777	4,096
Cap. Exp.	528	420	366	444	551	577	634	913	1,142	1,007
Cash Flow	2,986	2,586	125	2,068	1,861	1,617	889	1,106	1,625	1,352
Curr. Ratio	1.8	1.2	1.3	0.9	0.8	0.7	1.3	1.3	1.3	0.9
% LT Debt of Cap.	35.3	31.8	32.4	28.0	31.2	27.7	15.1	10.3	6.8	6.8
% Net Inc.of Revs.	25.5	22.7	NA	20.7	19.3	20.7	7.6	13.4	23.0	21.7
% Ret. on Assets	20.0	16.7	NA	10.6	9.0	9.8	5.4	9.8	16.3	17.7
% Ret. on Equity	53.9	46.2	NA	26.4	24.2	23.9	10.4	16.8	30.0	31.9

Data as orig reptd.; bef. results of disc opers/spec. items. Per share data adj. for stk. divs. Bold denotes diluted EPS (FASB 128)-prior periods restated. E-Estimated. NA-Not Available. NM-Not Meaningful. NR-Not Ranked.

OfÆce-Lilly Corporate Center, Indianapolis. IN 46285. Tel- (317) 276-2000. Website- http://www.lilly.com Chrmn & CEO- R. L. Tobias. Pres & COO- S. Taurel. EVP & CFO- C. E. Golden. VP & Treas- E. A. Miller. Secy- D. P. Carmichael. Investor Contact- Patricia A. Martin (317-276-2506). Dirs- E. Bayh, S. C. Beering, A. G. Gilman, C. E. Golden, K. N. Horn, C. La Force, Jr., K. L. Lay, F. G. Prendergast, K. P. Siefert, R. L. Tobias, S. Taurel, A. M. Watanabe, A. O. Way. Transfer Agent & Registrar- First Chicago Trust Co. of New York. Incorporated- in Indiana in 1901. Empl- 29,800. S&P Analyst: H. B. Saftlas.

Figure 4.7 *(continued)*

Eli Lilly and Company

NEWS HEADLINES

■ **04/17/00**   11:07 am... STILL HOLD ELI LILLY (LLY 69***).. Q1 EPS rose 18% to $0.63, $0.02 above consensus... Sales rose 13%, fueled by gains in Zyprexa anti-psychotic (+18%), Evista for osteoporosis (+85%), Gemzar anticancer, and diabetes treatments... more than offset sluggishness in Prozac (+3%)... working with Sepracor (SEPR) on enhanced version of Prozac... Robust pipeline also incls. treatments for cancer, diabetes, respiratory diseases, impotence, other medical conditions... Valuation in line with drug industry average... but overall group likely to remain out of favor due to Medicare & patent issues. /H.Saftlas

■ **04/17/00**   NEW YORK (Standard & Poor's)--Apr 17, 2000, LILLY (ELI) & CO., announced 1Q EPS $0.77 vs. $0.40.

■ **04/13/00**   UP 4 1/8 to 69 1/8... Co., SEPRACOR receive antitrust approval from FTC for their license ageement allowing to exclusively develop, commercialize R-Øuoxetine... Merrill upgrades to near term buy...

■ **04/13/00**   2:15 pm... ELI LILLY (LLY 68-7/8) UP 3-7/8, CO., SEPRACOR RECEIVE APPROVAL FROM FTC ON LICENSE AGREEMENT... MERRILL UPGRADES TO NEAR TERM BUY FROM ACCUMULATE... Analyst Steven Tighe tells salesforce believes concern relating to outcome of pending licensing agreement has been suppressing investor appetite for LLY... Says LLY clearly was successful in convincing FTC that R-Øuoxetine is different then Prozac, will not be used to delay or slow entrance of genetic competition... With litigation moving in positive direction to date, LLY's pipeline visibility increasing, sees opportunity for multiple expansion as well as appreciation due to EPS growth... Has $80 target./ Trombino

■ **01/27/00**   NEW YORK (Standard & Poor's)--Jan 27, 2000, LILLY (ELI) & CO., announced 4Q EPS $0.71 vs. $0.50 and annual EPS $2.30 vs. $1.87. Results for 1999 exclude income of $0.16 per share for the year and income of $0.01 for the 1998 4Q and year all from discontinued operations. Results for 1999 include charges of $26M and $87.4M for the 4Q and year from asset impairment.

■ **10/22/99**   NEW YORK (Standard & Poor's)--Oct 22, 1999, LILLY (ELI) & CO., announced 3Q EPS $0.67 vs. $0.46 and 9 mos. EPS $1.59 vs. $1.36. Results for 1999 incl. a charge of $128M for both periods related to acquired in-process technology and for the 9 mos. also incl. a charge of $61M related to asset impairment. Results excl. income of $0.16 for the 9 mos. 1999 and $0.01 for the 9 mos. 1998 related to discontinued opers. Results for 1998 9 mos. also excl. loss of $0.01 related to extraord. charges.

■ **10/20/99**   DOWN 4 1/2 to 65 3/8... Posts $0.62 vs. $0.53 3Q EPS from ops... Sees slight decline in worldwide Prozac sales... Salomon SB downgrades... S&P maintains hold... 5.

■ **10/20/99**   2:00 pm... STILL HOLD LILLY (LLY 65***), DOWN 5 ON DEPRESSING PROZAC SALES... Q3 EPS rose 17% to $0.62, in line... But Prozac sales off 13% on growing competition, wholesaler stocking in Q3 '98... Prozac accounted for 30% of '98 sales... larger share of proÆts... see further erosion in '00 as U.K. patent expires... Newer drugs doing well such as Zyprexa anti-psychotic, Gemzar anticancer, Reopro cardiovascular, Evista for osteoporosis, Actos diabetes treatment... LLY's guidance for '00 EPS in the $2.60-$2.65 range, below present $2.67 consensus.. Adequately valued at avg. drug group multiple. /H.Saftlas

■ **10/20/99**   12:30 pm... ELI LILLY

(LLY 65) DOWN 4-3/4, POSTS $0.62 3Q EPS FROM OPS; SEES DECLINES IN WORLDWIDE PROZAC SALES... SALOMON SB DOWNGRADES TO NEUTRAL FROM BUY... Analyst Christina Heuer tells salesforce Prozac continues to underperform, now expected to decrease 5%-10% in each year until 1st generic launch mid-04... Although R&D budget rankd near top of industry, believes co. does not have resources to be fully competitive... Thinks LLY should not be able to fully participate in proÆt margin expansion that had been expected to play larger role in pharma EPS growth as pharma sales growth moderates... Thinks $2.27 '99 EPS est. few pennies too high, cuts '00 EPS est. to $2.60./Trombino

■ **07/21/99**   July 21, 1999, Lilly (Eli) & Co. announced June '99 3 mos. EPS, $0.52 vs $0.44 and 6 mos. EPS, $0.92 vs $0.91. Results for the 6 mos. ended 1999 excls. EPS of $0.16 fr. discontd. opers. Results for the 6 mos. ended 1998 excl. an extraord. charge of $0.01.

■ **05/27/99**   UP 2 to 69... Credit Lyonnais initiates coverage with buy... Co. no news, does not comment on stock activity...

■ **05/27/99**   3:30 pm... ELI LILLY (LLY 69) UP 2, CREDIT LYONNAIS INITIATES COVERAGE WITH BUY... Analyst Adam Green believes 33x multiple, $88 target for LLY shares one year out justiÆeed... Cites deep pipeline that is, he believes, underappreciated, overshadowed by Prozac concerns... Says strong near- to intermediate-term EPS growth outlook of 18% in '99, 17% in '00 slightly better than outlook for overall group... Notes projected imminent launch of potential new blockbuster diabetes drug Actos... Also notes removal of unrealistic expectations for Evista's potential from valuation... Sees $2.28 '99 EPS, $2.67 '00, $3.04 '01./B.Brodie

(continued)

Figure 4.7 *(continued)*

Lilly (Eli)

INDUSTRY OUTLOOK

Despite a period of sluggishness during the Ærst few months of the year, drug stocks have outperformed the broader averages in recent months, as investors have renewed their interest in this recession-resistant industry in the face of rising interest rates and a projected slowdown in the overall economy. Past concerns over patent expirations and anticipated changes in Medicare have also waned. While the passage of outpatient Medicare drug coverage is expected to occur in 2001, the current thinking is that its net effect on the industry may be neutral to slightly positive, with any ensuing price discounting offset by higher volume. We recommend drug stocks with strong patent-protected drug portfolios and robust new drug pipelines. Selected issues also offer takeover appeal the consolidating global drug market.

On the negative side, managed care constraints and looming patent expirations remain challenges facing the industry. HMOs and other managed care buyers are scrambling to contain escalating drug costs, which represent their fastest growing expense category. New cost-containment strategies that have been implemented include requirements that members pay for larger shares of their drug costs and strong incentives for members to choose generics and less-expensive formulary-listed products.

The branded drug industry is also facing patent expirations over the next Æve years on drugs that generated close to $40 billion in sales in 1999. However, the industry has stepped up its R&D efforts, which are expected to generate a growing stream on new products to replace patent-expiring drugs. Last year, the FDA approved 35 new molecular entities (signiÆcant medical breakthroughs), Æve more than in 1998.

Despite managed care issues and patent expirations, the U.S. pharmaceutical industry is still one of the healthiest and highest-margined industries in the country. The industry has historically rejuvenated itself with the development of new premium-priced breakthrough therapies that have obsoleted older drugs and opened up entirely new markets. Drugmakers should also continue to beneÆt from a more industry-friendly regulatory environment, with the FDA committed to streamlining and making more efÆcient the overall new drug approval process.

Industry Stock Performance
Related S&P 1500 Industry Index

Health Care (Drugs - Major Pharmaceuticals)

Month-end Price Performance As of 04/28/00

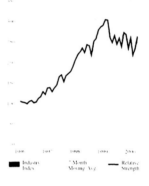

INDUSTRY: HEALTH CARE (DRUGS - MAJOR PHARMACEUTICALS)
*PEER GROUP: ETHICAL PHARMACEUTICALS - MAJOR

Peer Group	Stock Symbol	Recent Stock Price	P/E Ratio	12-mth. Trail. EPS	30-day Price Chg %	1-year Price Chg. %	Beta	Yield %	Quality Ranking	Stk. Mkt. Cap. (mil. $)	Ret. on Equity %	Pretax Margin %	LTD to Cap. %
Lilly (Eli)	LLY	75½	28	2.67	16%	-4%	0.72	1.4	A-	82,267	53.9	32.4	35.3
AstraZeneca PLC	AZN	43½	32	1.38	-2%	6%	0.82	1.6	NR	77,832	30.6	19.0	15.3
Aventis	AVE	58½	23	2.51	-1%	19%	0.63	0.8	NR	47,858	8.6	NM	28.3
Forest Laboratories	FRX	92	72	1.28	12%	82%	0.98	Nil	B+	7,768	11.4	20.3	Nil
Glaxo Wellcome	GLX	58½	36	1.61	-5%	-2%	0.75	2.0	NR	106,836	62.0	30.3	28.3
Merck & Co.	MRK	68½	27	2.54	5%	-7%	0.87	1.7	A+	157,817	20.1	27.0	6.0
Novo Nordisk	NVO	76	32	2.41	9%	44%	0.18	0.6	NR	9,643	13.4	19.3	8.6
PÆzer Inc.	PFE	43½	53	0.82	7%	10%	0.90	0.8	A+	166,797	23.3	19.2	5.5
Roche Holdings ADS	RHHBY	NA	NM	0.92	-11%	NA	NA	Nil	NR	NA	18.2	22.0	33.1
Schering-Plough	SGP	41½	28	1.48	0%	-16%	1.10	1.3	A+	61,343	46.0	30.5	Nil
SmithKline Beecham plc	SBH	65¼	35	1.89	-5%	-2%	0.86	1.5	NR	72,994	34.3	10.5	42.3

Figure 4.7 *(continued)*

Lilly (Eli)

WALL STREET CONSENSUS   12-MAY-00

Analysts' Recommendations

Stock Prices

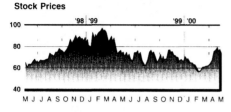

Analysts' Opinions

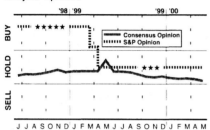

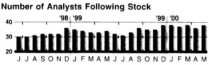

Number of Analysts Following Stock

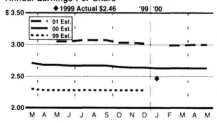

Analysts' Opinion

	No. of Ratings	% of Total	1 Mo. Prior	3 Mo. Prior	Nat'l	Reg'l	Non-broker
Buy	8	21	9	9	6	0	1
Buy/Hold	12	32	11	12	3	7	1
Hold	16	42	14	14	8	5	1
Weak Hold	0	0	0	0	0	0	0
Sell	2	5	2	2	0	0	1
No Opinion	0	0	0	1	0	0	0
Total	38	100	36	38	17	12	3

Analysts' Consensus Opinion

The consensus opinion reØects the average buy/hold/sell recommendation of Wall Street analysts. It is well-known, however, that analysts tend to be overly bullish. To make the consensus opinion more meaningful, it has been adjusted to reduce this positive bias. First, a stock's average recommendation is computed. Then it is compared to the recommendations on all other stocks. Only companies that score high relative to all other companies merit a consensus opinion of "Buy" in the graph at left. The graph is also important because research has shown that a rising consensus opinion is a favorable indicator of near-term stock performance; a declining trend is a negative signal.

Standard & Poor's STARS   ★★★
(Stock Appreciation Ranking System)

★★★★★	Buy	Standard & Poor's STARS ranking is
★★★★	Accumulate	our own analyst's evaluation of the
★★★	Hold	short-term (six to 12 month)
★★	Avoid	appreciation potential of a stock.
★	Sell	Five-Star stocks are expected to
		appreciate in price and outperform
		the market.

Analysts' Earnings Estimate

Annual Earnings Per Share

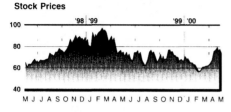

Current Analysts' Consensus Estimates

Fiscal years	Avg.	High	Low	S&P Est.	No. of Est.	Estimated P-E Ratio	Estimated S&P 500 P-E Ratio
2000	2.63	2.67	2.57	2.63	38	28.7	24.5
2001	3.00	3.15	2.83	2.95	34	25.1	21.7
2Q'00	0.60	0.61	0.59		25		
2Q'99	0.52 Actual						

A company's earnings outlook plays a major part in any investment decision. S&P organizes the earnings estimates of over 2,300 Wall Street analysts, and provides you with their consensus of earnings over the next two years. The graph to the left shows you how these estimates have trended over the past 15 months.

Source: Standard & Poor's.

Figure 4.8 Morningstar

Morningstar, too, scans company operations, and puts together mountains of data for investors to peruse. Morningstar sheets are available at the local library, brokerage firms' offices, or financial planners' offices. You can also subscribe by contacting the company at 800-735-0700.

All pricing data as of 04-30-2000. Reprinted by permission of Morningstar.

Symantec SYMC

Sector	Industry	Style	Stock Price	Market Cap $mil	Dividend Yld%
Technology	Software	●	62.44	3,709.4	0.0

Stock Type	Growth	Profitability	Financial Health	Valuation
Classic Growth	B-	B+	A	B+

Symantec develops software products for information management, productivity enhancement, software-development, and software-utility needs for the business-microcomputer market. Symantec derives more than 80% of its revenues from products that operate on Microsoft's MS-DOS operating system for IBM and IBM-compatible personal computers. In addition, the company offers products for use on the Microsoft Windows, Apple Macintosh, and IBM OS/2 operating systems. Symantec sold its Internet Tools business unit in December 1999.

Top 5 Fund Owners
Seligman Communi & Info
Legg Mason Special Investment
Fidelity Low Priced Stock
Brandywine
Seligman Global Tech

20330 Stevens Creek Blvd
Cupertino, CA 95014-2132
USA
408-253-9600
http://www.symantec.com

Growth

Growth rates%	1 Yr	3 Yr Avg	Industry	S&P 500
Revenue%	11.2	10.0	29.7	12.1
Net Income%	-11.0	NMF	52.3	14.3
EPS%	39.4	NMF	48.9	15.1
Equity Per Share %	11.6	19.7	50.3	13.2
Dividend %	NMF	NMF	100.0	10.4

Earnings Estimates

	Cur Qtr	Next Qtr	2000	2001
Mean Estimate$	0.58	0.60	2.10	2.53
High Estimate$	0.61	0.62	2.20	2.59
Low Estimate$	0.54	0.56	1.85	2.35

Projected 5 Year EPS Growth 25.6
Number of Analysts 6

Quarterly Income

	Jun	Sep	Dec	Mar
Revenue $mil				
Current	175.1	182.5	200.8	197.2
Previous	137.8	130.0	155.2	169.6
% Chg	27.1	40.4	29.1	10.4
Earnings Per Share $				
Current	0.41	0.43	1.41	0.49
Previous	0.13	0.03	0.28	0.43
% Chg	215.4	EUB	403.6	14.0

Financial Health

Balance Sheet $mil	1999	1998	Latest Quarter
Total Assets	476.5	563.5	792.4
Current Assets	328.5	315.5	511.6
Cash	225.9	197.6	404.5
Inventories	3.2	6.4	7.7
Noncurrent Assets	147.9	247.0	280.7
Total Liabilities $M	159.0	218.4	231.3
Current Liabilities	153.0	216.9	230.4
Long Term Liabilities	6.0	1.5	1.0
Total Equity	317.5	345.1	561.0

Cash Flow $mil	1997	1998	1999
Cash Flow from Operations	94.4	130.9	123.5
Capital Spending	27.2	26.3	25.1
Free Cash Flow	67.2	104.5	98.4

Segment Analysis

	% of Revenue			% of Oper. Income		
	1997	1998	1999	1997	1998	1999
Segment						
Security & Assistance	55	55	57	71	57	53
Remote Productivity	40	41	39	29	55	55
Internet Tools	5	4	NA	NA	NA	NA
	NA	NA	NA	NA	NA	NA
Region						
United States	66	63	60	NA	NA	NA
Foreign Countries	34	37	40	NA	NA	NA
	NA	NA	NA	NA	NA	NA

Company Publication

	1995	1996	1997	1998	1999	TTM
Annual Income						
Revenue $mil	431.3	445.4	452.9	532.5	592.6	745.7
% Rank All	23	23	24	24	30	22
% Rank Industry	8	8	9	9	11	8
Net income $mil	33.4	39.8	26.0	85.1	50.2	170.1
Earnings per share(EPS) $	0.64	-0.76	0.47	1.42	0.86	2.76
Continuing-Operations EPS $	0.64	-0.76	0.47	1.42	0.86	2.90
Dividend per share $	0.00	0.00	0.00	0.00	0.00	0.00
Payout Ratio %	0.0	NMF	0.0	0.0	0.0	0.0
Average Shares(mil)	49.1	52.4	54.3	56.0	56.4	59.4
Profitability						
Return on Equity(ROE) %	18.1	-22.1	11.5	76.8	14.5	30.3
% Rank All	22	66	33	6	37	5
% Rank Industry	29	68	26	11	21	5
Net Margin %	7.7	8.9	5.7	16.0	8.5	22.8
% Rank Industry	31	58	32	9	73	3
Asset Turnover	1.4	1.6	1.3	1.1	1.1	0.9
% Rank Industry	43	22	33	39	31	39
Financial Leverage	1.7	1.6	1.6	1.5	1.6	1.4
% Rank Industry	56	54	55	57	79	52
Return on Assets(ROA) %	10.9	14.1	7.7	17.9	8.9	21.5
Debt/Equity	0.1	0.1	0.1	0.0	0.0	0.0

Stock Performance

Current	62.44 Stock $	1995	1996	1997	1998	1999	04-00
52-Wk High	81.63						
52-Wk Low	17.75						
5-Year High	81.5						
5-Year Low	8.7						

Performance Quartile(within sector)	—	—	—	—	—
Total Return %	32.86	37.63	51.30	0.86	169.54	6.50
+/- S&P 500	4.67	60.58	17.95	29.44	148.50	7.29
+/- Benchmark	-4.67	-60.58	17.95	29.44	148.50	7.29

Total Returns

Trailing Period Performance	Total Return	% Rank Industry	S&P500	Bmark
1 Month	-16.89	78	-13.88	-13.88
Year-To-Date	6.50	28	7.29	7.29
1 Year	204.15	18	204.02	204.02
3 Year Avg	63.15	22	39.47	39.47
5 Year Avg	27.84	35	-3.41	-3.41
10 Year Avg	18.95	18	1.18	1.18

Valuation

	Rel to S&P 500		Rel to S&P 500		Rel to S&P 500		Rel to S&P 500		Rel to S&P 500		Rel to S&P 500
Price/Earnings	36.3	1.93	NMF	NMF	46.7	1.70	15.3	0.46	68.2	1.75	22.6	0.66
Price/Book	6.6	1.61	4.2	0.93	5.6	1.04	4.1	0.57	9.9	1.21	6.6	0.86
Price/Sales	2.8	1.56	1.7	0.81	2.7	1.00	2.4	0.71	5.8	1.53	5.0	1.39
Price/Cash Flow					12.9	0.75	10.0	0.45	27.7	1.19	17.5	0.61

Valuation Analysis

Business Appraisal		Forward Valuation	
Appraisal/Share $	33.0	Forward P/E	29.7
Appraisal Ratio	0.5	PEG Ratio	1.2
Predictability	High	Cash Return %	5.6

MORNINGSTAR   Stock Research

Source: Morningstar.

NUMEROLOGY

Numbers and statistics help investors judge shares and grasp what's going on in the market, if only because there are almost too many stocks to pick from. Over 9,000 companies trade on the New York Stock Exchange and the Nasdaq, and choosing good investments from the lot of them isn't going to be easy. Whether you leaf through the paper or talk shop with a broker, you're likely to be deluged in figures—price to earnings multiples, growth rates, earnings, and so on. Figure 4.9 outlines the typical newspaper listing. The following subsections explain in detail the numbers you should care about, as well as others that you should really worry about.

Figure 4.9   The Stock Listings

Here's what your daily newspaper puts out on stocks and stock prices.

52-WEEK HIGH	LOW	STOCK	DIV	YLD %	P/E	SALES 100S	HIGH	LOW	LAST	CHG.
62	10	Buttermaker	.5	1.0	25	360	51	49	50	1.3

Here's what it all means:

52-Week High	The highest price the stock listed has sold for in the last year.
52-Week Low	The lowest price the stock listed has sold for in the last year.
Stock	The company or company shares in question.
Div	The stock's dividend, or the amount of company profits management shares with shareholders annually.
Yld %	The stock's current yield or just what percentage the stock's dividend represents of the stock's share price. Yield is calculated by dividing a stock's price by its dividend.
P/E	How much a stock is valued in relation to company profits. P/E is calculated by dividing a stock's share price by its company's earnings per share.
Sales 100s	How many shares of the stock traded.
High	The highest price the stock fetched yesterday (if the figure appears in a daily newspaper) or during the week before (if the number is printed in a weekly publication).
Low	The lowest price the stock traded at yesterday (if the figure appears in a daily newspaper) or during the week before (if the number is printed in a weekly publication).
Last	The final price the stock fetched for the day (if the figure appears in a daily newspaper) or during the week before (if the number is printed in a weekly publication).
Chg.	The percent gain or loss the stock made during the day (if the figure appears in a daily newspaper) or during the week before (if the number appears in a weekly publication).

Share Price (Not Important)

A big or small price doesn't matter; whether a stock's price rises or falls, however, should be a major concern.

Day after day, the newspaper prints pages of company share prices—highs and lows, this week's top and the year's bottom. Stock prices have to be important, then, to warrant all the ink and newsprint, no?

It would certainly seem so. A stock is a commodity—a chunk of ownership of company. It trades on a marketplace: On the stock market, a network of buyers and sellers regulate a company's share price by supply and demand. So, applying some real-world common sense, if a high-quality ketchup made of the finest plum tomatoes on earth carries a $10.00 price tag per bottle at the grocery store, and a run-of-the-mill second-rate brand seems to be constantly on sale at 39 cents a jug, it only seems logical that a stock trading at $100 a share has to be far more valuable than one fetching just $20.

Oh, if it were but that simple. In practice, share prices by themselves don't tell you much about a company's worth. They only help you keep track of your investment over time. When comparing one stock to another, however, share prices aren't going to do you much good.

Take, for example, the Washington Post Company (stock symbol: WPO), owner of the venerable newspaper published in our nation's capital, and Cisco Systems (stock symbol: CSCO), maker of computer networking hardware, much of which is used to help the Internet go. In September 1999, the Post Company stock traded as high as $595 a share. Meanwhile, Cisco Systems (CSCO) had risen to $70 a share. Applying the everyday associations that are useful at the department store or local pharmacy, it would seem that whatever has been happening to the *Washington Post*, its subscriber base, and its ad sales were snaring Wall Street's attention and motoring the company's stock to the heavens. Using the same analysis, Cisco's business, as reflected in its share price would seem to be nothing spectacular. It might have well been solid, but the fact that its stock was hundreds of dollars below that of the Washington Post Company must have meant nothing was going on in Cisco's industry that would cause a seismic disturbance in the stock market.

Not so fast. Between 1994 and 1999, the Post on average reaped investors a 20 percent return annually, below the 26 percent gains the S&P 500 averaged during the same period. In the years between 1995 and 1999, its sales grew between 6.5 and 7.9 percent annually; its profits, as measured by earnings per share ranged from 16.9 percent in 1996 to an impressive 57.2 percent leap in 1998. Cisco? During that same period, Cisco shares brought gains to owners of almost 90 percent a year between 1994 and 1999. Its sales grew 67, 84, 57, and 31 percent in 1995, 1996, 1997, and 1998, respectively, while the company reported profits per share rising 33, 90, 12, and 24 percent in each of those years. The reason: With the Internet taking hold in the United States and abroad, Cisco's wares have been in high, high demand. Which stock would you have rather owned?

Bear in mind that share prices tend to be arbitrarily selected. When a company is first selling its stock to the public, it consults with investment bankers and other financial experts who help with the offering. At that time, the CEO and his or her entourage may decide that pricing shares at a low figure might keep grassroots interest high by attracting individual investors in numbers. That will make the stock relatively liquid, meaning it will trade briskly and often during the course of any day's session on Wall Street. The bigwigs might also scratch their heads, scribble out some calculations, and determine that management doesn't want individual investors piling aboard their stock. They'll opt to keep the stock more or less illiquid and will attach a high price to it.

Once the new stock hits the market and begins trading, other factors begin to guide its price up or down. Strong profits coming in year after year will likely push its shares higher, as will an increase in dividends, a shrewdly planned and executed divestiture of a division, or rumors of a takeover. A business sabotaged by its own ineptitude, or a stumble in its core activities, meanwhile might send its shares downward. If the price of shares goes so high that it seems unaffordable to investors, sometimes a company will choose to split its stock by issuing existing holders a new share for each one they already own. That way, the shareholders' investment remains untouched, except for the number of shares they own. And, the company stock now reduced in price, might well trade more actively.

Don't obsess on the number of shares you can or cannot buy. Instead focus on what's important: the sum you have invested. While you're at it, forget fretting over how large or small a corporation's share price is. Instead, hone in on how its stock performs—if it is going up or down, relative to its price at some starting point—over time. That you can check by examining gains or losses over periods of 1 year, 3 years, and 5 years. Feel free to compare those figures with other stocks, mutual fund total returns and, of course, the performance of a benchmark like the Standard & Poor's 500. That way you'll know whether your investment is working for you.

Total Return (Very Important)

This is an excellent gauge of how much a stock has made.

Think of the ways a stock can make money for you during the course of a year. Take the gains. Take the dividends. Add them together. What you get is a figure commonly called total return.

Often, perhaps too often, you hear experts, journalists, even investors talking on and on about a stock's gains. Such and such company's shares have risen 30 percent since the beginning of the year. Or perhaps another corporation has seen its stock slink off to a 5 percent loss in the matter of a week. By contrast, you'll seldom hear much mention of total returns. There's a good explanation for that. These days, companies aren't that generous with dividends. Corporate America of late has been stingy, sharing little if any of its profits directly with shareholders.

As a result, with dividends shriveling up over time, there's little if any reason to dwell on anything but a stock's gains. That said, we'd still encourage you to think in terms of total returns. Dividends are money that accrues in your account. Also, someday companies may revert back to their generous ways of old (the S&P 500 over the years has averaged a yield of over 4 percent, more than most bank accounts could boast these days).

Dividends or not, the math required to calculate total returns is straightforward. It's a matter of adding a stock's gain or loss for the year to its dividend payout (if there is one) and dividing that figure by a stock's share price at any point in the year.

Total return figures are generally measured for periods of time, generally a year or a few years, and can be compared with a benchmark like the Standard & Poor's 500. The Morningstar Web site (www.morningstar.com) gives investors a clear breakout of total return figures.

Earnings (Very Important)

Earnings are the bottom line when it comes to investing.

One of the most important measures of a company's profitability appears at the bottom of many accounting ledgers. That's because to come up with an earnings figure, company accountants start with its intake from selling goods and subtract all the overhead, cost of raw materials, and a lot of other costs of doing business.

What you get after pushing a pencil around is a statistic that's of the utmost importance to most investors. Earnings are a crucial measure of how business is doing. They tell you how well a company is run; they signal whether the company's industry is growing or shrinking; and finally, they often foreshadow the movement of a company's stock. Earnings that are going up often indicate that a corporation's shares are poised to increase in value; earnings on their way down often drag a stock downward.

For most publicly traded companies, a raw earnings figure is nonetheless huge—millions of dollars. It takes one more mathematical step to help shareholders better grasp what's happening to a company and how it relates to their stock. A corporation's earnings figure starts to make more sense when it's stated as a sum per share, derived by dividing its earnings by the number of shares a company has outstanding. You'll often see references to EPS (earnings per share).

A company's EPS yields a lot of information. Still, investors should not settle on just static earnings per share. The most desirable companies find ways to grow their earnings over time. Wall Street measures earnings growth by examining the percentage change up or down in EPS year after year. Then, to give the numbers some impact, the pros compare earnings growth figures both with the market at large, measured by an index such as the S&P 500, and with a company's industry peers, who have coped with the same conditions and markets.

They'll also look at earnings growth trends over time. Looking back, say at average annual earnings growth over the past 5 years, gives a good indication of how successful—or even reliable—management has been over time. A look at the future can be even more rewarding. Wall Street churns out earnings growth projections by the truckload. Firms like Zacks Investment Research or I/B/E/S gather up the earnings predictions and calculate averages for the analysts' prognostications. The mean estimates not only shed light on what Wall Street sees a company doing in the future, but also provide investors with a way to measure the performance of corporate management. Companies that beat the estimates are often rewarded with higher stock prices. Those firms that fail to meet projections often see their share prices hammered in the stock market.

Earnings figures are reported regularly in the financial press, including daily and weekly publications such as the *Wall Street Journal, Barron's,* and *Investor's Business Daily.* On the Web, you'll find plenty of ways to dig up earnings at an investing hub such as Investorama (www.investorama.com) or Dailystocks (www.dailystocks.com).

Market Cap (Somewhat Important)

Although it's not the most important number around, it can suggest how a stock might trade.

How much is a company worth? What value does Wall Street put on a company, or at least its shares? Professionals turn to a market capitalization figure or market cap to find out. The *market cap* of any given company is the product of straightforward multiplication: share price times the number of shares outstanding. The resulting figure is none other than a tally of what the investing public thinks of a company.

The pros like to use market caps to carve up the market into big companies, medium-sized ones, and small fry. They claim that stocks from each of the three groups has distinct characteristics and reacts to the economy and other factors differently.

Start with large capitalization stocks or *large caps* as they're commonly called. These companies include the mammoths of the economy. Among their ranks count behemoths like General Electric (market capitalization, $439 billion as of 1/31/00), AT&T ($156 billion as of 1/31/00), and Microsoft ($508 billion on 1/31/00). Large caps span many of the household names from the grocery store, gas station, or everyday life. They include Time Warner, DaimlerChrysler, and Citigroup.

Investing in large caps goes beyond simple name recognition. A lot of money managers feel there's safety in the big, well-known names. These, after all, are the companies that have had to weather ups and downs to get to be as giant as they are. They tend to have more stock, and more investors are familiar with their names and hence are likely to want to buy shares. That makes large caps more liquid. So, it's little wonder, then, that when there are questions about how the economy and stock market are going to fare, large cap stocks do well.

At the other end of the capitalization roster are *small caps*. Small, though, isn't necessarily bad, and frequently can be good for investors. Studies have shown that small caps actually outperform the elephants by 3 percentage points a year on average, although they tend also to be riskier investments. The small cap group includes a lot of young companies, rapidly growing firms in new fields where opportunities are cropping up like mushrooms. Small cap stocks tend to do well when the economy is booming.

Mid caps fall somewhere in between the two caps and may have a recognizable name or two buried in their ranks. And, their growth, while not as spectacular as the small caps, will often outdo their large cap cousins.

Sales (Important)

Sales are the engine that drives earnings.

You might wonder: Just where do profits come from? The short answer: sales, or revenues as they're also called—the amount of money a company takes in.

The basics of the everyday economy are familiar. People earn money by providing a product, good, or service. They then pay their bills with that cash, and whatever is left over is theirs to keep or spend.

Apply that same basic principle to the workings of a corporation. The intake of funds, the receipt of money for a good or service, is called sales.

It goes without saying that you'd like to see a company log some sort of revenues, or sales. More importantly, check that a company's sales are growing over time, that is, increasing year after year because that's a crucial gauge of what management is doing, and how well they are accomplishing their job. It indicates whether the widgets a company produces are already a hit or at least catching on with consumers (or whoever hands over the cash to your corporation).

Sales growth is important these days for another reason. Earnings can be boosted a number of ways such as by selling off portions of a company or by sending workers home and retrenching. The problem: The benefits of that kind of maneuver are short-lived. Eventually, the gains pocketed from selling off divisions and slicing payroll run out.

Sales increases, meanwhile, fuel profits directly. They represent income—the top line that fattens earnings and helps companies buy new equipment, buy other companies, or expand into new markets. Revenue growth implies that the strategies that are working for a company could continue to do so in the future.

Price-to-Earnings Multiple or P/E (Very Important)

A key gauge of a stock's worth, P/E tells you how shares are valued relative to the market and to their industry peers.

When you head to the store to buy steak, you check how much beef costs per pound. During the course of a month, you probably keep a running tally of how much you are paying per gallon for gasoline. Both serve as compass points most anyone keeps at the back of their mind while shopping about. They're simply a good gauge of how much something is worth and whether it makes sense to open up your wallet.

When you are dealing with stocks, a similar measure helps cut to the chase of a company's worth. It's called a price-to-earnings multiple, a term abbreviated as P/E or referred to as a stock's "multiple." P/Es don't require an advanced degree in accounting or the use of eight functions on your pocket calculator; to find out a company's P/E, all you have to do is divide its share price by either its earnings for a full year as reported to the public or by projections by Wall Street. You merely need to divide a stock's price by its earnings per share.

A P/E is useful in different ways. First, it allows you to compare a stock's value with that of the broad market. The pros typically look to the P/E of a benchmark, often the Standard & Poor's 500 as a starting point. Historically, the S&P 500 has traded between 9 and 30 times earnings tabulated for the 500 companies covered by the index. At times when the S&P 500 has a multiple in the lower portion of that range, Wall Street is likely saying that the market is either undervalued or that investors are taking a cautious stance toward stocks because of an economic slowdown. When the S&P 500 is priced at the high end of that historic range, shares are said to be overvalued or overheated. Investor confidence is running high.

Comparing a company's P/E to the broad market is just as simple. If its shares trade at a P/E higher than the market, or a premium to the market, are either overvalued or have earned their lofty multiple for a reason such as robust earnings growth. Stocks that are priced at a multiple below that of the market are possibly undervalued, or face some sort of future adversity that has scared many investors away.

A check against the market P/E provides just part of the story, however. The stocks of different industries or economic sectors with higher or lower P/Es often trade at a premium or discount to the market depending on the quality of their earnings and the dependability of their earnings growth. For example, Wall Street tends to see the fortunes of car manufacturers like Ford and General Motors rising and falling in lockstep with the direction of the economy. When the economy is growing, people have stable employment and put down money on major purchases, like a new automobile. When things don't look so good, and workers are being laid off, many consumers hesitate to make such a large purchase. Car manufacturers will see their profits shrink. Because of these cyclical ups and downs, automakers on average carry a P/E that's 60 percent that of the S&P 500.

Conversely, companies that make computer networking hardware more often than not trade at a premium to the market. Investors are excited by the earnings growth reported by companies like Lucent or Cisco Systems. Additionally, Wall Street thinks that a technology boom is certain to benefit companies that provide key products and services for computer users and corporations that invest a lot in computer equipment. Higher expectations lead to a higher multiple, and therefore computer networking companies, on average, trade at a multiple almost $3\frac{1}{2}$ times that of the stock market.

Depending on what kinds of "E" or earnings you use, P/Es can lend you insight on the past, present, or future. Plug in an earnings figure for the past 12 months, and you get a reliable standing for the company and its stock are right now. Use current-year estimates, and you get Wall Street's take on what to expect from the company this year. Push out a year or more, and "forward" earnings estimates help you gauge the future.

As convenient as P/Es are, there's a catch in using them. Portfolio manager Dawn Alston-Paige for the investment firm Loomis Sayles, warns that companies can reconfigure earnings in several ways, according to how they report items like the depreciation of assets. Still, bearing that in mind, you should keep tabs on a company's P/E, and use it in conjunction with a few other measures listed here.

PEG Ratio (P/E Multiple Divided by a Company's Growth Rate) (Important)

This is a good gauge of how much a fast-growing stock is worth.

There's yet another way that Wall Street looks over P/E numbers, especially when companies are a hit in the stock market. Often, fast-growing technology corporations are so popular with investors that it's hard to judge just how expensive they are by looking at P/E multiples alone. The professionals then take P/Es one step further by dividing them by earnings growth rate projections to obtain what is commonly called a PEG ratio. Investors look at PEGs to see if they're paying too much for a hot stock's projected growth, or if shares of a fast-moving company are still a bargain. Many pros say that they like to see a company's PEG in the 1 to 1.5 range. That's to say a company whose P/E is equal to its projected growth rate, or whose P/E is 1.5 times its growth rate is either reasonably priced or not too expensive. Push a PEG up to 2 or more, and a professional investor is likely to think twice, maybe three times before putting money into a stock.

Dividends and Yield (Very Important)

How much money does management want to share with you directly?

There's one catch to investing in stocks: You have to be patient and wait for a payoff. Yes, your savings account may pay a meager sum of interest, is compounded daily, but stocks are a different beast. All the while that you own shares, however, you have little if anything to show for your gains, whatever value your shares may have accrued over time. You can hold shares through thick and thin, weather a stock market crash, or rejoice over a bull market. But, through it all, you will not have any money to show for your stake until the day you cash in your shares.

One way a company can make owning its shares more like your trusty bank account, though, is by paying a dividend. To do so requires merely that management hand over a set portion of its profits to shareholders, usually every quarter.

Dividends tend to come regularly over time, and are parceled according to the number of shares you own. And to better illustrate what kind of return they provide shareholders, Wall Street usually expresses the annual dividend income a corporation passes over to shareholders as a percentage of a company's stock price, a figure called a yield. It's calculated by dividing the yearly dividend by a stock's price.

For example, Ford Motor (F), was scheduled to pay $1.80 a share to shareholders in four installment of 45 cents each in 1999. When Ford's stock stood at $49 a share, its dividend yield was thus 3.7 percent.

Dividends are a tonic that many money managers seek. Many professional portfolio managers will tell you that a dividend represents much more than a way to share wealth with shareholders. It allows Wall Street a direct peek at a corporation's fiscal health. It takes steady profits to come up with regular payments to shareholders, and management that misses a dividend payment or cuts down on the amount it gives shareholders can bet its stock price will suffer.

On the other hand, a consistent dividend, or one that rises over time, is a positive signal. It shows a company is generating enough cash to handle payments to shareholders each and every quarter. It's also a sign that management is confident of future growth and knows that profits aren't about to dry up anytime soon. "If you have a company that increases its dividend steadily and consistently, you can be sure it's enjoying great earnings growth," says Joseph Lisanti, senior editor of Standard & Poor's investment newsletter, *The Outlook.* "Dividends are real. You can't fake them."

Dividends provide shareholders with another benefit. Because dividend-paying firms spread their profits around and generate regular income for shareholders, their shares are generally less volatile than others in the market. They also tend to suffer less during market downturns than other stocks, and for good reason. If the stock market neglects a company, a dividend serves as compensation for shareholders until shares rise in price.

Many money managers will tell you that a stock's yield can clue you into more than a company's fiscal health. A high yield relative to the market is often an indication that a stock is undervalued, possibly because investors have overlooked its business. A low yield in comparison to that of an index like the Standard & Poor's 500 can be an indication that a stock is overvalued.

When you're mulling yields, be sure to keep a couple of numbers in mind. The first is 4.5 percent, the average yield of the S&P 500 over time. The other is 1.5 percent, the current yield of the S&P 500. The experts would tell you that today's low payout, could be interpreted a number of ways, almost the way tea leaves are read by a fortune teller. A grim take is that stocks in general are too expensive and due for a drop. Another explanation is that companies are using the extra cash they generate to boost productivity by upgrading equipment or even by buying out other companies. Which view is right? Investors will eventually know.

Some of the biggest anchors of American industry have a history of paying regular dividends that have increased over time. General Electric

THE SHORT AND THE LONG OF IT

There are most investors, and then, there are the "shorts."

Most investors put money into the market, hoping the value of their investment climbs. Shorts don't. Instead, through a odd twist in the market, they can actually make money if a stock loses value.

Shorting a stock involves a couple of steps. Say Gravy Train Inc. stock is trading at $50 a share, and a short—as the folks who short a stock are called—is convinced the company's shares are overvalued. First, a short will borrow shares, more often than not from a brokerage. Say our short picks up 10 Gravy Train shares for $500 and promises to return to the broker 10 of the company's shares by some specified time in the future. The short now sells the Gravy Train stock and pockets $500, knowing that he or she is obligated to buy 10 Gravy Train shares to complete the deal. Three months from now, if Gravy Train stock stumbles down to $30 a share, our savvy short can buy the 10 shares to return to the brokerage, spending $300, and pocket a handsome $200 in profit. If Gravy Train rises to $60 a share, however, the short has to scrape together $600 to close the deal and lose $100 in the process. Shorting is a risky venture, especially when the stock market is climbing, and is best left to the professionals.

That's not to say that you have to ignore the shorts altogether. They often have the scoop or at least a well-educated hunch on a gap between a stock's actual value and its current price. A burgeoning short interest that increases over time can often be a tip that investors have soured on a company. A short interest that seems to be dwindling could be an indication that the trouble has passed (see Figure 4.10). While you can't read the minds of shorts, though, you can see a tally of how many shares of a company's stock are being shorted in publications such as the *Wall Street Journal* or *Barron's*, or online at the Web site Dailystocks (www.dailystocks.com).

(GE) has paid out an uninterrupted dividend for just over a century. Pharmaceutical maker Pfizer (PFE) has paid a dividend every year since 1901.

Not every company around treats investors to dividends. Some young corporations find that their money is best earmarked for expansion. New hires, new facilities, and new equipment are needed to grow quickly. And, with higher earnings in sight, many executives feel that shareholders will be more than satisfied with stock price gains based on higher profits. Indeed, money manager Randall Eley of the Edgar Lomax Company says he prefers

Figure 4.10   The Short Interest Listings

Here's what you're likely to see in the financial press on a stock's short interest.

NAME	5/15/01	4/15/01	PERCENT CHANGE	AVG. DAILY VOLUME
Xylophonium Inc.	600,000	800,000	−25.0%	1,000,000

Here's what it all means:

Name	The company you're looking at.
5/15/01 and 4/15/01	The short interest on two given dates, used to track an increase or decrease.
Percent change	How much the short interest in a stock has increased or decreased during the past month.
Avg. daily volume	Average daily volume is a tally of the number of shares you can expect to change hands on any given day.

newer companies to plough any excess money back into the business. "At that point, management should really be trying to reinvest in the business," he says. "Dividends are good discipline for older, better-established companies," he adds. "It keeps management thinking about how to best use its money, and often discourages the top brass from pecking about for buyouts and takeovers that are just too expensive."

You'll find yield and dividend information all over the Web, especially at many of the sites listed at Dailystocks and Investorama.

Volume (Important)

This figure helps you track the movement of big institutional investors and how they're putting their money to work.

Before discussing volume, it's a good idea to quickly review the laws of supply and demand. When demand is high relative to supply, prices often creep upward. When supply is high relative to demand, prices can slip.

Those basic tenets guide most every market around, including the stock market. One way to gauge how the supply/demand seesaw is affecting any stock is by looking through its trading volume.

Volume is nothing more than the number of shares that change hands over a certain time period—most often a day. Yet, even though it's just a simple count of how much of stock A was sold by investors (or how much was bought, if you want to look at it that way), volume figures can sometimes lend insight into investor sentiment about a company.

Debt-to-Capital Ratio (Important)

The lower a company's debt, the less strapped it is by credit payments. The pros look for a clean balance sheet—or companies with a debt-to-capital ratio of 40 percent or less.

A string of credit card payments is likely to prevent anyone from saving much or even acquiring the finer things in life. The same goes for big corporations. A growth company that has the banks looming over its shoulder will have less money to put into research, new factories, or even share buybacks. With that in mind, many investment pros will tell you that a debt-to-capital ratio of 40 percent is a reasonable cutoff. Above that, a company may not exactly be gasping for air, but is likely devoting a great deal of energy to financing its debt. Here's another way to consider corporate debt: The same cash used to pay off loans and interest could be going toward day-to-day business. It could even make for a nice dividend distribution. So, look for companies that have managed to contain their indebtedness to 40 percent or less; that are likely to be better-managed and perhaps even more profitable.

Price-to-Book Value (Important)

A measure of a company's rock-bottom worth.

What if a company ceased to be? What if it shut the doors, called it quits, and let the cobwebs stretch out on its factory floor, its computers, its fax machines? Rust or not, it still would have some value to the outside world, and some price could be devised to set on its worth. That calculation of a firm's rock-bottom value is called its book value.

Price-to-book value, or just "price to book" as some of the pros label it, seeks a relationship between a company's share price and that rock-bottom worth. That way, professionals know how much the stock market values a company's assets—how much management would bring in if operations were closed down and everything (buildings, factories, office equipment, and the like) sold off. And Wall Street uses just such a figure to see if a company is expensive or cheap, overvalued or undervalued.

Historically, the S&P 500 has averaged a price to book of 2 to 3.5; in the inflated market at the end of the 1990s, the index's average filled out to a bloated 7 to 8.

Price-to-book value figures can be found on the Web at sites such as Zacks Investment Research (www.zacks.com). Additionally many sites such as Investorama, Dailystocks, Yahoo and others will provide access to price to book numbers, too.

Return on Equity or ROE (Important)

Used to separate the cheap stocks from duds, ROE shows how efficient management is with your investment.

Earning per share figures are a great measure. And a company that's reporting sizable increases in earnings is often doing the right things to keep its profits climbing. It's investing in new equipment, sprucing up its computer network, hiring new employees, and bringing on key personnel. Other times, though, managements will fritter away the money they bring in. The folks in the executive suite are out of touch; their businesses are declining; their marketshares are evaporating.

You'll want to find out just how savvy the corporate heads are and to that end there's an excellent measure to see if the executives are actually putting the money you've invested in their stock to good use. Return on equity or ROE, helps show how successful a company is at its business. Investment pros will tell you that a high ROE indicates that a corporation is working to get the most out of funds they have to invest in technology, new manufacturing processes, or key personnel. Michael Manns, a portfolio manager with the investment arm of American Express Asset Management says he's happy with companies that have a 20 percent ROE. "We like to invest for the long term, and when you see an ROE above 20, you've got a pretty good idea that management knows how to put shareholders' money to work."

Beta (Somewhat Important)

It is not the most critical number around, but beta is a pretty good measure of how queasy a stock might make you over time.

Simply put, a stock's beta is a calculation of how much its price will go up and down relative to the S&P 500 index. If shares in the S&P 500 run up or down 10 percent during a given time period, any stock that matches that kind of movement will carry a beta of 1. Stocks that move 5 percent during the same time period will have a beta of .50 and those that jump about twice as much or 20 percent will have a beta of 2.

Stocks in fast-moving industries—biotech, healthcare, technology—typically carry high betas. For example, in 1998, database company Oracle's beta stood at 1.43, Micron Electronics carried a 1.65, while Intel's was a surprising low 1.15, an indication that the semiconductor maker's shares aren't as skittish as the rest of the sector. Low beta stocks? Those have typically been more staid shares, such as utilities including NYNEX (.80) and Texas Utilities (.70).

While betas typically aren't published in the newspaper, investors can find the statistic in stock guides such as Standard & Poor's and Value Line, which are available in many libraries. Your broker, as well, should be able to supply you with a stock's beta.

HINTS FROM HEADQUARTERS

Insider Trading

There's another way to make investment decisions or check up on stocks: Follow the leaders and track insider trading. Anyone who has half a memory of the 1980s is sure to hear the term "insider trading" and gasp. That's because an infamous kind of illicit market tweaking and manipulation, called insider trading, landed a few of Wall Street's heavies behind bars and strapped others with hefty fines.

You might be surprised, then, to find out that insiders—the head honchos at corporations far and wide—are actually allowed to trade in their company stock legally. What's more, you can learn a lot about how business is doing simply by tracking the moves of the top brass. Top executives from the chairman down can buy or sell their company's shares, just as long as they tell the Securities and Exchange Commission (SEC) what they're doing in what the government agency calls a "Form 4." Those SEC documents are public records that all investors can check. And, if you're feeling a little lazy, you'll be glad to know that a number of Web sites scour over government inside trading papers and release the info to investors, free of charge.

Talk about a surefire stock tip. It's only logical that the folks at headquarters would know what's going on at the company. They're visiting sales staff, looking up and down factories, and shooting memos back and forth. They're keeping tabs on rivals in the marketplace. And most importantly, they're looking over sales and profit figures all day long.

That same team of executives, officers, directors, managers and the like can buy and sell company shares on the open market as they please, within the limits of the law. You can bet that if business is good, they're thinking their corporation's share price is in for a nice climb. So, as sure as spring turns to summer, they will snap up their firm's stock. Conversely, if the company is getting beaten up, if competitors are walking away with marketshare, or if the company stock looks a little too expensive, it's not uncommon to see the same cufflink and power suit set selling shares. When it comes to selling, however, don't rush to conclusions. The top executives frequently receive stock options and sometimes unload shares to pay for a new house or help get their kids through college. More often than not, though, their sales are a forewarning that some hard trekking is fast approaching.

These days, thanks to Internet access and investor Web sites that sprout up like toadstools, insider trading info is relatively easy to dig up. Form 4 disclosures often appear in publications such as *Barron's* and the *Wall Street Journal*. You can also check Yahoo! (biz.yahoo.com) or Daily-stocks (www.dailystocks.com) for records of insider trading.

Insider buying and selling aren't the only clues money managers seek out to better understand what is happening at a given corporation. They feel that insider ownership is equally important; a strong signal that the folks in the corner office have incentive aplenty to keep up the good work. Randall Eley, portfolio manager and head of the Edgar Lomax Group, an institutional investment firm, says he's encouraged when he see that the chieftains hold 3 percent to 4 percent of the shares of a large corporation or as high as 10 percent for a smaller firm. "We like to see management invested in its own stock," says Eley. "That way we know they have an incentive to see those same shares rise in value. In a way it's a daily reminder to keep a close eye on business."

Tracking insider ownership is a relatively easy task as well. Corporations are required, in their annual 10-K reports, to list a roster of top brass and how much stock they hold.

Conference Calls

Companies take the business of keeping investors informed seriously. That's especially true when it comes to big brokerage firms and powerful pension companies, which can champion a stock if it makes them money or blacklist it if they're unhappy with how their shares are faring. As a result, almost every publicly trading company (corporations whose shares trade on the stock market), has set up a special office to keep the lines of communication open. This corporate division is called a variety of names, depending on the company you're talking about. Most often, though, it's known as the Shareholder Services unit or something similar.

There in their cubicles, the employees toiling down at Shareholder Services try their best to keep investors supplied with annual reports and earnings releases. But there's a special function provided to the mighty brokerages and pension investors that individual investors haven't been able to enjoy until now: conference calls.

The word "enjoy" should be interpreted loosely because conference calls can often be tedious, drawn-out affairs. Whenever a company has major news to announce or simply informs investors and media of its earnings results for a given quarter, it may choose to make a presentation in a conference call, allowing the influential members of the investment world to listen in.

As dry as they seem, conference calls can be awfully important. During a presentation, analysts will grill company management on what's going on and how business prospects look. And, just as often, analysts will get clues on a company's fortunes from a conference call, and then either recommend a stock to the brokerage's clients or recommend that clients stay away.

These days, individual investors are getting in on the conference call act. To listen in, you'll first need to know the special telephone number that connects you to the call and the time that it is scheduled. There are a couple of ways to get the skinny on conference calls for companies whose shares you own. The old-fashioned way is to call company headquarters and bug Shareholder Services. A second way is to check the Motley Fool Web site (www.fool.com/Calls/Calls.htm). The Motley Fool(s) are investment commentators who have made a living by helping individual investors learn more about the market. Their site lists conference calls, the telephone number you need to call to participate, and even commentary on past calls.

Addition by Division

Stock splits are another hint a company can give investors that it feels its shares are likely to increase in value.

On the surface of things, a stock split may not sound like good news. If you're a shareholder, though, it probably is reason to be pleased.

This much is certain: A stock split is painless. It occurs when a company gives out a certain number of shares to holders for each share they already own. The arrival of new shares on the market lowers the price of the company's stock. Still shareholders don't suffer since they receive whatever number of shares that is a multiple of their current holding during the split. Net-net, there's no change in the value of a stock owner's stake in a company; it's a break-even proposition.

On July 1, 1999, shares of the pharmaceutical company Pfizer went through a 3-for-1 split. What happened? Well, Pfizer officials granted shareholders two additional shares for every share they owned of the company's stock. If you held 50 on June 30, your account would have tripled, leaving you with 150 shares. At the same time, your stock's share price would have fallen to a third of its value the day before. Sure enough, Pfizer, which had ended the day before the split at a price of $109, started before market trading session of the very next day at $36.33 a share. Pfizer shareholders had three times as many shares, but their total stake in the company was worth the same amount.

If shareholders come out with the same value of stock, just more shares, why the fuss? Some experts claim splits, in fact, aren't that big of a deal. They say that a split is the equivalent of cutting a pie in sixteen slices

Figure 4.11   A Stock Split

BEFORE	AFTER
50 shares of TNT Corporation	100 shares of TNT Corporation
$100 per share of TNT Corporation	$50 per share of TNT Corporation
A $5,000 stake in TNT Corporation	A $5,000 stake in TNT Corporation

instead of eight. You have the same size crust and just as many blueberries, only more pieces (see Figure 4.11).

Maybe so. Still, corporate minds like to split company shares after they've risen quite a bit in value. Higher priced shares often don't trade as actively as cheaper stocks. Less expensive shares, though, can often attract more small investors who do not have large sums at their disposal, but are willing to buy a more reasonably priced stock. And every economics student knows more demand relative to supply can force prices upward. True enough, share prices tend to scoot upward the minute a split is announced. Check for splits at Yahoo! (biz.yahoo.com) or at Dailystocks (www.dailystocks.com).

PUTTING IT ALL TOGETHER—HOW THE PROS TAKE NUMBERS AND RESEARCH AND GENERATE GREAT STOCK PICKS

The Great Divide

There are Democrats and Republicans. Our world is divided between optimists and pessimists. Some people at the dinner table turn out to be meat eaters, others are vegetarians. So, given the variety of temperaments and preferences out there, you can well imagine that when it comes to investing, there are different angles and schools of thought that take their own unique approach to choosing stocks.

Wall Street is divided up into several camps, too. First there are the pros who are fundamental investors. A company's fundamentals turn out to be several things—some numbers, some factors, most of which are listed in the Numerology section of this chapter. The factors are essentially no-brainers. Fundamental buffs like companies with good managements. They like companies in industries that are doing well, or are expanding. They like new products that haven't yet been fully appreciated.

Contrast the fundamental school with investors who use what is commonly called technical analysis. Wall Street looks at "techies," "techs," or whatever you want to call members of the technical analysis school as odd-balls of a sort. The reason: Practitioners of technical analysis use charts to make a lot of their investing choices. They claim that patterns in a stock's price chart can help predict the future or tell just what investors' sentiment is toward a stock or toward the market.

Most professionals would tell you that they are fundamental investors. That's fine, but there are some ideas in technical analysis most anyone can use. After all, if you use all the best ideas, you're sure to come up with the best picks.

LEARNING THE FUNDAMENTALS

By now, you've probably come across references to fundamental investing's two schools: "value" and "growth." On Wall Street, the two are essentially polar opposites-differing philosophies on how to choose the best stocks possible.

Portrayed as the more conservative, the more staid of the approaches, value stock picking hinges on finding companies mired at a stock price below their true worth. A value portfolio manager will then buy into the underappreciated shares, confident that the market will one day will realize it has overlooked a good deal. At that point, investors will bid up the price of the value stock.

The growth school, on the other hand, targets companies whose profits are booming. Growth managers say that if a company can increase its earnings faster than the market, it will attract investors, who will in turn bid up the price of the growth stock in question.

Which is better? Neither, to be honest. Stock picking, like all other trends in the market goes in cycles. Studies have shown that growth might be in favor for a few years when the economy's hot and companies see profits piling up. Then, inevitably, the economy cools. Growth highfliers stumble and value shares take off as investors scour the market for underappreciated shares.

For proof, just look at the results of the Standard & Poor's Barra Large Cap Growth and Large Cap Value, benchmarks the pros use to monitor growth and value investing. In the first half of the 1990s, the S&P Barra Growth index had particularly strong years in 1991 and 1995; in both years it logged a total return of over 38 percent. In 1992 and 1993, however, value investing had the upper hand. The Barra Large Cap Value index logged 10.5 percent and 18.6 percent gains, respectively, during those two years. The Barra Large Cap Growth index, meanwhile, rose just 5.1 percent in 1992 and 1.7 percent in 1993.

Each school has its own fan club and fanatics, but no matter how you may now be leaning as an investor, we suggest that you look at both and see what makes sense to you. Think it over, and choose the best of both worlds or stick to the one that appeals the most.

VALUE: LOOKING FOR THE OVERLOOKED

If you read investing books or leaf through the financial press, you'll find that value stock picking is typically likened to bargain hunting. Value managers start by looking for cheap stocks. To help gauge what a company's shares should fetch, they look at a price-to-earnings multiple or P/E, a figure calculated by dividing a company's share price by its earnings per share. Their thinking is that by buying companies for a P/E below that of the S&P 500 or the greater market, they're digging up cheap stocks that will likely be worth more when the rest of the stock market realizes that the shares in question should fetch more than their current price.

There's more to value than a low price-to-earnings multiple, however. Dawn Alston-Paige, a portfolio manager with Loomis Sayles who's a value picker, looks for companies the market has abandoned or ignored, provided there's some reason for the stock to turn around and make money. If she spies a way for company management to increase earnings, along with a cheap P/E, she's likely to give the shares a double take. "We're always looking for cheap stocks, but we're also looking for something that will ultimately help the shares gain value," she points out. "Value investing rules help us choose stocks, but we're also looking for a little earnings growth to help get things going."

Then, there's Randall Eley, a portfolio manager for the Edgar Lomax Group who wants to cushion his investments from as much risk as possible. Eley says a low P/E is nice, but he's also looking for a sizeable dividend yield, and a low price-to-book value to signal a good time to buy shares. "When we look at stocks, we first like to ignore earnings growth," he says. "That way, we're choosing a company that will make us money even if its profits don't increase. Then, if earnings increase, we get a nice extra boost for our investment."

Value Hunting

Value managers will likely look at four figures to help decide whether they should invest in a stock and when they should take a stake. They are, in order of importance, (1) *price-to-book value*, (2) *price to earnings*, (3) *return on equity*, and (4) *dividend yield*. These factors were discussed earlier in this chapter. Price to book is a reliable measure of a company's rock-bottom value. As mentioned, historically, the S&P 500 has averaged a price to book of 2 to 3.5; in 2000's inflated market, the index's average is now a bloated 7 to 8. Value managers typically gravitate to companies with a price-to-book of 4 or less. For your own hunting, price-to-book value figures can be found on Web sites such as Zacks Investment Research (www.zacks.com).

For price-to-earnings values, look for companies whose stocks trade at a P/E below that of the market. As with price-to-book value figures, aim for a third off from the market's going rate. Currently, with the S&P 500 trading at 28 times projected 1999 earnings, you should look in the neighborhood of 19 times earnings or less.

The return on equity should be on par with the market or slightly better. Again, look for a discount to the S&P 500's current ROE of 20; aim for a ROE of 15 or better.

Management's reward to the investor is the dividend yield—a steady stream of dependable income. Value investors measure a company's generosity by its yield, its dividend divided by its share price. Look for a yield on par with the S&P 500 or better. Currently, the S&P 500's corporations pay out an average yield of 1.2 percent annually, or 60 cents for every $50 share. Randall Eley looks for his portfolio to offer a payout roughly twice that figure or 2.4 percent annually.

The Intangibles

In addition to studying the critical value investing numbers, experts suggest that you should mull over other criteria when you screen for shares, some of which can't be boiled down to hard and fast statistics. That's why it's a good idea to look at annual reports and anything written about the company in the current business press.

It's that kind of fact finding that Alston-Paige says she relies on when screening stocks. With extra work she may find a catalyst—something to help prod earnings growth from the company and add to the value of a corporation's shares. "We like our stocks at a discount, that's for sure," she says, "but we're not aiming to have dead money sit around in our portfolio." Figure 4.12 provides you a value checklist.

GROWTH

As far as investing styles go, growth has been where it's at over the past few years. In fact, growth stock pickers—the portfolio mangers who hunt the market for companies with rising profits and sales—couldn't have asked for a better economic backdrop over the latter half of the 1990s. A booming economy kept corporate earnings, the bounty that growth managers cherish, chugging along and climbing as high as 20 percent annually. Low inflation helped keep money flowing into the stock market. And newspaper headlines seemed to spotlight massive mergers and acquisitions daily.

Figure 4.12 A Value Investing Checklist

When value investors search for stocks, they focus on a few key numbers. Here are some of their criteria and how value investors use them.

Price to book	*What it is.* Price to book is a measure of how a company's stock price relates to its most basic assets such as its equipment, buildings, and tools. It's calculated by dividing the worth of a company's stock by the worth of those possessions and assets.
	What it tells value investors. Price to book gives value investors an idea of a company's base value. It indicates how much a stock would be worth if everything that could possibly go wrong for a corporation actually did.
Price/earnings multiple	*What it is.* The most basic gauge of how much a stock is valued relative to its profits, P/E multiples, as they're commonly called are often high on the list of a value investor's criteria. P/Es are calculated by dividing a stock's share price by its earnings or profits.
	What it tells value investors. P/E multiples show how pricey a stock is compared to the market as a whole and to its peers.
Return on equity or ROE	*What it is.* Return on equity or ROE helps show just how management is putting shareholders' money to use. The higher the ROE, the more bang the bosses at headquarters are getting for bucks they've received from investors.
	What it tells value investors. The higher the ROE the more assured value investors are that their bet on a company's future worth is likely to turn out well. A low ROE could signal the fact that a company's fortunes have soured somewhat and that many investors in the stock market believe a turnaround isn't coming anytime soon.
Dividend yield	*What it is.* A dividend is corporation management's way of sharing profits directly with shareholders. It's calculated by dividing a company's dividend by its stock price.
	What it tells value investors. Value investors look at a dividend yield two ways: (1)How much can they earn by holding a company's shares? (2) Is the yield high in comparison to the market indicating that a company's shares might be undervalued?
Intangibles	*What they are.* Value investors love a cheap stock but want to know why a company has been shunned by the market. More important, they want to see that a corporation's management is taking steps to remedy whatever problems have beleaguered company shares.
	What it tells value investors. Evidence of a turnaround clues value investors in on a good opportunity. Shares of a company might be cheap now, but there's reason to think they'll rise in value sooner rather than later.

Add it all up and you have a paradise for growth investors. For proof, just look at the Standard & Poor's Barra indexes for both growth and value, widely accepted as the benchmark for both investing camps. Since 1995, the S&P Growth index has outpaced Value every year by a couple of percentage points. In 1998, however, the Growth index truly excelled, with a 42.16 percent total return walloping the 17.47 percent Value mustered the same year. You could also think of it this way: A $1,000 investment in 1995 would now be worth $3,324, judging by the S&P Growth index; that same initial sum would be worth $2,717 judging from the S&P Value index, a respectable sum, but still second-best.

To understand why growth has come out a winner, look no further than a lineup of companies and industries portfolio managers in the camp have come to love. Start with high-tech industries such as computers, networking hardware, and telecommunications equipment. In those sectors, companies like Dell Computers (up 5,000 percent since the start of 1995), Cisco Systems (up 1,370 percent over five years), and Lucent Technologies (up 555 percent since hitting the market in 1996) have all reaped humongous share price gains as the PC and Internet have become integral in our lives. Thanks to major breakthroughs and blockbuster treatments for depression or impotence, pharmaceutical companies have also been good to growth managers, too. Over the period between 1996 and 1999, Johnson & Johnson, Merck, and Pfizer have trekked on to gains of 241, 266, and 457 percent respectively.

That's not to say that growth investing has conquered the world, or that value investing as a school should be placed on life support, as some newspaper articles have argued from time to time. Some of the best growth portfolio managers out there will tell you that every style eventually has its season to bask in the sun, and that later both growth and value sometimes are stuck in the shade. "Go over the past few years, and growth has done phenomenally well," says Lou Holland, a seasoned pro who runs institutional and mutual fund portfolios for his Chicago investment firm Holland Capital Management. "We veterans know, however, that growth stocks, and the market in general have risen so much, that it's hard to find good picks these days."

Growth Tools

Growth managers love to center on a company's multiple (its P/E), and look at several factors when trying to determine whether a stock deserves its current price. Investment professionals consider the industry a company is in and the multiples of competitors in the same business. A second factor is the dependability of earnings. Wall Street has a fondness for companies that grow earnings year in and year out, so much so, growth managers say, that investors are willing to pay a premium or a higher multiple for that predictability.

The Edge

For growth managers, coping with an inflated market means one thing: finding an "edge" or a way to spot good possibilities before hordes of investors bid up its share price.

Securing a head start on the market for growth pickers boils down to finding growth candidates early. Instead of rooting about like value players for underappreciated and underpriced shares, growth managers try to find companies where earnings growth is about to take off or "accelerate." By getting in before the growth spurt, professionals like C. Kim Goodwin, portfolio manager for American Century, are able to buy in at a reasonable price.

A good example, says Goodwin, is Wal-Mart, which for much of the 1990s had delivered steady earnings growth on the order of 13 percent to 15 percent a year. In 1998, though, thanks to a big international expansion and a move to set up a chain of superstores throughout the United States, Wal-Mart's growth leaped up to 27 percent. Wal-Mart's stock rose 80 percent. "Our mantra in this business is simple," says Goodwin. "Money follows earnings, period."

Growth Gauges

Growth investors look for the following figures when they invest in stocks: earnings growth, earnings acceleration, PEG ratio, sales growth, and return on equity (see Figure 4.13). Whenever they're searching for stocks, growth investors key in on several numbers, including (1) earnings growth, (2) P/E to earnings growth, and (3) sales growth.

Earnings growth is the foundation of growth investing.

Growth managers will tell you they've had their seven-layer cake a la mode, and eaten a good portion of it, too. Corporate earnings growth of late has been nothing short of phenomenal, peaking at 20 percent year-over-year in 1995. And while for the past five years, earnings growth for the S&P 500 has skipped along at a 10 percent rate, Lou Holland says things are bound to cool down soon to the 7 percent to 8 percent range. That said, a good growth screen should aim for stocks that can increase earnings faster than the broad market, perhaps by 20 percent to 50 percent. Put into numbers, if the S&P 500 is slated to grow earnings 10 percent in the upcoming year, a growth manager is probably looking for a 12 percent, 15 percent or even greater increase in profits from the companies he or she holds.

Figure 4.13   A Growth Investing Checklist

Growth investors like their stocks to meet the following criteria.

Earnings growth	*What it is.* Earnings growth per share, or EPS growth, shows investors how well a company is increasing its profits.
	What it tells growth investors. To gauge a company's prospects going forward, growth investors like to focus on earnings growth projects for the next year, 3 years, or 5 years. A company whose EPS growth is higher than the market overall or its industry peers will attract more growth investors than a corporation that is merely keeping up.
PEG ratio	*What it is.* A P/E to earnings growth, or PEG, ratio is calculated by dividing a company's price-to-earnings multiple by its growth rate. As an example, take a company whose stock that is trading at 20 times its earnings per share and that is projected to grow earnings at a 20% rate over the next 5 years. Pros would say it has a PEG of 1, that is 20 divided by 20.
	What it tells growth investors. Growth investors look at a stock's PEG to determine how expensive a stock has become. A high PEG tells growth enthusiasts that the market has bid up the price of stock relative to its outlook. A low PEG is a sign that a stock with good earnings growth ahead is cheap—it simply may not have gained much notice yet.
Sales growth	*What it is.* Sales growth shows how a company's revenues or sales change from year to year.
	What it tells value investors. Earnings growth can come one of two ways. Some companies are simply worldbeaters, the type that are in hot markets and doing a great job of attracting customers. They are likely paving the way for further earnings growth in the years ahead. Others are simply going through maneuvers such as mothballing factories, sending workers home, or spinning off divisions. In those scenarios, earnings growth might not be sustainable. To tell how durable a company's earnings growth is, investors look to sales. Sales that are growing indicate that earnings should be on their way up, too. Stagnant sales indicate that earnings might not keep climbing much longer.
Intangibles	*What they are.* Growth investors keep an eye on a company's market share in certain key products to see how competitive it is. They also look for a "product pipeline," new innovations or products that are likely to attract new customers and spur sales growth.
	What they tell growth investors. Growth investors love a company that is pushing its competition aside. Increasing market share shows a company is doing better than its peers. New products in hot sectors are likely to keep sales and earnings growing.

123

A P/E to earnings growth (PEG ratio) is also an important tool. Growth managers use it to determine whether a stock is overvalued.

The reason: As much as they're impressed with earnings, growth managers tend to be at least a little value conscious. If the stock market bids up a company's share prices to the heavens, there's little reason to attract new investors. So as a practice, while growth managers may not angle for companies with P/Es below the market average, they put a cap on how high a multiple they're willing to pay. To do so, typically, the growth camp weighs P/Es against earnings growth rates. Some, like Michael Manns, a portfolio manager with American Express go so far as to divide a company's P/E by its projected earnings growth to get what's called a PEG ratio. Manns says that while a PEG of 1 is the sign of a bargain growth stock, he's willing to go a bit higher— say a PEG of 1.5 or even 2—for companies that have been dependable in the past. "At 1.5 I tend to get a little queasy," he says. "And paying a P/E two times a company's growth rate is merited only in the case of a company with exceptional management, high barriers to entry in its business, leadership in its products and 15 percent or better earnings growth 5 years back."

Next, there is sales growth. Over the past 10 or 20 years, renegade owners have blazed their way to the top of companies. They've sold off factories, sent workers packing, spun off divisions on their own, only to see fabulous results in the stock market.

Growth? Well, over the short term, those kinds of actions are bound to raise both earnings and share prices. But ask C. Kim Goodwin, and she'll tell you that for the long haul a company needs to create something substantive for the future. Her measure: positive sales growth.

"If you ask me, sales growth really confirms corporate earnings," she says. "To my eye, sales growth shows all the positives we look for in a company—good products seizing market share, margins rising, or even dominant products in a given sector." And as a gauge, Goodwin points out, sales will often separate stocks on their way up from those headed south. "In this day and age it's hard to find large companies that can augment sales growth, but when you do, it's often a sign of bigger and better things to come."

Intangibles

Growth investing, just like its value counterpart, requires research beyond a collection of favorable numbers. Take a look at a company's annual report and read through whatever magazine articles you can gather up on the Internet or at your local library. Another resource, says American Century's Goodwin is a company's Web site where you'll often find annual reports and a lot of good background information on its businesses and prospects. "I think you should look at research as a continuous project," she says. "You should monitor stocks just like anything you put your money into—the family car, your air conditioner."

TECHNOLOGY STOCKS

The tech stock bug? The market certainly has it. It's so widespread, in fact, that everyone—penny-pincher, daredevil, or cautious observer—knows the symptoms. It starts with a fascination in all things speedy and new, from the Internet to laptop computers. Then, there are the sweaty palms investors get whenever there's a mention of a company like America Online (NYSE: AOL) or Intel (Nasdaq: INTC). That's followed by bouts of wishful thinking, particularly anytime those investors read about the 50 percent, 100 percent, sometimes even 200 percent annual gains achieved regularly by stocks like Amazon.com (Nasdaq: AMZN) or Cisco (Nasdaq: CSCO).

The truth can finally be told. Locked away in the recesses of the human psyche, in each investor's soul, there's a deep longing for technology stocks. And when it comes to growth stocks, there's nothing like talk of technology shares to get the blood of most anyone racing.

Face it. Everyone would have bought shares of Compaq (NYSE: CPQ) or Microsoft (Nasdaq: MSFT) 5 or 10 years ago, if only people had known how rich those stocks were going to make investors. The question on everyone's mind is this: Just how in the world do you figure out what makes technology stocks tick?

That's no small matter, indeed. Tech companies are hard to understand, what with the heavy-duty jargon that describes what they do. Confusing terms like wafer boards and software upgrades can make most investors feel like a Fred Flintstone hurled unceremoniously onto the set of the Jetsons.

Then, there's the simple fact that technology shares don't act like other typical stocks. Many software, hardware, semiconductor, or Internet shares just don't fit those neat, understandable price-to-earnings multiples used with other industries. An Internet start-up or biotechnology outfit can often trade beyond the ozone, with a P/E ratio of 200 or 300, at a time when the S&P 500 fetches maybe 20. Sometimes, a tech company, for all of its cutting-edge innovations hasn't yet turned a profit. And to really set your head spinning, there are the sad tales of investors who plunked down thousands on a speculative issue, only to see their investment evaporate at the first sign of a crisis.

So what's the use, then? Well, start with the fact that the personal computer and all its trappings are here to stay. Companies that shuttle shoppers on and off the Internet or hammer out semiconductor codes on silicon wafers will make a lot of money for both management and shareholders. The world of biotechnology is making fascinating discoveries and medical breakthroughs almost daily.

Translated into raw numbers, there's a veritable gold mine to be had in the right tech stocks. Consider some of the winners: In 1999, that includes Qualcomm, which finished the year up 2,619 percent or JD Uniphase, a fiber-optic equipment maker that rose 830 percent for the year. Cisco Systems was up 131 percent for the year.

How Much, How Many, How Little?

Perhaps the biggest problem technology stocks pose for investors is just how to value their worth. For ordinary companies suck as Ford Motor (F) or General Electric (GE), you start by looking at earnings per share and how quickly or slowly those profits are growing. To help compare a company against the broad market, you look at price to earnings or P/E multiples—a stock's price divided by its earnings per share. And to determine whether a stock looks like a bargain, you compare a stock's P/E to that of the Standard & Poor's 500 or Dow Jones Industrials.

The pros use the same yardsticks for technology shares, but make special adjustments. Many money managers reason that tech companies can generally grow earnings faster than ordinary retailers, financial companies, or industrial powers, and therefore their shares stand a greater chance of appreciating over time. For that ability to increase in value, tech shares are typically allotted a high P/E multiple in the stock market.

A good example is Cisco Systems. Wall Street analysts have felt that the computer networking company will increase earnings at close to a 30 percent clip for approximately 5 years ahead according to Zacks Investment Research. That figure dwarfs the 10 percent earnings growth rate projected for the S&P 500 over the same time, and gives Cisco a good chance to reward investors with gains that surpass those of the stock market over this period. Since that potential keeps Cisco shares in hot demand, the networking company's stock trades at a much higher price-to-earnings multiple—as high as 4 times that of the S&P 500.

That difference alone makes it difficult to compare the P/E of tech stocks with that of other companies. Instead, when looking over tech stocks, money managers tend to use P/E multiples to differentiate stocks of companies in the same industry. Because these firms face the same challenges and same markets, a tool like a P/E can help distinguish which stock is the better deal.

Just how much is a company's predicted growth worth? To figure that out, money managers again turn to a tech company's P/E multiple and size it up against a company's projected growth rate—the PEG mentioned earlier. According to Michael T. Manns, the American Express portfolio manager who oversees $800 billion, this is the rule of thumb: A technology stock looks attractive as long as its P/E is no more than 1.5 times its growth rate.

Above 1.5, and chances are the stock's price is too high. Below that, and you may well have a bargain on your hands.

A final measure to use is price to sales. Often young technology companies aren't yet putting up great earnings when they're taking the market by storm. Sales or revenues, however, often give Wall Street a good indication of what's to come. "The way a lot of these tech companies are going to fuel earnings is by accelerating the top line," says Kim Goodwin, portfolio manager of the American Century Twentieth Century Growth Fund. To gauge just how costly a tech company is on the market, investment pros often compare its price-to-sales ratio. It's a relatively easy figure to come up with: First, take a company's stock price and multiply it by the number of shares it has outstanding. Next, divide the figure by a company's sales.

Then what? Price-to-sales figures generally aren't useful outside of industry circles. However, they're a great way to look at competitors to see how they stack up.

Follow the Leaders

Perhaps the soundest piece of advice for investing in tech stocks is also the easiest: Stick to companies that dominate their industries, for example, Cisco Systems. Cisco's equipment has been a favorite of companies establishing computer networks and working on the Internet. As a result, Cisco dominates the business worldwide.

Investing in leaders makes sense for several reasons. First, what the mammoths say, generally goes. When AOL decides to hike prices on monthly Internet access, it's highly unlikely that subscribers will go anywhere else to surf. Second, the big players all have installed bases and deep-rooted customer relationships making it hard for upstarts, no matter what innovation they offer, to push the leaders aside. So if Cisco Systems has sold your local phone company on tons of computer networking equipment, chances are it has won over a customer for a long time.

Then, consider that big players can fend off all comers. How? Well, if a competing technology pops up, a company like Cisco has the resources to buy out inventors and claim it for its own. Manns says he'll afford tech leaders a high PEG rate, on the assumption that the big players will pump up growth overtime through mergers.

Finally, portfolio managers point out that, the leaders have staying power when the markets get topsy-turvy. "You'll pay a little more for a leader in terms of P/E, just because you know they have figured out how to weather the top and bottom of the cycle," says Goodwin. "When it's your money invested, you want that kind of dependability. In effect, you're paying for reliable growth."

BEGINNER'S LUCK

If you're a novice investor, just learning to make sense of the market and how it works, then, there's probably nothing more intimidating than stocks. Taking a stake in a company by owning shares can be a convoluted process that costs a lot to boot. Step 1, you have to contact a broker and arrange to buy shares. Step 2, you can count on digging up a sizable commission to pay for the transaction, anywhere from $19 to $60 above the price of the shares you're tucking away in your portfolio. Factoring in that kind of expense, you really need about $2,500 or more up front to make it worthwhile.

There's an easier way into the market for first-timers and for folks who already own shares: direct stock plans (DSPs) and dividend reinvestment plans (DRPs). Companies that offer DSPs and DRPs are essentially cutting the broker out to give you a cheaper way of owning their shares without having to ante up a large block of cash. What's more, under both plans, you can opt to make steady, small purchases of shares, and can even arrange to have regular withdrawals taken from your checking or savings account to do so. That way, you can build a sizable position in a stock or a few companies' shares over time. Often enough, you can start up with little (say, $50, $100, or $250) or no money, if you're willing to agree to regular purchases of shares. And, by buying shares directly from the company, you can often save a bundle on brokerage commissions. Some companies, however, charge a processing fee of a few dollars on transactions, although it's a lot less than the commission you'd hand over to even a discount broker.

There's another plus. Both DRPs and DSPs allow you to reinvest dividends. In other words, should your company pay a dividend, whatever distributions you receive can be reinvested in partial or full company shares. As already pointed out, compounding is a great way to fatten your savings. For an example, look at the S&P 500 Index over the past 10 years. An investment of $1,000 in the index alone would have grown to $3,160 during the 10-year period ended May 31, 1999. But, plow the dividends back into your account, and that sum jumps a full 43 percent to $4,520 over the same amount of time.

DSPs and DRPs have similar names and in many ways are alike. Still, we prefer DSPs to DRPs. That's because DRPs often require you to buy at least one share from a broker before joining the company's plan. DSPs, however, let you skip the middleman and get your initial shares from the company itself.

BEGINNER'S LUCK (CONTINUED)

Today, there are over 400 companies with DSP plans, including Sears (NYSE: S), Wal-Mart (NYSE: WMT), and Merck (NYSE: MRK). According to Standard & Poors, that number should bolt to about 1,000 by the end of next year.

There are several ways to find out if a stock that has piqued your interest offers a direct purchase program. One way, albeit hit-or-miss, is to call a corporation's investor relations department. On the Internet, Quicken, the personal finance software maker, has a Web page devoted to DRPs and DSPs (www.quicken.com). Another good resource is the *Directory of Dividend Reinvestment Plans,* published by Standard & Poor's (55 Water Street, New York, NY 10041) for $39.95.

DO IT YOURSELF STOCK PICKING

Dear Mr. and Ms. Individual Investor, your Internet miracle is here. It comes in a complete online package that's easy for investors to use. It's great for experts and novices alike. In short, it's something akin to the gift of fire. It's the stock screen.

Don't laugh. Stock screening programs readily available on the Internet do a lot to live up to that kind of billing. They offer you the very same tools professionals use to sift through the market and choose stocks.

Don't be fooled, either. Screens may look mild-mannered, but they have a lot of power. The best online versions cull mountains of stats on price-to-earnings ratios and sales growth. They harness computers to grind through the heavy mathematics of investing, slicing through forests of stock market data to unearth the best shares.

And it isn't just the power of screens that makes them so special. A sizable portion of their wonder lies in sheer speed. In the time it takes to type out a few keystrokes to input criteria, you can tailor a portfolio of stocks that fits your needs, your taste for risk, and your plans for the future in one sitting. Better yet, many Web sites don't require you to have a degree in computer engineering or any great level of investing expertise to get started. And if that hasn't yet won you over, consider the price in many cases: free.

You probably remember seeing crusty old prospectors in the movies panning through mountain streams in search of gold. They'd dip into the river's silt, swirl the mud and water about a bit, skim the contents and collect the shiniest rocks. A stock screen works much the same way prospectors did. Its software scoops up data on thousands of stocks that trade publicly on the New York Stock Exchange, American Stock Exchange, and

Nasdaq. Next, it sifts through the numbers according to requirements or criteria you plug in, discarding the stocks that don't meet your goals. If you're looking for companies that are growing earnings 20 percent or more a year, yet are trading at a price-to-earnings multiple of 30 or less, a screen will ferret out a list of candidates for your researching pleasure.

That's a marked break with the past. Not that long ago, the average individual investor's stock-picking efforts amounted to a hit-and-miss venture. You'd have to wade across mounds of prospectuses, peel past an infinite array of numbers or rely on dumb luck, based on a tip from a friend. Or, if you wanted to shell out extra money in trading commissions, you might get a few recommendations from your broker. Otherwise, if you had a spare $30,000 or so, you could get a company like Factset Data Systems, the Connecticut screening company that caters to huge institutional money managers, to do the job online screens accomplish today gratis. There are many sites on the Web where you can screen for stocks. When you are surfing for a stock screening program remember two things: Keep it simple and make sure it's free.

Next, look for all the help you can get. If you're just getting the knack of how stocks are valued and how the market sees things, there are online sites that provide a decent bit of hand-holding. Be forewarned, however. At the very least, you'll need to know how to use some of the numbers listed in the Numerology section of this chapter. A little homework will pay dividends, though. By just noodling with a stock screen, you can quickly learn and assimilate the same concepts used by pros at the big investing firms.

Looking for All the Right Parts

Screens all start with a database. That's because no matter how large or small they happen to be, stock screens at their root are large pools of information. They include a library of company names and one- to four-letter ticker symbols. Screens are also loaded with company-specific facts and figures. There are earnings growth rates, for one, to help point out how quickly the CEO of a given outfit is conquering the world. Heaps of price-to-earnings ratios help indicate whether shares are cheap or expensive relative to the market or even a specific industry.

That's dandy, but you might be asking yourself just where those figures come from. Often stock screens tap into companies that poll industry analysts at Wall Street brokerage firms such as Merrill Lynch, Salomon Smith Barney, and the like. Firms like I/B/E/S, Zacks, and First Call, to name a few of the most reputable in the field, then combine numbers, tabulate averages, and provide "consensus" figures, averages of what Wall Street projects for a firm. In turn, a good screening program serves up those kinds of numbers for after all, a screen is only as good as the facts and figures it's weeding through.

Remember, too, that fresh data ensures that your screen will be up to date. Numbers on Wall Street have a way of changing overnight. One day, a darling company, Acme Rocket Corp. might release news to the press that its marvel of a booster engine didn't make as much money during the last quarter as expected. Almost automatically, analysts will sharpen their pencils, rush headlong through their books, and lower their estimates of revenues, earnings, and perhaps even the rate they feel a company can grow profits. The market takes those assumptions seriously because they help determine how much a stock is worth now and in the future. And inevitably, the figures stockpiled by consensus estimate firms will probably dip as well. So, to provide the most accurate figures, a good screen updates its reservoir of numbers regularly.

Off from the Starting Block

Among screens on the Net, there are four winning sites where you needn't pay a dime for the goods. All update regularly and use solid sources for their data. Perhaps the simplest and most straightforward can be found on Quicken's site (www.quicken.com/investments/stocks/search). There, you can screen the entire market, or industry by industry, using a no-nonsense format. Marketplayer (www.marketplayer.com), is by far the most comprehensive in its criteria choices. However, Marketplayer's site can be daunting at first, if you're just cutting your teeth. A lot of the terms (e.g., forward P/E, meaning a company's price-to-earnings multiple for the upcoming year) can be a bit much for initial investors. It's advisable to first go to the simple screening heading in the left margin of the site or try your hand at a few of the model screens provided at the site. Another solution: Click on the support heading in the left margin, and send a query to Marketplayer via e-mail.

DailyStocks (www.dailystocks.com) not only offers a choice of screens, it has links to a diamond mine of company and stock information. Again, the terminology can at times get meaty; as an entry point, click at the heading "Quick Pre-Screened." There you'll find a number of preset screens to help you get up to speed. Finally, you might want to check in at www.stockscreener.com, run by Hoover's company information site.

Recipes for Success

Once you have found the horsepower, a screen with the fabulous ability to parse and pare the market, what do you do? Well, even if you're the stock expert of all time, it probably makes sense to first take a test drive by running a few of the prepackaged screens a site offers. At DailyStocks' pre-screened window, for example, it's possible to call up a list of shares below $10 in price with an average annual growth rate of 20 percent or greater.

After a few runs with the training wheels on, you'll probably want to start off on your own, with a few of your own creations. While screens are full of features that help whittle the seemingly insurmountable scope of the market down to size, many screens can be surgically precise as well, preening through your choices to pinpoint anywhere from one to a few stocks.

Where to start? One surefire method is to copy the moves of the pros. The discussion of value and growth stock picking in this chapter lists a few suggestions. And, in many cases, it's possible to mix and match criteria depending on your preferences or even whims.

Keep in mind a couple of additional sources for ideas. *Black Enterprise's* Moneywise section features a monthly column called "Private Screening." There, you'll find hints and techniques used by African American portfolio managers. A second place to look is in the weekly publication, *Barron's*, where institutional and mutual fund portfolio managers alike love to strut and boast about their strategies. Finally, mutual fund prospectuses can offer a wealth of investment strategies as well. A hint: Dig up a few of a fund's holdings, and you can quickly determine what biases a manager might use in selecting stocks.

Only the Beginning

You've screened and screened again. You've found a few stocks that have caught your fancy. You might be tempted to call it a trading day and be done. Don't. Even a rookie portfolio manager will tell you that once the screening is done, his or her work has just begun. Even after you've narrowed the investing universe to workable dimensions, you still have to look a bit closer at companies and their respective industries. In financial parlance, that's called a "bottom-up approach."

True enough, you probably can't sit down to a power lunch with management; the truth be told, many institutional portfolio whizzes don't get that privilege. But, you'd be wise to read up in financial magazines to see what's going on at headquarters. The reason: Company data, no matter where it comes from, is fallible. If you read the financial pages of your local newspaper, you've no doubt seen instances where earnings or sales fell short of expectations. Since company CEOs don't have to sit down for a polygraph test, any further due diligence falls into your lap.

TECHNICAL TICKS—REVENGE OF THE CHART READERS

The failings of human nature are all too evident when it comes to outsiders. All too often, folks who approach life differently are chased away, labeled as outcasts, or just plain ignored. Practitioners of a peculiar form of stock picking called technical analysis have suffered that same sort of treatment over the years.

That's because a lot of professionals on Wall Street scoff at the claims some of the practicers of technical analysis make. And wouldn't you? Some members of the technical analysis camp claim they never look at a company's fundamentals—its growth rate, its P/E ratio—and they still get a good sense of what its stock is going to do. Others claim that charts of a company's stock price movement follow certain patterns again and again, shapes the technical analysis folk call "head and shoulders formations," or "candlesticks," or "double-bottoms."

For all the bizarre claims and oddball names, though, there's a decent amount of logic behind some technical analysis. To crawl into a technician's mind, you have to know a thing or two about stock charts. One variety, price charts are often published in newspapers and magazines. A stock's price is mapped out on the vertical axis of the chart. Days, weeks, months, and sometimes years are etched out on the horizontal portion of the chart. Follow the lines from left to right, and you get an idea of what a particular company's shares did as time moves forward.

Other charts that don't always appear in magazine articles, can nonetheless be useful to investors. One, a volume chart, is a diagram that shows how many shares of a company stock changed hands during a given day, or "trading session," as the pros say. High-volume days occur when many, many buyers and sellers swap stocks for cash, and vice versa. Low-volume days are those when not much trading is going on.

Combine price and volume charts, however, and suddenly you have a keener insight into the stock market as a marketplace where goods exchange hands and prices go up when demand is high relative to supply and down when supply is greater than demand.

By poring over chart after chart, technical analysis users delve into the supply and demand for any given stock. These days, that's important because institutional investors—pension funds, mutual funds, brokerage firms and the like—make a big splash in the market. If several mammoths like a stock, chances are its share price will go up—demand will rise, outstripping supply. By the same token, if most of the moneyed legion turn cold on a company, dumping shares by selling their stakes, supply will outstrip demand and share prices will fall.

Technical analysis allows you to observe in a very simple and easy-to-understand way just how major investors view a stock. All you have to do is take trading volume and price movement into account. Add them together, and suddenly you'll see new possibilities.

Say a company's share price is rising, a phenomenon easily spotted on a chart. If that same stock's trading volume is higher than usual, chances are the movers and shakers have an interest. They're buying a lot of shares. If the same price rise is accompanied by little in the way of trading volume, then the recent gains might not have enough steam to sustain their momentum.

Now, look at a falling stock. If a company's share price is dropping and volumes are high, you could be witnessing a stampede of big investors out of a stock. If a stock is descending, and volumes are low, it could be a sign that big investors have enough confidence to stick it out.

This is in no way a recommendation that you scrap fundamentals like P/E ratios or growth estimates. Instead, think of the relationship between fundamental and technical analyses in much the same way as you'd approach buying a new car. Fundamental analysis is no different from kicking the tires, looking under the hood, and taking the sedan around town on a test drive. Technical analysis? The equivalent in this analogy is a thorough check of the overall car market. If you learned that Detroit's auto sales were sluggish and that a major sale was likely to take place, you'd probably want to stall your purchase for a bit. Or, heed the words of Randall Eley, one of the top value managers around. Eley's in no way going to abandon his comparisons of yields, price-to-book ratios or P/Es. "You absolutely must go over the fundamentals to decide whether or not you want the stock," he says, adding, "but technical analysis sometimes gives you a sense of just when might be the best time to buy."

The only props you need for a little technical analysis of your own are simple stock charts, the kind you can fetch on Web sites such as Big Charts (http: www.bigcharts.com). So, assuming you're wedded to the ways of fundamental analysis, here is a basic primer of technical analysis, a list of simple tips that could make it well worth your while to ponder a chart now and then.

Support and Resistance

What they tell you: Where institutions think a stock's a good buy, or at what level they feel it's time to sell.

A technical analysis whiz who first sets eyes on a stock chart will often draw a horizontal line through two peaks or two bottoms during the past year's trading. A horizontal line connecting two troughs or low is dubbed a "support," a figure where one or more institutions have determined there is a good buying opportunity, a rise in demand that thereby lifts a share price. The line connecting the two peaks represents what chartists call a "resistance," a point where some institutions decided to cash out, creating a rise in supply that deflates a stock price.

Whenever a support or resistance point is broken, technicians perceive it as a signal that the market's sentiment on a company's shares has changed. Once a stock pierces a resistance or ceiling, it's often buoyed by enough demand to keep it rising for a while; individual investors can interpret this as a good time to buy, should they like the company's fundamentals. Crashing through a support price signals the opposite: There's an indication that some institutions out there have turned bearish on a stock, perhaps signaling a good opportunity to sell.

Elementary though it may be, this is important stuff for the chartist, because it shows a range of prices where most investors are willing to trade in the shares. The stock's support level is a point where the stock is expected to pique bargain hunters' interest. The higher line is called investors' resistance because any advance in price is expected to be cooled by profit-taking (see Figure 4.14).

Figure 4.14   Support and Resistance Points

In technical analysis, support points show investors a share price point where institutional investors think a stock might be a bargain. Resistance points represent share prices that might seem too dear or too expensive to big institutions.

The trading pattern of shares of cigarette maker Philip Morris during 1996 and 1997 helps illustrate support and resistance points. For much of that period, Philip Morris stock traded in a range between $85 and $108. At times when the stock fell in price, it never crept below a "support" level of $85 a share, a sign that enough investors felt the stock was a good value at that price and moved to buy Philip Morris. Other times, when the stock rose, it bumped up against a "resistance" point at $107 to $108 a share, an indication that many investors believed the stock was too expensive at that price.

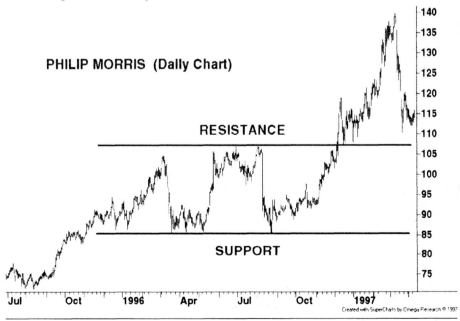

Source: Salomon Smith Barney.

Trend Lines

What they tell you: The direction where many investors feel a stock is headed.

Another trick of the technical trade is a variation on the old puzzle book game, connect-the-dots. On a chart where a stock's price is rising, draw a line through as many drawbacks or troughs in the chart as possible while remaining below all the stock's gyrations. On a chart where a share's price is falling, go only through the successive peaks that the stock manages to reach, just so all the stock's price fluctuations remain above the line. The result is a trend line, a vector that technical analysis buffs say indicates the

Figure 4.15   Trend Lines

Trend lines tell technical analysis buffs whether a stock is gaining buyers or being sold off by many big investors. Technical analysis users say the trend helps them see how the market at large feels about a stock.

During October 1998 and July 1999, Motorola moved steadily upward. A trend line (an upward sloping line in this case) could be drawn to connect the series of higher lows made by the stock during that period, and during the period between October 1999 and March 2000. According to technical analysis, the moment the trend's pattern is broken, a stock's upward momentum has ebbed. In July 1999, that meant Motorola was set to hover in a holding pattern. In early 2000, however, the stock was in for a steep drop.

Source: Salomon Smith Barney.

primary direction the stock's price is moving toward. On the way up, should the chart continue above that line even while touching it periodically, you have a good indication that a majority of the investors out there feel the same way about the shares. The minute the trend line is broken through, however, is the moment that the market has soured on the stock in question (see Figure 4.15).

Moving Averages

What they tell you: What direction a stock's price seems to be headed; how bullish a majority of portfolio managers are.

Although moving averages are simple to understand, technicians say they are an important reading of the market's overall bent on a particular stock. The calculation required is straightforward: You choose a set number of days, often 50, 100, or 200, find a stock's closing price for each trading session, and average the total. Technicians then compare the average to the stock's current price, an indication whether institutional investors are currently bullish or bearish on a stock. It works much the same way as a trend line. A stock trading above its moving average is seen to be on a bullish upswing; one that's below could well be floundering.

Pension managers are in charge of the investment decisions behind huge sums of money and are constantly on edge over the stocks they are banking on. That means they will stick with the highfliers, but laggards—say a stock that hasn't moved much in the previous 200 days—are likely to get weeded out after a prolonged period of underperforming the market.

WEB SIGHTINGS
TECHNICAL ANALYSIS CHARTS ONLINE

The best place to start eyeballing charts is a Web site that's aptly named Big Charts (www.bigcharts.com). Plug in a stock ticker, and the Big Charts site will instantly draw up a chart of price and volume activity for the shares in question for the past day, week, month, 5-month, or year period. The site's database stretches back as far as a decade. Click on a button labeled "Interactive Charting" and you can dig up moving averages as well. What's more, the site provides market analysis, stock quotes, and industry overviews.

Volume

What it means: A sign showing how the majority of institutions out there feel about a stock.

One of the most frequently quoted aphorisms of technical analysis is "volume reinforces the trend." Translation: Shares that are rising in price, will continue to do so only as long as demand, or volume, remains high and pushes up on the stock. Company shares that are falling will continue earthward as long as trading is brisk. In that case, supply outstrips demand. If a stock has hit a new 52-week high on below-average volume, or if the number of shares trading daily has started to flag somewhat, there's a good chance it

Figure 4.16   Volume Bar Chart

The stock market, just like any other place where buyers and sellers meet, is swayed by supply and demand. A volume bar chart helps investors clue into those two influential forces. High volume means a lot of shares traded hands on any given day. If a stock is going up, a day of heavy volume could well mean that a stock is attracting a lot of interest. If volume is large on a day when a stock is going down, it would indicate that investors are losing faith in a stock.

The latter seems to be true for Motorola shares in 1995 and 1996, when heaving trading volume on days when the stock hit low points indicated that investors felt the company's shares weren't due for much of a rebound. Motorola suffered a drop in price from $82 to about $44 during 1995. The sell-off climaxed in January 1996 with very high volume. The stock recovered during the following months to as high as $68 in 1996, but the rebound proved to be short-lived that year.

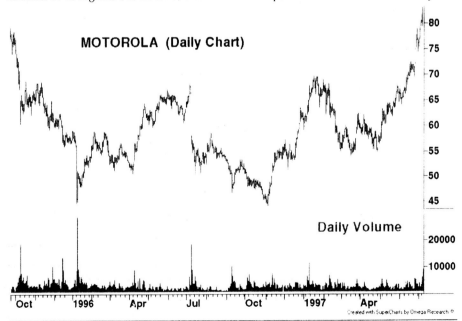

Source: Solomon Smith Barney.

won't keep the peak for too long. By that same logic, if a stock hits a 52-week low on heavy volume, there's a good chance it's due for a nice bounce, and perhaps even a ride upward (see Figure 4.16).

Head and Shoulders, Double Bottoms

What they tell you: A good point to sell or buy a stock.

Leaf through any text on technical analysis and you're sure to spot a chapter or two on patterns dubbed the "head and shoulders" or "double bottom." Despite the odd names, both refer to a relatively common phenomenon that

Figure 4.17   Head and Shoulders, Double Bottoms

Technical analysis users talk about quirky phenomena such as "head and shoulders" patterns or even "double bottoms." A head and shoulders often indicates the highest price a stock has been able to attain. Past that price, investors have been reluctant to invest. A double bottom is a low point for a stock. Investors have shown that they feel the shares in question can't get any cheaper, and could well be in for a rebound.

The stock price chart for aircraft manufacturer Boeing shows a head-and-shoulders pattern between June and August of 1990. From summer through the fall, Boeing's stock rose up to $62 a share but never broke through the mark. When Boeing shares began to slide in August, volume picked up and the shares began a steep descent.

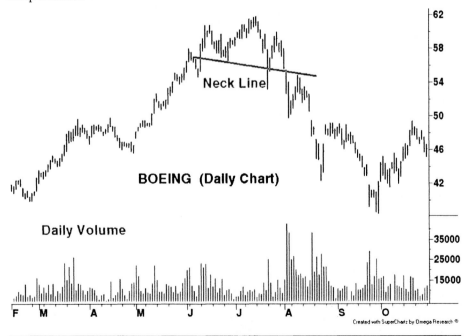

Source: Solomon Smith Barney.

occurs when a stock grazes a resistance or support level several times. When a share price graph scrapes up against a resistance line a few times, it's labeled a head and shoulders because of its three successive peaks. The fact that not a single rise of the stock was able to push through the resistance level is a poignant indicator that a company's fortunes aren't strong enough to convince investors that its shares are worth more than that resistance point. And rest assured that a good number of even the most fundamentally attuned portfolio managers will look over their numbers twice before buying in.

A double bottom is based on the same logic, except this time in relation to a support level. Technicians reason that a stock that has bounced one or two times off a support line isn't likely to fall further. The reason is that the stock seems to have lured enough institutional investors to keep it from slipping further (see Figure 4.17).

BLACK MARKET: THE BLACK ENTERPRISE INDEX OF BLACK STOCKS

You show your support of African American owned businesses. You buy from black vendors, spend your money at African American establishments when you can. And now, you want to take a stake by buying stock in an African American firm.

Actually, you'll have quite a selection of companies from which to choose. There is Granite Broadcasting, which owns and operates television stations from coast to coast. There's OAO Technologies, a firm that outsources IBM computer software work. Carver Bancorp is a financial institution in New York. American Shared Hospital Services makes medical equipment (see Figure 4.18).

Figure 4.18   The Black Market—Black Stock

COMPANY (TICKER-EXCHANGE)	LINE OF BUSINESS
American Shared Hospital Services (AMS: American Stock Exchange) Four Embarcadero Center Suite 3620 San Francisco, CA 94111 415-788-5300	Has pioneered advanced medical devices for x-rays and magnetic resonance imaging.
Ault (AULT: Nasdaq) 7300 Boone Avenue North Minneapolis, MN 55428-1028 612-493-1900 Web site: www.aultinc.com	Makes power conversion equipment that is sold to companies that manufacture communications and medical equipment.

Figure 4.18 *(continued)*

COMPANY (TICKER-EXCHANGE)	LINE OF BUSINESS
Broadway Financial Corp. (BYFC: Nasdaq) 4800 Wilshire Boulevard Los Angeles, CA 90010 323-634-1700	Holding company for a savings and loan in South Central Los Angeles, California.
Carsons, Inc. (CIC: New York Stock Exchange) 64 Ross Road Savannah Industrial Park Savannah, GA 31405 912-651-3400	The maker of hair care products.
Carver Bancorp (CNY: American Stock Exchange) 75 West 125th Street New York, NY 10027 212-876-4747	Holding company for Carver Federal Savings Banks which operates branches in and around New York City.
Chapman Capital Management Holdings (CMAN: Nasdaq) 401 East Pratt Street, Suite 2800 Baltimore, MD 21202 410-625-9656 Web site: www.chapmancompany.com	Brokerage and investment management firm. Operates two mutual funds: DEM Equity and the Chapman U.S. Treasury money fund.
Granite Broadcasting (GBTVK: Nasdaq) Web site: www.granitetv.com 767 Third Avenue 34th Floor New York, NY 10017 212-826-2530	Operates television stations around the country.
OAO Technology Solutions (OAOT Nasdaq) 7500 Greenway Center Drive Greenbelt, MD 20770 301-486-0400 Web site: www.oaot.com	Provides outsourced data management and information technology services and software services.
Pyrocap International (PYOC: Nasdaq) 15010 Farm Creek Drive, Suite 102 Woodbridge, VA 22191 703-551-4452	Makes fire extinguishers and products that control the foul odors of waste sites and farms.
Radio One, Inc. (ROIA: Nasdaq) 5900 Princess Garden Parkway, 8th Floor Lanham, MD 20706 301-306-1111	Operates radio stations targeting African American audiences.
United American Healthcare (UAH: New York Stock Exchange) 1155 Brewery Park Boulevard Detroit, MI 48207-2602 313-393-0200	Manages HMOs in Tennessee and Michigan.

Black Enterprise follows the group of African American stocks by means of its Black Stock Index, published regularly in the pages of the magazine.

The group has certain characteristics you should take into account. For one, the stocks listed are primarily small companies with small cap stocks. They are thinly traded, meaning the number of shares that change hands on any given day is small, and because of that, their prices are subject to surge up or down. Also, during the latter portion of the 1990s, small cap stocks

Figure 4.19   The Black Market—Prominent Corporations with African American CEOs

COMPANY (TICKER - EXCHANGE)	LINE OF BUSINESS
Avis Rent A Car (AVI: NYSE) CEO—A.B. Rand 900 Old Country Road Garden City, NY 11530 516-222-3000 Web site: www.avis.com	The world's second largest car rental company.
Federal National Mortgage Association (Fannie Mae) (FNM: NYSE) Chairman & CEO—F.D. Raines 3900 Wisconsin Avenue NW Washington, DC 20016 202-752-7000 Web site: www.fanniemae.com	U.S. government-sponsored company that invests in mortgages.
Maytag Corp. (MYG: NYSE) Chairman, President, & COO— Lloyd D. Ward 403 West 4th Street North Newton, IA 50208 515-792-7000 Web site: www.maytagcorp.com	Makes household appliances.
Symantec (SYMC: Nasdaq) Chairman, President, & CEO— J.W. Thompson 10201 Torre Avenue Cupertino, CA 95014-2132 408-253-9600 Web site: www.aymantec.com	Makes PC and antivirus software.
American Express Corp. (AXP: NYSE) President & COO—K.I. Chenault World Financial Center New York, NY 10285 212-640-2000 Web site: www.americanexpress.com	Financial services company with a famous credit card.

took a drubbing as investors flocked to big, well-known companies. That hurt the results of the Black Stock Index members, and put a damper on their stock performance. If you feel strongly about backing a Black Stock, by all means go ahead. Before jumping in the fray, however, make sure you have a solid foundation in a mutual fund or two, or have a decent-sized stake in the shares of a large company.

Breakthroughs

If you're a community-conscious investor, you can now take another tack. Purchase stock of companies with African American CEOs, or with prominent African Americans who are heads-in-waiting. Within the past few years, the choice has expanded: As of this writing there are four companies and counting, many with names you'll recognize immediately. Start with Maytag Corporation, the household appliance manufacturer headed by Lloyd Ward, or Avis Rent A Car, whose Chairman and Chief Executive is A.B. Rand. Fannie Mae, the mortgage investment firm led by F.D. Raines, is another good example, as is Symantec, the software firm that makes Norton antivirus cures for PCs. Symantec's Chair and CEO is J.W. Thompson, an African American. Three of the stocks—Avis, Fannie Mae, and Maytag—trade on the New York Stock Exchange; the fourth, Symantec is listed on the Nasdaq.

Meanwhile, at financial services giant, American Express, Keith Chenault is currently president and considered CEO in waiting by most observers of the company.

Buy stock in one of these companies, and you can make your support known. At the same time, you'll be investing in a large-cap company. Unlike some of the Black Stock Index members, the large caps with African Americans in top positions are somewhat less volatile stocks. They'll probably fluctuate less in value than the smaller-capitalization members of the *Black Enterprise* index, and could each make a good core holding in your portfolio, if you so choose (see Figure 4.19).

NEXT STOP

You might think the world of investing begins and ends with stocks. And while they may certainly be exciting, there are other very useful investments out there, including bonds, that serve an important function in an investor's portfolio. Read on.

5

BONDS—THE STABILITY EVERY PORTFOLIO NEEDS

Bonds aren't the most exciting investments around. What they lack in sparkle, however, they compensate for with a steady, dependable flow of income. Over time, bonds have won a reputation as the sort of mild-mannered, milquetoast investments your stockbroker would recommend to your grandparents or to the local pastor. And in general, bonds fit that kind of billing. They pay investors interest through thick and thin, a dependable, predictable stream of income that's far greater and more reliable than the money stocks can guarantee in the form of a dividend. On top of that, if you hold a bond until it matures after a set term (in the same way that a certificate of deposit or money market account matures), you'll receive the amount you originally invested back in full.

Stability comes at a price, though. While you probably won't lose a thread off your shirt investing in bonds, in all likelihood you'll never see the beefy gains the stock market has racked up the past few years. Statistics show that over time, bond investments tend to return investors 5 percent to 6 percent annually, compared with an average annual 11 percent for large company stocks and 13 percent for small company shares. Start with a $1,000 investment, park it in a bond paying 5 percent annually, and you won't break $2,000 in a decade: You'll have $1,629 to be exact. A small company stock or mutual fund averaging a 13 percent annual return would have turned your $1,000 into $3,395.

That said, any good portfolio has an anchor in investments that won't lose their value and can still produce income no matter what happens. Treasury bonds and municipal bonds meet those specifications because they not only pay interest regularly, but also promise to return your original investment in full on maturity.

Figure 5.1   Bonds Are for You If . . .

- You've earmarked a certain amount of your long-term portfolios in stocks and stock mutual funds to make the gains you'll need for retirement or other long-term needs.
- You want to safeguard some of the gains you've made in the stock market.
- You want a steady, reliable stream of income from the money you put aside.
- You have a goal to finance in the near future and want to make sure the money you've saved will be there.
- You can keep your money invested for a set period of time and resist the temptation to cash out too soon.

The dependable income put out by bonds provides a bankable return that comes in handy when the stock market decides to head into a dive. Bear markets tend not to make investors any money and can often take a big bite out of the funds you've put away in stocks. Treasury, municipal, and corporate bonds, meanwhile, keep on paying. It's no surprise, then, that the minute stocks look shaky or foreign economies start to teeter, investors flock to the bond market as shelter from the storm.

Some years, too, there's an added reward for opting to put at least part of your money in safe and sound bonds. Whenever experts look for interest rates to fall, previously issued bonds often get a boost in value. That can translate into a nice bonus if you opt to cash in your bond investment. The downside: When rates rise, a bond's underlying value can drop. Either way, though, the bondholder can always opt to take the staid route by holding a bond until it matures. This keeps the original investment intact, protecting it from any loss in value, while still providing interest payments (see Figure 5.1).

THE LOWDOWN—WHAT IT'S ALL ABOUT

When it comes to bonds, there are some things you should expect. There are also some things you can forget.

On the forget-it list, you can pretty much write off making the kind of gains from a bond portfolio that the stock market saw during the 1990s. If you had put $1,000 into an S&P 500 index fund on January 1, 1990, you would have been sitting on $4,350 by mid-year 1999. Meanwhile if you had opted for a 10-year Treasury Bond paying 7 percent interest on the same date, your $1,000 investment would have grown only to $1,967.

Over time, the difference between bonds and stocks has followed pretty much the same course. According to calculations published by the Securities Industry Association, you can expect an average annual total return of 5.3 percent from long-term Treasury Bonds, Uncle Sam's portion of the market,

REALITY CHECK

Financial planner Percy Bolton can't seem to sell many of his clients on bonds no matter how well they work into clients' portfolios. Not that it should come as a surprise. After the stock market's tear in the late 1990s, most everyone is looking for the next "dot.com" express or Internet stock ready to head to the galaxy.

Bolton, though, has watched investment fads come, grab hold of investors, and then go. He'll tell you, first off, that the 20 percent gains are great, but there comes a time when you just can't risk losing a large sum of money in the stock market. If you're retired, you want to know that your nest egg is earning money and that as much of your principal as possible is safe and secure, should the market go up or down. Or, if you're about to pay for your kid's college tuition, you don't want to awaken one day to find that share prices have shaved 10 percent off your savings. It's cases like these, Bolton says, that make bonds so valuable.

"When stocks are running off 20 percent to 50 percent yearly increases, it's hard to convince people that there are a lot of advantages to mixing bonds or bond mutual funds into your portfolio," he says. "But there comes a time when we all want to lessen the volatility of what we own. When it comes down to preserving capital, there's often no better choice."

Bolton can also count off other reasons why bonds still make sense. There's the fact that they move up in value when stocks drop. Or, in some cases, the income from bonds can be tax free.

So Bolton keeps on trying to convince whomever he can. He'll preach that stocks are the way to go, but that bonds are still worth considering. "Hey, we'll see investors do an about-face the minute the market turns," he predicts. "And believe you me, the market can sometimes turn fairly quickly." Bolton has seen that before, and as a result he's parked some of his own retirement money in a bond mutual fund—the PIMCO Total Return Fund, which has consistently earned high ratings from Morningstar, the Chicago financial publishing firm. "Every portfolio has to have some balance," he points out. "The stocks are great, but I'm going to carry something safe as well, and there's nothing quite as sure as bonds."

which many analysts use as a benchmark for the group. Stocks, on the other hand, have more than doubled that figure; they averaged 11 percent annual gains during the period from 1926 to 1999. Project that average over a 10-year period, and you'll see that stocks bring a 184 percent return on your money; bonds bring only 63 percent over the same period.

What the numbers won't explain, however, is the beauty of the bond. Bonds are great for capital *preservation*. When you buy bonds, hold them, and allow them to mature, they not only protect a certain sum within your portfolio, they also generate a modest, yet important return. What's more, that income comes in regular, steady payments. In many cases, the guaranteed amount is larger than almost any other kind of investment can provide. That's why bonds are a favorite with people who have to rely on a steady return through thick or thin.

A bond works something like this: you hand over your money to a borrower—the U.S. government, a city or state government, a corporation—and get a piece of paper in return. That sheet, or bond, guarantees you a certain income, paid twice a year, based on an interest rate applied to your principal or the amount you lent. The professionals often call bonds "fixed-income" investments, because the stream of income they provide is unwavering over the duration of the bond. It's indeed income that's "fixed."

After a set, predetermined amount of time, you get the original amount you handed over to the borrower—in full. Retrace the steps, and you've not only safeguarded your savings, you've made a little money on top of it. The stock market? Well, as great of an investment as stocks have been over time, they're prone to pass through some high peaks and a few valleys along the way to wealth. That's no big deal if you have a long time to reach a goal and don't have to tap into your savings. That's nothing short of a tragedy if you were planning to cash in and apply the money you had salted away for Junior's first year at Harvard.

True, you'll definitely need to keep a sizable portion of your portfolio working in stocks whether you're a green 20 years of age and fresh out of college, or 70 years old and already scouting about for resort towns after you've left your job. When it comes to investing, the stock market's statistics don't lie—shares are the only way to grow what you set aside for mammoth responsibilities like retirement, for a new home, or for college tuition. At the same time, you'll want to lock in a portion of your gains from the market and still reel in some kind of return, especially as the time fast approaches for you to tap the funds you've stockpiled.

There are other selling points for bonds. One is that they can help cushion an investment portfolio from the harrowing gyrations that stock prices sometimes undergo. True, bonds can fluctuate in value, especially as interest rates rise and fall, but their prices tend to be less volatile than those of shares. Bonds also act as a strong counterweight to stocks; they often increase in value or hold steady when stocks are declining. Finally, as a perfect fallback, when bonds mature, investors get the face value of the bond, or their principal back in full.

It might help to picture your portfolio as a kennel. Think of stocks as sleek greyhounds. They're there to chase the rabbits and pounce on quarry like quail or pheasant. Bonds, meanwhile, are less glamorous, but just as useful in their own way—a golden retriever of an investment. The bonds you own won't race off and snare fabulous gains, but they will bring the paper in every morning and fetch what they can.

NOSTALGIA

Bonds are quite possibly the first investments you have known. Perhaps your grandparents or parents bought savings bonds for you to fund your education. They stressed that the bond would retain its value and at the same time pay interest, a surefire way to not only protect what you had gathered up but to increase its value over time as well.

You grew up, though, and over time didn't hear much more about bonds. They lack the headline-grabbing ability of stocks, and maybe what is a potentially reliable investment doesn't deserve a lot of attention, anyway. Whatever the reason, the talk around most any office watercooler from Manhattan to Detroit is unlikely to be about safe, sound bonds and their way of protecting wealth. More often, the chat probably gravitates toward zooming and zipping Internet shares. It could be that your neighbors or co-workers are caught up in initial public offerings (IPOs) and stock options, the kind of whizbang investments that are the stuff of dreams. The bond? In this day and era, it doesn't seem to have enough sex appeal to hold our interest for long.

That's not to say that there is no intrigue in bonds. As explained later, investors might use zero-coupon bonds to angle for capital gains that rival stocks. Then, there are spicier bonds available for investors who hanker for something with more "bite." A variety that should appeal to the more adventurous sort is the *junk bond*. These high-risk holdings pay a higher return than government or even conventional corporate bonds. (Be forewarned: There's always the risk that the company that issued a junk bond might default or miss interest payments.)

Another bolder bond category is emerging market debt, issued by countries such as Russia, Malaysia, or Cameroon. It's a subgroup that not only carries the flavor of faraway lands, but also higher rates of interest and higher risk as well. Back home in the United States, there are municipal bonds, or munis, issued by local governments to cover new schools, street lights, water purification plants, and a host of other projects. And while we're on the subject of public debt, there are also the bonds put out by agencies like Fannie Mae or Sallie Mae, which tap lenders like you and me to help fund mortgages or student loans.

HOW IT WORKS

A bond is nothing more than a formal IOU issued by a branch of government or floated by a corporation. Either way, it's a loan dangled out before investors like yourself. It carries terms for repayment. And, like any loan, a bond carries certain conditions to protect lenders and at the same time make their investment worthwhile for investors.

Imagine any time that you've ever lent money to friends, neighbors, or family. You probably stipulated that you'd get your money back after a certain period of time. In the world of fixed-income investing, the return of an investor's principal occurs on a predetermined date, months, or even years off in the future. Once that great day arrives, the bond expires or "matures," a way of saying that the loan agreement comes to an end. At that point, an investor with a bond with a "face value," or principal, of $1,000 will get $1,000 back.

Sometimes, friends who borrow money not only pay you back, but reward you for your trouble as well. In the world of bonds, there's no getting around paying investors something for their money. That reward comes in the form of a yield, a percentage of the principal paid yearly to investors as interest. Yield, or *coupon* as it is sometimes called, is calculated by dividing the interest doled out to bondholders by the face value or principal of the bond itself. Therefore, a $10,000 bond, yielding 7 percent, will pay investors $700 a year in income. Remember, bonds are called fixed-income investments because the dividend they pay holders is preset and doesn't vary over the life of the bond.

Many factors come into play when an issuer floats or offers a bond to the investment community. First, there's the current level of interest rates to consider. Rates are ultimately influenced, if not guided, by the Federal Reserve, depending on whether the government agency wants to promote economic growth or cool it down and stem inflation. Keep in mind, too, that rates in general edge up or creep down over time—they never remain stationary. The same holds true for the bond market's benchmark, the 30-year U.S. Treasury note, an issue that is used as a compass point for the world of fixed income. As the yield of the 30-year Treasury rises, bond yields, too, will inch upward. As the 30-year's payout drops, bond yields will drop as well.

Another factor that comes into play is the issuer's ability to make interest payments as well as pay back the money it has borrowed. When the city of Baltimore or Procter & Gamble floats a bond, the market will take into consideration either entity's reputation for honoring its bond debt. Investors will also factor in a bond issuer's overall solvency. That's because investors who put their money in bonds, no matter how much trust they're willing to extend borrowers, want some notion of a bond issuer's ability to pay them back. Investors rely on several ratings agencies to examine and weigh in on the borrower's standing. Firms such as Standard & Poor's, Moody's, and Fitch make a good deal of money reviewing corporate and government bonds, and passing judgment, usually in the form of a letter grade—A being the highest ranking on down to D, the lowest. For your information, federal debt, such as Treasury bonds, is generally regarded as the highest quality fixed income investment around.

How do ratings affect investors? Well, in the bond market, the rule of thumb is that the lower a company's or government's rating, the higher the interest it must pay out to convince the investment community the extra risk it carries as a debtor is worth the financial market's attention.

Fixed income investing has a lot in common with your mortgage or car note. There's a base sum that the lender invests or hands over to the borrower. In fixed income circles, that's called the bond's face value. There is interest to pay on your note; on bonds it is often labeled a coupon. The interest you pay on your car loan or receive for a bond often varies according to the length of the loan, or the date the bond matures. One thing that affects your rate is how much loans in general fetch. Something else the loan officer—or bond investors—consider: your credit ratings (what companies like TRW and Equifax think of your chances of paying the loan back in full and on time). The higher your rating, the easier it is to get credit on good terms (i.e., lower interest payments). The lower your rating, the more difficult it is to secure a loan, and the higher the interest rate you'll probably have to take on.

WHAT'S IN IT FOR THEM

Float a bond. Fund the future.

That's the way many a corporation or community views the bond market, and for good reason. For one, a bond can secure a large amount of cash at a fixed price—that is, a set amount of interest to pay over the life of the loan or the bond.

The bond market doesn't have to rely a catch phrase like that because it's already quite popular, thank you. According to the Bond Market Association, in 1999 there was over $11 trillion in corporate, government, and muni bonds outstanding, either stacked high in investment accounts or on the market. It only stands to reason that any investment that can guarantee holders a 6 percent or greater return a year is going to attract its share of attention.

The advantages of funding projects, construction, or day-to-day operations with bonds are remarkably similar to the considerations we all take into account when signing loan papers. In real life, scraping together enough cash to cover big-ticket items—a car, a house, a year's worth of college tuition—is often impossible. A mortgage, a car note, or a student loan, allows people to enjoy the benefits of an expensive good or service now and to pay smaller amounts over time to do so.

Bonds work the same way. Borrowers need only pay back a set amount every year, far less than the total amount of the bond issue. And when interest rates are low, those payments on average stand to be small. Hence, a lot of bond issues are presented to investors. Low rates mean that borrowers like bond issuers will have a relatively modest cost of capital (i.e., the amount they'll have to pay to use lenders' money).

Corporations have additional reasons for floating bonds. Issuing stock, the other popular way of raising money, carries with it a host of responsibilities. Chief among them is control of the company's direction—shareholders, after all, can vote on many issues. Then there are pressures on executives to ensure that company profits and performance meet big shareholders' expectations. Pension funds and investment firms that buy stock often lean on corporate heads to keep profits up, boost earnings, increase a stock's dividend payout, shed units, or trim costs. Then again, issuing additional shares to raise money can decrease or dilute the value of the stock a company already has available to the investing public. A larger supply out on the market tends to drag down stock prices.

Bonds, by comparison, are a low-impact way to gather up funding. True, they're strapped with stipulations. To make payments on time and decrease its debt load, a corporate management is naturally going to keep its eye on its bottom line. But compared with floating stock, the burden of bonds can be relatively minor.

The Ratings Game

That's not to say that corporations, or communities for that matter, take their bond payments lightly or load up on bonds. There's plenty of incentive for private and public borrowers to take their commitment seriously and limit their indebtedness. Bond issuers carry a rating supplied by companies like Standard & Poor's and Moody's, which regularly look over the books of companies and state and local governments. Ratings agencies review numerous items before assigning an investment grade. They examine how much debt a borrower carries or how a bond issuer kept to its payment schedule in the past. Why? Prospective bond buyers want to know the odds of an issuer possibly defaulting or backing out of the payments. The worst-case scenario doesn't materialize often, but investors want to gauge the likelihood that it could take shape.

Corporations and local governments alike are wise to take their rating seriously. The better the rating of a bond issue, the less risk the investment community sees in lending money to a corporation or locale, and as a result, the lower the interest rate the borrowers have to pay. That's important: A fraction of a point in interest can cost a mayor or a CEO millions of dollars.

Needless to say, professionals have staked out stretches of the bond spectrum. Treasuries and other U.S. agency debts are seen as so sound, so

reliable, that the federal government needn't stoop to the level of other issuers. Its bonds are a grade above "A" Below that lofty level, "A" or "AAA"
bonds (depending on the rating system in question) are seen as the next best
thing to a guaranteed interest payment and return of principal.

Beware crossing the threshold into B debt and lower strata. At that
point, you've entered "junk bond" territory. Junk bonds offer up higher
yields, but are also burdened with the possibility that their issuer, corporate
or governmental, could very well reveal to bondholders that it can't make
payments. The higher the return, the higher the risk you incur, as previously pointed out.

Should you opt to buy individual bonds, professionals tell you to never
stray from A level debt. A venture into lower rated issues can be hazardous
and is better left to a money manager running a mutual fund that specializes
in junk debt.

Brokers and Their Spread

You've seen how a bond issuer benefits from your investment in their
"paper," as bond market professionals like to call fixed income investments.
Another party is waiting to profit from your purchase of a bond, however:
your brokerage along with its liaison, your broker. Together, they lie between you and the financial markets, helping you place orders for investments and make trades. It's not charity work. And for their trouble, they
will take a cut off your bond investment called a *spread.*

A spread is easy to understand. In all financial markets, there are sellers and buyers. In the case of a stock transaction, a seller lets it be known
that he or she is willing to part with a holding for a certain sum, often
tagged as an "asking price." A buyer broadcasts that he or she is willing to
pay a certain amount for an investment, known as a "bid." Your broker,
meanwhile is there to negotiate the difference between the two parties, and
to snare the investment you've said you want, for an agreed sum. As compensation for the work involved in helping the transaction along, a broker
earns a commission, a set fee.

Bonds work a bit differently. First of all, cast any thought of a commission out. On a typical bond purchase, your dealer will find his or her take in
between the bid price, typically the price he or she paid for the holding, and
the ask price, or just how much they expect to collect from you, the investor.
In the investment business, that differential is called a spread.

When it comes to buying bonds, there are no hard-and-fast rules covering spreads. Brokers don't get a set sum for each bond transaction. Instead,
they usually shape and reshape their take on a transaction according to a
few factors including how much they value your business and how much
they think you can pay. Still, there seem to be some general, if hazy, ground
rules on spreads. Brokers, for example, take on a bond trade according to

how much money you're investing and the maturity of the bond. And if there are rules of thumb to apply here, they go as follows: First, the bigger the sum you have to invest, the less the proportional slice your dealer will carve out of the transaction for himself or herself. Second, the longer off the maturity, the more proportionately your broker will take. That said, call 12 brokers for the same bond deal, and you're likely to hear 12 different offers, each with its own spread.

To get the best deal, compare prices by calling around. Also, ask brokers how much they'd charge to both sell a bond and buy it back from a client. The difference between the prices will help you pinpoint the spread and any other charges that might accompany it.

Finally, you might opt to either leave individual bonds alone or buy bonds directly from the U.S. government (described in Chapter 6).

INTEREST RATE UP, BOND DOWN— INTEREST RATE DOWN, BOND UP

You might say bond investors have a love-hate relationship with interest rates.

At the very least, rates and bonds are perched on opposite ends of a seesaw. Rates go up, and bond values go down. Rates drop, and bonds appreciate in value.

Of course, if you invest in bonds to protect your principal and at the same time bring in a steady income, the ebb and flow of interest rates isn't going to concern you much. You'll hold your bond until it matures. Until then, your trusty bond will continue to generate income at its coupon rate— its original interest rate—until it matures. Then, you'll get your original investment back. It's that easy.

Beyond that, it's easy to see how bond investors would love rates because every bond ever issued carries an interest rate that dictates how much bond issuers must pay bond investors on the sum of money borrowed. The higher interest rates are when a bond is issued, the higher the rate the bond itself carries. And, the higher the bond's yield, the better investors feel—it's easy to have a favorable opinion about money coming to your door every six months.

But that doesn't explain bondholders' displeasure when rates go up. That stems from the fact that the return paid out by fixed income investments is set or fixed at a certain level. When you invest in a bond, you settle on a rate of interest that doesn't waver for the life of the bond. A $5,000 investment in a bond with a 7 percent coupon will bring you $350 or 7 percent of your principal in interest in two installments of $175 a year. Year after year, you can expect no more, although you certainly won't receive a penny less, either.

Because a bond's return is nailed to a set amount, however, a bond's underlying value (how much it would fetch on the open market should you sell it before it matures) will rise and fall as interest rates climb or drop during time.

To draw a loose comparison, think of what happened to the value of your 1999 sedan the minute the spanking new 2000 model rolled into showrooms. Sometime in the autumn of 1999, factory-fresh automobiles came off the assembly line and were shipped to car dealerships far and wide. Your 1999 Alpha Centauri four-door coupe, replete with air conditioning, state-of-the-art speakers, and a fancy dashboard, of course, had dropped in value the minute you turned the ignition for the first time and drove off the dealer's lot. It fell still further as soon as a comparable, arguably more attractive version, the 2000 Alpha Centauri, became available to drivers.

Now, take a newly minted 10-year $1,000 bond yielding 7 percent interest (a rate that would produce $70 yearly income for every $1,000 invested). Unlike the 1999 Alpha Centauri, time may not determine just how much that bond is worth prior to maturity. So what steers that particular bond's value upward or down year after year? Interest rates.

Suppose, for example, that interest rates were to rise after you had bought that same 10-year bond. To keep investors interested in putting money into Treasuries, the interest rate Washington would attach to new bonds would have to be higher than the current 7 percent yield. The second that new bonds carried a 7.5 percent stated yield, however, would be the very instant that your bond, yielding 7 percent would drop in value. It would still hold some sort of worth, especially since whoever held it would be entitled to its return over time. Still, if you asked 10 investors coming to the market for the first time which they preferred, most everyone would opt for the new higher yielding issue.

To keep up with current interest rate levels, you could expect your bond's current value to drop to a point where its yield would fall in line with the market's present rate—7.5 percent. The original bond, yielding 7 percent or $70 per $1,000 of principal would drop to $933.33—if and only if you were to sell it ahead of its maturity. At that level, the bond's principal would ensure that $70 of interest, paid annually to the bond holder until the investment matured, would represent 7.5 percent of the bond's principal.

Should you elect to keep a bond until it matures, these occasional fluctuations in its value won't matter a bit to you. That's because your coupon will remain the same. Not only that, but the issuer of the bond will be required to return your full principal.

Bonds can increase in value, too. When interest rates fall, bonds carrying higher yields rise in value. For example, take the very same 10-year Treasury with a coupon of 7 percent. Now suppose that interest rates drop. Soon 10-year Treasuries are carrying a coupon of 6 percent. Your $1,000 bond will now increase in value—to $1,166.66—simply because it generates more income than comparable debt issued after the rates dropped. Figure 5.2 shows the fluctuating value of bond principal relative to interest rates if you sell a bond prior to its maturity.

Figure 5.2   Bond Values and Rates—What Happens
When Rates Go Up and When They Drop

When rates increase, bond principals sink.

	VALUE OF A $1,000 BOND AT A 7% COUPON IF INTEREST RATES INCREASE				
BOND MATURITY	.5%	1%	1.5%	2%	2.5%
2	$991	$982	$973	$964	$955
5	979	959	940	921	902
10	965	932	900	870	841
20	949	901	857	816	778

When rates decrease, bond principals rise.

	VALUE OF A $1,000 BOND IF INTEREST RATES DECREASE				
BOND MATURITY	.5%	1%	1.5%	2%	2.5%
2	$1,009	$1,019	$1,028	$1,038	$1,047
5	1,021	1,043	1,065	1,088	1,111
10	1,036	1,074	1,114	1,156	1,200
20	1,056	1,116	1,181	1,251	1,327

Source: The Vanguard Group.

Longer Maturity, Higher Risk

Rate changes can make the unflappable bond more volatile. In fact, bonds can be a potentially risky holding for holders who, for whatever reason, cannot wait until their investment matures.

Now figure another factor into the equation: time. The longer the period you hold a bond, the more outside variables swirling about the economy can come into play and alter the value of your investment. During periods of great inflation, the Fed might lift rates to cool the economy down and slow price increases. Under other circumstances, the Fed might opt to lower rates to help jolt the economy out of a recessionary funk. Either way, over the course of any given year the Federal Reserve Bank might elect to tighten the money supply and raise rates or ease money to lower interest rates.

Apply those factors to the bond market, and you'll find that bonds with a short maturity—6 months to a year—are less likely to undergo as many shifts and changes that might alter their value as those with intermediate maturities of between 2 and 5 years. Following that logic, bonds with a longer maturity—ranging as far out into the future as 10 to 30 years—will be even more vulnerable to changes (see Figure 5.3). In the past 30 years, any number of events or policies have shaken up the economy, and ultimately

Figure 5.3 Bonds—The Long and the Short of It

MATURITY	WHAT THE PROS CALL A BOND LIKE THIS
1 to 3 years	Short-term
3 to 10 years	Intermediate-term
10 years or longer	Long-term

the bond market. Rate hikes by the Federal Reserve, oil prices, recessions, and federal budget deficits, to name just four, have each rocked bond yields and stirred up the fixed income market. They've each triggered volatility for bond investors, and having done as much, have generated risk for bond investors who opt to sell out.

At the same time, the financial markets often compensate investors who angle for higher potential returns by choosing high-risk investments. The same holds true for the bond market. Over time, changes in the economy, inflation, or the mission of the Federal Reserve all stand to alter the projected return offered up by a bond to the investing public. It follows then, that most often the longer a bond's maturity, the higher its yield. For example, Ryan Labs, a New York bond analysis firm, says that over the past 10 years, the 3-month Treasury bill has averaged a total return of 5.35 percent annually; the 30-year Treasury, meanwhile has averaged 7.35 percent. Bear in mind, as we have pointed out, that bonds with longer maturities will also undergo wider swings in value when events crop up to alter the outlook for bonds (see Figure 5.4).

Figure 5.4 The Bond Payoff

Typically, when it comes to bonds, the longer the maturity the greater the return. The following data cover Treasuries through the 1990s.

MATURITY	RETURNS (%)
3 months	5.35
6 months	5.46
12 months	5.91
2 years	6.38
5 years	6.84
10 years	7.05
30 years	7.35

Source: Ryan Labs.

THE YIELD CURVE

Investment professionals surveying the bond landscape, look no further than a graph called the yield curve.

The yield curve amounts to a type of electrocardiogram of the bond market. It plots bond yields on its vertical or x axis, against various bond maturities on its horizontal or y axis. That way, portfolio managers, professional investors, or bond market traders can see in a glance how much income individual bonds promise to yield, in a line from the shortest maturities (under a year) to the longest (30 years).

The pros will tell you that there's more to the yield curve than just connecting the dots, however. That's because they can read a lot into the shape and slope of the line drawn through points where interest rates and durations intersect. A steep curve shows that bond investors will get much more yield for investing in longer maturities. A more gentle, even slope is a sign that you'll get little if any reward for taking on the risk of a bond that won't mature until far in the future. "A steep yield curve tells me that inflation and other factors that could adversely affect the bond market are under control in the short term and that bond investors think things look more uncertain further out in the future," says Mark Lay, a portfolio manager who specializes in bonds for his own institutional investment firm, MDL Capital Management. "The message I get is that intermediate or short-term bonds are a better bet at that point."

Figure 5.5   Yield Curves

The yield curve is a barometer of the bond market. It slopes upward gently, has a steep slope, or slopes downward. On the yield curve, look for bond maturities on the horizontal axis. Look for interest rates—yields—on the y axis.

Gentle slope
The yield curve typically shows investors how much more yield they receive for longer maturing bonds. Normally, the bills and shorter-term bonds on the left offer lower yields, whereas bonds with longer maturities pay higher yields.

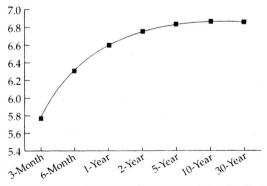

Figure 5.5   *(continued)*

Steep slope

Other times, when the long-term outlook for the economy or inflation becomes uncertain, even with the economy currently running well with stable prices, the yield curve becomes steeper. Short-term bonds will offer lower yields. Longer-term issues, however, will need to raise the amount they pay holders.

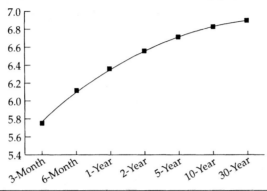

Downward slope

Conversely, if the long-term outlook for the economy is good, yet there's some short-term turbulence in the months or year ahead, you may see a downward sloping yield curve. Short-term bonds will pay higher rates to compensate investors for risks in the near term. Bonds with longer maturities will pay lower yields since prospects in the future, as the bond market perceives them, are good.

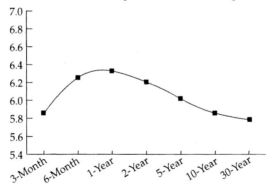

Then, there are odd situations when the yield curve slopes downward. What's its message then? "The bond market has scanned current conditions and is sending out the message that near-term circumstances are a bit more iffy, while the long-term economic picture is a good one for the bond market," says Lay. "Under those conditions, I'm probably going to be more attracted to intermediate- to long-term bonds."

So the next time you tune into the business news or an investment advice program, you'll know that a steep yield curve means there's enough

---

WEB SIGHTINGS
THE YIELD CURVE ONLINE

For daily updates on the yield curve, click on the Web site for Bloomberg (www.bloomberg.com), the financial news company. Bloomberg's financial markets page (www.bloomberg.com/markets) presents a fresh yield curve daily, and for a close-up, you can visit a page for U.S. Treasury bill, bond, and note data at (www.bloomberg .com/markets/C13.html). There, you'll find the latest rates for Treasuries and a yield curve chart to look over.

---

risk out in the future to warrant a higher interest rate for bonds that stretch over longer periods. A flat yield curve, meanwhile could indicate that there's near-term risk or the possibility that interest rates could rise soon. Finally, the rare downward sloping yield curve might show that investors are quite concerned near term, and are less worried about future events. Figure 5.5 depicts gentle, steep, and downward curves.

ONWARD

With a grasp of the bond market's inner workings in hand, it's time to see what's out there for you. In Chapter 6, you'll learn about the bond market's bountiful selection, and at the same time find out what choices make sense for you and what might not.

6

BONDS

Municipal Bonds, Savings Bonds, Corporate Bonds, Zero-Coupon Bonds, Junk Bonds, and More

Bonds may serve one purpose, but they come in a variety of forms, some more risky than others, and some more exotic than their cousins. Treasury bonds, for example, are U.S. government debt, plain and simple, backed by Washington, D.C. Then there are the tried and true savings bonds that most people remember from childhood. Municipal bonds are floated by our communities, our towns, to fund everything from new swimming pools to schools. Junk bonds are often issued by corporations looking to aggressively finance bold new projects; they pay higher interest than most bond peers, but also carry a greater amount of risk. Before you enter the bond marketplace, you need to learn how to distinguish one bond family from another. This chapter will help.

TREASURIES

You could well think of Treasuries as the Fort Knox of investments. If there's anything close to an ironclad bond out there, it's Treasury debt, Uncle Sam's IOU. It might help you to think of it this way: Treasuries are a loan out to the world's sole superpower, the government that looks over the world's strongest economy with a budget of over $1.5 trillion. Sounds pretty sturdy, doesn't it?

There's another reason Treasuries have a sterling reputation. Through feast or famine, through times when the economy knew no bounds, and leaner periods when things weren't so good, the U.S. government has never once defaulted on its debt. Put your money in Treasuries and you're virtually assured that you'll get two predetermined payments of income a year. In addition, there's practically no worry whatsoever that you'll get your principal back in full. It's not surprising, then, that the world flocks to Treasuries at the slightest sign of political unrest or economic uncertainty.

Treasuries have the same characteristics as any other bond. Like their fixed income cousins, they represent a loan—in this case with investors like yourself acting as lenders and the federal government cast in the role of the borrower. In return for your funds, you get a set rate of interest and a promise from Washington that you'll receive the face amount of the bond on maturity. You also get the highest rated bond issued by the highest rated debtor around. And, to top it off, you pay no state or local tax on the interest income you receive.

Treasuries come in several maturities, each with its own name. Treasury bills—commonly known as T-bills—are issued for one year or less. Treasury notes are the next step up. They mature in 2 to 10 years. Finally, there are Treasury bonds, which mature in more than 10 years.

One thing to keep in mind: There are set minimums for Treasury investments. You'll need at least $1,000 to invest in T-bonds and T-notes; for T-bills, you'll need to scrape up $10,000 to invest.

As with other bonds, the amount of interest Treasuries pay varies according to their maturity. The longer the period investors have to tie up their money, the greater the reward they'll need and, typically, the higher the yield they will receive.

Where to Buy Them

You're making a major purchase. You have two places to shop. One's a big retailer, with plenty of salespeople to pay. The other is a factory outlet, where the very gadget was assembled. When it comes to most any trinket, tool, shirt, skirt, or shoes, most shoppers would choose the second of those possibilities—the source. That way, you can cut through layers of middle management and overhead. And as a result, logic has it, you save.

If you're thinking of taking the fixed income plunge any time soon, you'll be glad to know that a factory outlet of sorts can save you a fair amount of money on you next purchase of a U.S. Treasury note, bill, or bond. It's none other than the Federal Reserve Bank, the Treasury Department's own clearance warehouse. There, Uncle Sam, is more than willing to process the transaction gratis which will save you a nifty sum. Consider: By dealing with even a discount broker, the purchase of a 5-year Treasury, at $5,000, yielding 7 percent, could well cost $20 in fees. Your first-year yield would amount to $350, yet you would have surrendered 6 percent of your income in

Figure 6.1 Buying Treasuries Direct

There are several places you can call to get in on the government's Treasury Direct program, a plan that lets you buy bonds straight from Washington without paying a broker.

1. Call the Bureau of Public Debt toll-free at 800-943-6864 or in Washington, D.C., at 202-874-4000. You can also visit the Bureau's Web site at (www.publicdebt.treas.gov).
2. Use the following list to contact your local Federal Reserve Bank for information and applications.

FEDERAL RESERVE BANKS	RECORDED MESSAGE	VOICE LINE
Atlanta	404-521-8657	404-521-8653
Baltimore	301-576-3500	301-576-3300
Birmingham	205-731-9702	205-731-8708
Boston	617-973-3805	617-973-3810
Buffalo	716-849-5158	716-849-5000
Charlotte	704-358-2424	704-358-2100
Chicago	312-786-1110	312-322-5369
Cincinnati		513-721-4787
Cleveland		216-579-2490
Dallas		214-922-6000
Denver	303-572-2475	303-572-2470
Detroit	313-963-4936	313-964-6157
El Paso		915-544-4730
Houston		713-659-4433
Jacksonville	904-632-1178	904-632-1179
Kansas City	816-881-2767	816-881-2409
Little Rock		501-324-8272
Los Angeles		213-624-7398
Louisville	502-568-9240	502-568-9236
Memphis		901-523-7171
Miami	305-471-6257	305-471-6497
Minneapolis	612-340-2051	612-340-2075
Nashville	615-251-7236	615-251-7100
New Orleans	504-593-3290	504-593-3200
New York	212-720-5823	212-720-6619
Oklahoma City	405-270-8660	405-270-8652
Omaha	402-221-5638	402-221-5636
Philadelphia	215-574-6580	212-574-6680
Pittsburgh	412-261-7988	412-261-7863
Portland	503-221-5931	503-221-5932
Richmond	804-697-8355	804-697-8372
Saint Louis	314-444-8602	314-444-8665
Salt Lake City	801-322-7844	801-322-7900
San Antonio	210-978-1330	210-978-1303
San Francisco	415-974-3491	415-974-2330
Seattle	206-343-3615	206-343-3605
Device for Hearing Impaired		202-874-4026

commissions. Think of it another way. That small commission would actually lower the first year's yield on your Treasury to 6.6 percent.

To get in on the savings, all you have to do is enroll in the government's Treasury Direct program. That way, you open an account with Washington and buy bonds with no midlevel sales force involved. To get an application, connect online with the Bureau of Public Debt (www.publicdebt.treas.gov) or call the Bureau of Public Debt Public Information Center in Washington, D.C., at 202-874-4000 or toll-free at 800-943-6864. You can also call your local Federal Reserve Bank (see Figure 6.1). You'll get a kit in the mail, complete with an application form and a booklet entitled *Buying Treasury Securities*. For accounts above $100,000, you'll pay $25 a year in fees. Otherwise, it doesn't cost you a cent.

MUNICIPAL BONDS

Think of municipal bonds as a tax shelter. That's because they offer investors a great way to earn a bond's regular income and avoid paying taxes on the return.

Munis, as they're also called, are a lot like Treasuries, but different in some fundamental ways. Whereas Treasuries are chunks of the U.S. government's debt, munis are portions of the money borrowed by state and city governments and agencies to provide goods and services to constituents such as paved roads, schools, buildings, or community parks. There's another difference: Many municipal bonds are exempted from federal income tax. And if the bond is issued in the state where you live, you won't owe a cent in local or state taxes, either.

Although most munis pay less interest than Treasuries, keep in mind that you owe no federal tax on the interest you earn off munis. So, before you dismiss munis flat out in favor of Treasuries or other bonds, do some number crunching to even the playing field. And to better compare the two, find out just how a muni's tax-free yield stacks up alongside the taxable yield of other fixed income investments (see Figure 6.2).

The mathematics is a snap. You'll merely need to divide a muni's yield by 1 minus your federal tax rate (for couples filing joint returns that is 15 percent for up to $42,350, 28 percent for up to $102,300, 31 percent for up to $155,950, 36 percent for up to $278,450 and 39.6 percent for any sum above that). For example if the muni bond pays 4 percent, and you're in the 36 percent tax bracket, its taxable equivalent yield is 6.25 percent or 4 divided by .64. In other words, for a couple making $160,000 a year, a muni bond paying 4 percent, is providing the same amount of income as a "regular" bond with a 6.25 percent coupon.

Bear in mind, too, that different municipalities, states, and local agencies have varying debt obligations and tax structures. As a result, rating

Figure 6.2   Tax-Free Muni Yields versus Taxable Bond Yields

At first glimpse, the municipal bond yields don't seem like much. Figure in their tax savings, calculate the equivalent yield of a taxable bond, and suddenly they look a lot more attractive. This chart shows how much taxable bond yield you need to equal a muni-bond's payout, according to your tax bracket.

| | MUNI YIELD | | |
| | 4% | 5% | 6% |
TAX BRACKET	TAXABLE BOND EQUIVALENT		
15%	4.71	5.88	7.06
28%	5.56	6.94	8.33
31%	5.80	7.25	8.70
36%	6.25	7.81	9.38

agencies, like Moody's, Standard & Poor's, and Fitch will grade each issuer accordingly from A to D. And, as with all paper or bonds, the lower the grade, the higher the amount of yield a borrower has to supply to attract investors.

For individual investors, munis can be complicated. They're also difficult to research. For starters, you'd have to study local governments, examine their budgets, and look over their reputations. Since this research can be exceedingly involved, it's advisable to opt for muni bond funds, many of which are offered in a variety of state packages to help you get the biggest tax boost possible. Bond mutual funds are discussed in Chapters 7 and 8.

Here's a tip on municipals if you're still looking into buying individual bonds: Some cities—New York, Chicago, Washington, D.C., and others—sell bonds directly to investors, in much the same way that the U.S. government markets Treasuries through its Treasury direct program. Check with City Hall to see if your local government has a direct purchase plan.

SAVINGS BONDS

In all the talk about Treasuries, munis, junk bonds, and emerging market debt, it's easy to overlook the Old Yeller of the group—the savings bond. The Series E bond originated at the beginning of World War II to fund the war effort and became so much a part of the American social fabric that savings bonds still seem patriotic in a sense. They are investments that your parents might have picked up in anticipation of your college education. In fact, you might have received some from your grandparents when you were still in diapers.

Whether savings bonds are part of your childhood memories or not, you might think twice before sneezing at them. Savings bonds are investments every bit as sterling as Treasuries, although they tend to pay slightly less interest. And since they have the full backing of the U.S. government, you can rest assured that you've lent your money to the most reliable creditor of all time, Uncle Sam. In addition, you won't have to shell out state and local taxes on your gains; the IRS taps your gains on savings bonds, but only when they mature.

Savings bonds come in a few varieties. There are Series EE/E bonds, which sell at 50 percent of their face value (e.g., you pay half—say $100—for a bond that will be worth $200 once it matures). Series EE/E bonds gradually increase in value over time, according to an interest rate that is adjusted every May and November. Their yield is calculated as 90 percent of the pay of 5-year Treasuries over the previous 6 months. Even if rates bottom out, you're guaranteed a minimum 4 percent annual interest on your investment. A Series EE/E, also has a variable maturity, depending on its rate of interest. To determine how long a given Series EE/E will take to reach its face value, use the Rule of 72 (see Chapter 3). Take the number 72, divide it by the interest rate of a Series EE/E and you'll have a rough idea. For example, a Series EE/E paying 6 percent will take roughly 12 years to mature. Series Es are available in denominations of $50, $75, $100, $200, $500, $1,000, $5,000, and $10,000, and can be cashed in after 6 months.

Then, there's the Series EE/E's cousin, the Series HH/H bond. The Series HH/H is more like the common bond; it pays interest semiannually and matures in 10 years. The face value of the bond never rises nor falls; instead, holders can expect two payments of interest income a year, based on a fixed rate set at the date you purchase the bond (Series HH/H bonds have paid 4 percent since 1993).

The government also offers a hybrid savings bond, the Series I. The yield of the Series I bond fluctuates according to the rise and fall of inflation as measured by the Consumer Price Index. The rate of return is adjusted twice a year, on May 1 and November 1. Like its cousins, the Series EE/E and HH/H, the I is exempt from state and local taxes. Federal taxes, however, are

---

WEB SIGHTINGS
GOVERNMENT PROGRAMS

For more information on Treasuries or savings bonds, visit the government's online Web site. There you'll find instructions, answers to most of your questions, and a rundown on just how to get started in government programs. The address: www.publicdebt.treas.gov.

THE LADDERED BOND PORTFOLIO

It's pointless to try timing the stock market. Trying to pinpoint purchases of bonds in synch with crests and troughs of interest rates is equally futile.

The bond market, just like the stock market, is swayed by innumerable forces. One minute, a war breaks out in the highlands of a faraway country. Labor statistics show that wages are rising and inflation could soon prompt the Federal Reserve to raise rates. Whatever the reason behind fluctuations in bond yields, no one, not even market professionals can accurately predict time and again just what's happening to interest rates. True, they'll often correctly analyze prevailing trends and give educated guesses on the general direction of rates and the market. Nevertheless, for all their painstaking labor, their predictions still are rough.

The moral for individual investors like yourself: Forget timing the market. Instead, there are ways to hedge your investment in bonds to protect your investment from the ups and downs of the market. One method is to opt for bond mutual funds. Like stock mutual funds, bond funds rely on the investment acumen of professionals who manage a portfolio of bond holdings. It's their job to keep abreast of market developments and aim for the highest possible return for fund holders.

Another hedging technique that is popular with bond professionals is the laddered portfolio. Charles Self, a portfolio manager for the ABN-Amro says the structure isn't all that complicated, although it requires a large sum of money. Essentially, the trick is to divvy up an investment into small chunks to be used to purchase bonds—say Treasuries—that mature every year for a succession of years (see Figure 6.3). Say you want to guard $20,000 for a 5-year period, yet hope to reap a decent sum of income. The laddered portfolio will work well in this instance if it includes $5,000 bonds set to mature in 2, 3, 4, and 5 years. "That way if interest rates go up, you'll be able to cash out of the shorter bonds and still take advantage of higher yields or you can hold on to the bonds until they mature." If rates go down, Self says, the longer duration bonds will increase in value.

Figure 6.3   The Laddered Bond Portfolio for an Investor with $10,000

A laddered portfolio is simple: All you have to do is divvy up the money you have invested in bonds between bonds of varying maturities.

$2,000	12-month Treasury bill
$2,000	2-year Treasury bond
$2,000	3-year Treasury bond
$2,000	5-year Treasury bond
$2,000	10-year Treasury bond

assessed only when you cash in the bond itself. Series I's are available in denominations of $50, $75, $100, $200, $500, $1,000, $5,000, and $10,000, and can be cashed in after 6 months.

STRIPS

Pinch yourself. It almost sounds too good to be true: The safety of a U.S. Treasury bond coupled with the potential to keep up with the stock market's gains. Yet that coupling of security and return are offered in something of a hybrid investment, called Treasury STRIPS (an acronym for Separate Trading of Registered Interest and Principal of Securities).

Normally, U.S. Treasury bonds act as a ticket to get regular income for a set investment. If you purchase a $1,000 with an annual coupon rate of 6 percent, you'd expect to get a $30 payment twice a year, constituting the $60 in interest you'd be entitled to. The thing that sets STRIPS apart is that bondholders agree to skip the biannual income payment. Instead, in a case roughly equivalent to this example, they would put down $200 with the promise of receiving $1,000 at a time in the future, say 10 years or so.

"I see STRIPS as a great way to save for a kid's college education," says Mark Lay of MDL Capital Management, a money management firm. "Instead of buying savings bonds, you might opt to purchase Treasury STRIPS with a 13- or 14-year maturity when your son or daughter is 3 or 4 years old at 50 or 60 cents to the dollar."

While Treasury STRIPS should be considered a long-term investment, statistics show that they have the potential for sizable gains as well. Studies by Ryan Labs, a leading bond research firm in New York, show that the 15-year Treasury STRIPS has about the same volatility as the S&P 500 stock index. Not only that, but the STRIPS has the potential to provide total returns that can match the index.

Two things to keep in mind: STRIPS are available only through your broker, so expect to pay a commission. Second, keep in mind that increases in the value of your STRIPS are taxable.

AGENCY BONDS

Start with the security of Treasury bonds. Add a touch more punch, in the form of higher yield.

What do you get? A winning combination if you ask agency debt investors. That's because the bonds offered up by federal agencies such as the Federal Home Loan Mortgage Corporation (Freddie Mac), the Federal National Mortgage Association (Fannie Mae), and the U.S. Post Office, have both attributes going for them.

Admittedly, nothing is as safe and sound as a Treasury bond. Still, agency bonds are essentially put out by the same rock-solid borrower—the U.S. government. Like Treasuries, agency bonds pay interest every 6 months and have virtually no credit risk. Washington implicitly stands behind the debt obligations of various government agencies. That way the rating on all agency debt is virtually triple A. To sweeten the deal, agencies historically have paid a yield that's a point or more higher than that of Treasuries.

There are two ways to pick up on agencies. First, you can buy them through an investment bank or brokerage firm, at the price of the bond plus a commission, much like purchasing stock. Also be ready to shell out a large initial sum, $5,000 or so depending on the bond. A second way in is through a mutual fund that focuses on agencies.

If you're thinking of individual bonds, keep in mind that the market for agencies is small and less liquid than the market for other varieties of bonds. That means it may be difficult to unload a bond once you've bought it. Should you opt for agency bonds, it is best to invest in individual agency bonds as a substitute for Treasuries. You should be prepared to hold them until they mature and set your sights on their relatively generous yields, when you want to preserve savings for a specific target such as college or retirement. Ask your broker to price both an agency bond and a comparable Treasury, and factor in the brokerage fees in both cases when comparing yields.

Another thing to check when buying agencies is how the income you'll receive from your bond investment is taxed by local, state, and federal authorities. For example, Fannie Mae and Freddie Mac bonds are taxed at all three levels. At the same time, interest on bonds issued from other agencies—including the Federal Home Loan Bank, Student Loan Mortgage Association (Sallie Mae), Tennessee Valley Authority, and the Federal Farm Credit Bank—are generally not subject to city and state tax. That can make a big difference in how much of your agency bond income you get to keep and how much you have to hand over to the IRS or the state taxation authorities in high-tax states such as New York and California.

If your horizons are narrower, select a bond mutual fund that targets the agency market. Mutual funds are also a great way to get into agencies if you don't have a large sum at your disposal. For a minimum initial investment of as little as $500, you can get into a government bond fund that invests in agencies.

HIGHER RISK, HIGHER RETURN? BONDS OFF THE BEATEN PATH

Here is a brief rundown on some of the many varieties of bonds out there in the market. Be warned, however, that whether you're talking about corporate bonds, convertibles, emerging market debt, or junk bonds, you're venturing into uncharted territory for individual investors. The bonds in the upcoming pages are complex issues that require the type of research most individual investors don't have time for. Additionally, they trade on narrow markets, with little volume. For you, that means the spreads you'll be asked to pay for individual issues will be wide, and could very likely cut deeply into your returns. Also, these bonds off the beaten path carry a lot of risk. There is the threat that a corporation or overseas nation will be beset by a crisis. That could put both your invested principal and interest payments in jeopardy. If you still have an inclination to jump into junk bonds or convertibles, do so through a mutual fund. That way, a professional or team of professionals will sift through a good many choices to find a portfolio of bonds that might work together well. Because funds spread their bets across a group of holdings, they have a defense from any wild gyrations one bond might undergo.

Corporate Bonds

Local, state, and federal governments aren't the only borrowers who turn to bonds to raise cash. Corporations, too, issue debt as much a part of doing business as issuing stock or selling goods and services. Companies that put out bonds get a sum of investors' money in exchange for a promise to provide biannual interest payments and later return the money they borrowed in full to their creditors, the bondholders.

Where does the money go? Corporations put the proceeds from issuing bonds to work in several ways. That might include the upgrade of a factory, the purchase of new equipment, or the replacement of a computer networking system. Management might elect to pay off other debt that carries a higher interest rate. The money might be used in the takeover of a rival corporation or to cover the day-to-day costs of doing business.

Corporate issues, like munis, can be a complicated affair. Potential investors need to research how indebted a company is; how much money a corporation is currently bringing in, and just how likely it is that management might find itself so strapped it cannot pay creditors back.

Some companies, like people, are riskier borrowers than others. Some are already loaded in debt. After a crisis or a change in fortune, others might find themselves pinched for cash and unable to pay back creditors without much pain. Again, the bond market relies on experts at ratings agencies to do some of the legwork.

When it comes to investing in corporates, leave the work to professionals running a mutual fund. In addition to the complex factors that affect ratings, the corporate bond market isn't as big or as easy to trade in as the stock market. Translated into dollars and cents, that means you, as a small investor, are probably in for some very wide spreads, both when you buy paper and when you sell it back. Rather than risk losing a major portion of your gains in trading or getting involved in a dubious issue, it is wiser to leave the complicated stuff to pros.

Junk Bonds—High-Yield Bonds

Talk about vivid descriptions. Junk bonds have a name that conjures up all sorts of imagery, but doesn't necessarily do much to help you grasp what they're about. They might sound dirty, scary, or even undesirable. That's why a lot of Wall Street pros call junk bonds by a friendlier name—high yield fixed income securities. A junk bond is nothing more than a bond that carries a rating of B or less. It's a risky investment, issued by a borrower whose history or financial state is less than pristine. That could be a corporation that has piled on the debt recently and could be in for a nasty fall if its business sputters or the economy falls. It could be a company whose results have been shaky, whose stock has fallen considerably, and that teeters on the brink of bankruptcy. Or it could be a firm trying to set itself straight and regain its standing.

Whatever the story behind the junk rating, a junk bond has to reward holders to justify the risk they're taking. That kind of compensation comes in the form of a higher yield, sometimes several points higher than comparable A-rated debt.

Often enough, the risk is all too real, however. Issuers of junk bonds can default, and often do, leaving bondholders empty-handed. That's why it's a good idea to entrust junk bond investing to mutual fund managers, should you find the high-risk, high-reward junk bond intriguing.

Emerging Market Debt

Another risky bond group is commonly lumped together as emerging market debt. Investment pros call virtually any nation whose economy is either on the rise or struggling to advance an emerging market. And, the list of counties huddled under the emerging-market label is as long as it is diverse. There's India, Botswana, Morocco, Malaysia, Chile, Brazil, and on and on.

Emerging market debt includes debt issued by governments in the developing world. It often pays a higher interest rate than U.S. government securities, and even corporate debt. It can also be a risky venture. There are questions about the soundness of the nation's economy, and whether it can withstand the ups and downs of global cycles. Then, there are currency issues. If you hold a bond issued in a nation whose currency suddenly drops in value, your bond's worth will drop as well. Issues like these make emerging-market debt tricky—reason enough for you to limit your sights to mutual funds that specialize in that type of bond.

Convertible Bonds

Somewhere between stocks and bonds, there exists a hybrid called the convertible bond or convertible. What makes convertibles interesting is that they combine attributes of both stocks and bonds. At their core, they're a bond, a deal allowing a company to borrow money in exchange for a yield and repayment of principal. And true enough, companies that issue convertibles promise to pay holders a set amount of income.

There's a wrinkle, however. By giving investors the option to exchange the bonds for a set number of shares, convertibles offer up an opportunity to take advantage of whatever gains a company's stock makes. Put together, the two qualities—bondlike steady income payments and a stocklike chance to see your underlying investment grow—provide investors a good hedge at a time when stocks might seem expensive or the direction of interest rates might be uncertain.

Why? Let's say Acme Corp. issues convertibles yielding 10 percent annually. If Acme shares begin to zoom on the stock exchange, you simply convert your bond into shares. If Acme stock seems lethargic at best, you can simply stick out your bond investment and see a regular 10 percent payment on your money.

A mutual fund is perhaps the easiest way to tap into the convertible market. As in stock investing, mutual funds offer investors benefits such as a diversified portfolio that limits their exposure to any one investment. Also, since volume in the convertible market is thin and since convertibles' value depends on complicated calculations of yield and conversion value, they can be difficult for individual investors to trade profitably.

NUMEROLOGY

You might think bonds are pretty straightforward. Well, yes and no. There are still some numbers you should keep in mind or refer to when examining bond investments.

Yield (Very Important)

The first thing you'll want to find out is just how much income your investment is going to bring you. For that, you needn't look further than a bond's yield. Stated in a percentage, a yield lets you quickly figure out how much of a return you stand to make from your investment compared with the amount of money you put in.

Yields are calculated by dividing the investment's yearly payout by the amount of the investment. Put into numbers that means a $1,000 bond with a 6 percent yield will typically generate two payments of $30 a year, or $60 of income.

Maturity (Very Important)

You could say that bonds, unlike diamonds, don't last forever. When you purchase a bond, you've entered in a sort of contract with the issuer—be it a corporation, a local government, or the federal government. The agreement's terms are clear-cut: For lending your savings, you're to receive interest payments of a set amount yearly for a certain number of years. At the end of that set period—anywhere from a few months to 30 years—your bond is said to mature and you get your principal or the amount you originally invested back in whole.

Remember, you don't have to hold a bond until its maturity. Just as there's a market for stocks where investors can buy shares of a company to sell their stakes to other investors, there, too, is a market for bonds. Should you decide to sell a bond before its maturity, however, you're in no way guaranteed to get your principal back. In fact, if interest rates have been rising since the day your bond was issued, you risk losing money; you'll likely receive a selling price less than the principal you originally invested. Of course, if interest rates fall, you could be in for a windfall, a profit above the principal you first put out.

In the bond business, the longer the maturity under consideration, the riskier the investment. Over time, war, earthquakes, typhoons, government changes, inflation, and a host of other factors lurk behind any and all bond investments. And should any combination or all those factors affect interest rates, they will surely affect your bond investment if you cash in prior to your holding's maturity. One way to sidestep the roil and rumble: Hold on to your bond until it matures, and get your principal back in full.

Par Value (Very Important)

How much money do you receive when a bond matures? When a bond expires and a borrower or bond issuer must repay the money holders loaned them, they are paying back what is called "par value."

Yield to Maturity (Good to Know but not Essential)

If you purchase a bond that was issued to another party, say another individual investor or a brokerage firm, you should be on your toes. Why? Well, probably many circumstances have changed since the bond was originally issued. Interest rates may have risen or fallen, and as a result, the bond will sell at a higher or lower price than its par value. The investment you are dealing with could be quite a bit different now that it has changed hands.

There's help, but only if you ask for one crucial figure: Yield to maturity. A yield to maturity calculation is complicated; it throws in factors such as the par value of the bond you're buying and whether it has changed. It takes into account the amount of interest you're bringing in from your investment. Yet, despite the unwieldy mathematics, you should be able to secure a figure from the broker, either discount or full-service, that is selling you the bond.

Coupon (Essential)

What determines just how good of an investment your average bond is? Its interest rate, of course. Bond issuers promise to pay holders like yourself a certain amount based on several factors. There's the general level of interest rates. If rates are high, issuers have to give their bonds, or their paper, an interest rate that's comparable to the market. Then, there's the issuer's credit rating. The higher the rating, the less a corporation or government has to cough up to investors. The lower the rating, the riskier the issuer is seen in the bond market's eyes; most probably, then it will have to compensate investors with higher than average rates.

30-Year Treasury (Essential)

Investors have indexes like the S&P 500 or the Dow Jones Industrial Average to check up on the stock market. For bonds, most professionals rely on the interest of the 30-year Treasury as their compass point. The 30-year is a good guide for a couple of reasons. First, it's issued by the U.S. government, and if there's anything like a sure thing in investing, it's a Treasury. At the same time, 30 years is the longest duration or maturity for any bond issued by the United States, and the longer the duration, the greater the risk underlying any bond investment. Together, these two factors—the government's standing and the elongated maturity—make the 30-year such a good gauge of the market. The pros keep in mind that corporate and even municipal bonds won't have the Treasury Department's reputation, and thus will have to pay out higher tax-adjusted yields. And, when they're sizing up the market, they'll also keep in mind that shorter-term paper (bonds with lesser durations) will most probably pay out less of a coupon.

The Lehman Brothers Aggregate Bond Index (Important)

In the world of bonds, the Lehman Aggregate Bond Index offers up a good yardstick to judge just how bonds are doing in general. The Lehman index combines a variety of bonds into one figure, used to chart the crests and valleys of the bond market. It's not absolutely necessary to track the Lehman, especially if you follow a buy-and-hold strategy with bonds and stick with your investment until it matures. It's nevertheless a good number to know as you're getting into an investment, or a good comparison for bond mutual funds.

ONWARD

Chapter 7 focuses on mutual funds, perhaps the best investment starter kit around. Mutual funds get your money into the hands of an investment professional, who can spread it across a portfolio with enough variety to absorb bumps in the financial markets, yet with enough horsepower to get your savings off and running.

7

THE BASICS OF MUTUAL FUNDS

A Professional Portfolio with a Cushion from Risk Built In

Hearken back for a second to the twentieth century. Think about the best goods and services that came your way during that not-so-distant era. You'll find that nearly every company involved shared a simple formula for success. First, they took something quite complex and made it suddenly seem facile or very much within grasp. Then, each opened up new vistas to the masses by offering everyone a way to get in on the fun without expending too much time, effort, or money.

A good example from the past is the Model T. A means to zip back and forth to work, the grocery store, or school was bound to be a hit. Nonetheless, it took Henry Ford's assembly line a while to make a great idea affordable and considerably more accessible. As soon as that happened, travel became easier, and faraway places suddenly seemed closer. In no time, there was a garage beside every home, and a car inside every garage.

The same is true about the Internet. There's no argument that a link to all points around the world is a fantastic way to speed the flow of information. Still, for all its glory, the Internet was nothing more than a good idea for many of us—until the proliferation of affordable personal computers that could retail for under $1,000.

Well, there's a product whose problem-solving practicality and easy access for one and all has done similar wonders for Wall Street. We call it the mutual fund.

Mutual funds make the financial markets, those complex, often scary playgrounds for brokerage firms and high rollers, a lot simpler. They provide

REALITY CHECK

Bob Crenshaw, 46, needed a little prodding to get into mutual funds, but some 20 years later, he's more than glad he got it and got started, too.

Back in 1980 when Crenshaw was working on a Master's Degree in Management at the University of Redlands in California, a classmate Dexter Henderson, would rave on and on about the stock market and how to invest. Crenshaw, who lives in Walnut, California, and sells dialysis machines for a medical device company, sat back and listened to Henderson describe opportunities he had tucked away in a burgeoning portfolio of mutual funds and stocks. "I was just watching what he was doing; he was certainly financially secure and it seemed as if he was accumulating a nice sum . . . anyone would be curious and would want to find out how he was doing it."

Crenshaw had to know what was so good and how he could get in on it, too, so he started picking Henderson's mind. His friend walked him through several steps. He talked about buying properties and selling them again in the market. But no matter what twists and turns their skull sessions took, Crenshaw noticed that Henderson's plans always started with mutual funds.

Crenshaw signed up with the Janus Venture fund to start. He agreed to have $100 a month tapped from his checking account to build up his balance with Janus. Over time, he branched out. Whenever he got a raise at work, Crenshaw increased the amount he invested, eventually bringing on two additional funds, the Invesco Industrial and American Century's Ultra fund. He's stuck to it, too, funneling a steady $100 a month to each fund. The result: Crenshaw has over $60,000 stashed away in the three funds, and by reading up on prospectuses and annual reports, he's becoming something of an investment whiz in his own right. "I started off slowly, but this was a great way to pick up on the market over time," says Crenshaw. "And then, to learn more about what was going on, I made sure to read through the prospectuses and material they sent me, so I could see how the portfolio manager of each fund thought."

Crenshaw picked up enough to start investing in a few stocks of his own by 1988. He's since picked up shares of companies like Ford, Amgen, and Oracle. "I first want to have a secure base, in funds, though—to establish a foundation before I move to the next level. When you compare them to stocks, funds are not real volatile so you get a base that's steady . . . hopefully one that's going up in value."

a team of portfolio managers to monitor your investments. They also require a relatively small amount of money to start. And, they help everyone from the most sophisticated investor on down to newcomers tap into the stock market—or bond market.

Put it all together, and you have a hit on your hands. In fact, to say mutual funds are enjoying something of a boom is as close to a gross understatement as you can get. At the beginning of 2000, the fund industry had a whopping $6.8 trillion in assets according to the Investment Company Institute (ICI), an industry group based in Washington, D.C. That's up over fivefold from 1990, when the industry had $1.07 trillion in its coffers. Morningstar, the Chicago company that keeps close tabs on funds now lists over 11,000 to choose from; and with investors clamoring to get their money into funds of every kind, the number is sure to keep growing. The list of choices certainly has. If you're looking for growth stocks, thousands of funds out there have portfolios brimming with shares of Cisco Systems or Qualcomm. If Gold Stocks are your cup of Earl Grey, you'll find a bushel or so ready for your investment savings. There's even the Cincinnati Fund, which invests its assets in companies that are big in the Queen City.

Meanwhile, money keeps rolling in daily. According to the ICI, investors pumped some $194 billion into stock and bond mutual funds in 1999, a sum that breaks down to almost $531 million a day.

FUND FEVER

No doubt, you'd have to spend a good amount on plane fare or take a long trip on secluded seas to escape the growing influence mutual funds seem to have on our culture, on our lives. Most everyone now knows of Fidelity Magellan, the best-known mutual fund, and certainly the largest with $100 billion in assets as of 1999 (that's up a staggering 66 percent from just three years earlier). Today, mutual fund portfolio managers are making their way into our everyday lives in magazine articles, on financial broadcasts on CNBC or on our television screens during the nightly news. Leaf through a few publications at the newsstand. You'll surely find ad after ad about funds from Janus, Scudder, or Fidelity in *USA Today.*

You don't have to look too hard for the reasons mutual funds are getting all this attention. Americans have hefty financial burdens—from retirement funding to the cost of college tuition, now six figures and climbing fast. We need all the help we can get (See Figure 7.1).

Low Maintenance, High Finance

Mutual funds are the quintessential low-maintenance investment. They have well earned this reputation by taking a lot of the fuss and worry out of

Figure 7.1   Mutual Funds Work for You If . . .

- You're new to investing and looking for an easy way to get into the stock market and build up an initial position.
- You haven't got a lot of time to analyze stocks or bonds and would rather have a professional do the grunt work for you.
- You're a nervous sort who prefers leaving the heavy-duty decisions to an expert.
- You're looking for a diversified portfolio that's shielded from occasional market volatility.
- You'd like to expand your investment portfolio into a foreign country or into a new type of stock without risking a large amount of money on one holding.
- You're learning about the market and would like to see how a professional investor thinks.

financial markets. They don't require a lot of work: Fund shareholders don't have to worry about researching stocks or what investments to choose. They don't have to sleuth out industry trends or examine growth prospects for competitors. There's no muddling about accounting ledgers or balance sheets.

Instead, the grimy, sweaty numbers that make up the biggest obstacle in investing are handled by a portfolio manager or team of professional analysts. Whether they work together or alone, portfolio managers typically spend hours sifting through myriad statistics. They roll up their sleeves and slog through annual reports and mounds of industry data. They monitor the stocks, bonds, and cash in the fund's coffers. They pore through annual reports and meet with company chief executives before deciding on a stock for their portfolio. And they also determine when it's the best time to cash out and sell a stock or bond, whether a holding has climbed in value as much as it can or when things for a company pick have gone awry.

Another plus: Mutual funds are one of the single most inexpensive ways to take out a stake in the stock market. For an initial investment of $500, for example, it's possible to get a piece of a diversified portfolio, with holdings in a wide array of investments. In fact, of the over 11,000 mutual funds tracked by Morningstar, the Chicago firm that analyzes and rates funds, 8,000 have a portfolio of over 40 stocks or bonds. With its wealth spread across that many investments, if one stock or bond hits the skids, the mutual fund has enough of a stake in other stocks and bonds to cushion the blow.

Imagine, if you will, what it would take to amass a portfolio like that, and you'll get a sense of just how inexpensive mutual funds are in comparison. The average individual investor would pile up a huge sum in brokerage commissions to get in on 40 stocks—assuming you went to a discount broker. Say you paid $20 a trade, relatively low as commissions go. A 40-stock portfolio would rack up $800 in commissions just at the start. On the other hand, by combining your money with the investments from hundreds of other folks, a mutual fund enjoys economies of scale that keep its transaction fees low—small enough, in fact to forgo charging individuals like yourself every time a stock or bond is bought or sold. That's a good thing, too, for most funds shed old stocks and bonds and buy new ones at a healthy clip.

Don't forget that funds also wield clout. Let's face it: Armchair investors seldom get to chat with corporate executives about corporate strategy or possible mergers in the business. If you got on the phone and rang up Lou Gerstner, chief executive of IBM, chances are your call would be screened and diverted to someone who'd convince you that as much as he prized your call, the boss of the computer company was unlikely to get back to you any time soon.

On the other hand, collect a few billion in assets (as many mutual funds have done), and suddenly you find that a slew of CEOs are willing to break bread and talk shop. Essentially, that kind of interaction with corporate officials like chief financial officers and investor relations heads chalks up to another day at the office for most fund managers. To run a fund, you have to meet regularly with the high-and-mighty of corporate America to put a face and management style to the earnings numbers and profit projections for any given company. So, during any given week, portfolio managers usually while away a good portion of time talking to executives about business strategies and reviewing financial results, not only to grasp what a CEO sees in the future but to suss out what kind of experience the top brass has and to learn what executives are doing to increase shareholder value.

Finally, even though you should invest with a long-term objective and leave your money in a mutual fund to let it build up over time, it's good to know that funds are liquid investments. If an emergency pops up, you can call a fund company and access your savings. By law, all mutual funds must be ready to buy back shares on any given business day.

A Key Benefit: Little Bother

Your job as a fund shareholder? In all, it's pretty easy when you get down to it. It begins with keeping every record of each transaction you make in the funds you own—not too difficult because fund companies will provide a printout of transactions, from new investments to any withdrawals. That kind of thorough record keeping is invaluable when tax time comes around or when you sell your shares in a fund. Other than that, in most cases you needn't do much more than follow your fund's record and track how your investment is doing. That's relatively easy. First, a fund's management often sends you prospectuses, literature, quarterly reports, and newsletters to keep you abreast of how things have gone. Second, the financial press maintains close tabs on the fund industry, if only to talk to portfolio managers about what's hot and what's cold in the stock market.

There is some downside to owning a mutual fund, although in perspective, it's minimal. As mentioned, you need to keep records of how much you invest in a fund and when. A second scratch in the paint is taxes. Funds tend to distribute their earnings yearly. In effect, that passes the fund's tax burden on gains to shareholders, and the Internal Revenue Service comes ringing your doorbell on April 15, not the mutual fund's. Finally, because a fund's money is spread across a group of investments, the outsized gains of one or more shares in its portfolio are dampened by the performance of the entire portfolio of investments the fund holds. Still, whenever that sense of missing out on something big haunts you, remember that same dilution of the market's ups and downs works in your favor should the stock price of a holding cave in.

All in all, despite these little bumps, mutual funds have all the makings of a secure toehold in the stock market. Read on, and we'll tell you how to get into the game.

PUTTING YOUR MONEY IN THE HANDS OF THE PROS

Sort through all the financial magazine articles, the mutual fund prospectuses, even the splashy ads featuring comedians and former portfolio managers like Fidelity Magellan's Peter Lynch. When you push aside the window dressing, a mutual fund is nothing more than a way to get your savings in the hands of an investment pro that you like. When you invest in a fund, you've entrusted your money to a money manager or team of experts with the hope that the professionals running the show are going to garner you a healthy return by buying stocks or bonds or other profitable financial tools.

The mutual fund you choose pools your money with the sums it has gathered up from other investors from spots far and wide. In return for all the money they've put into a mutual fund, investors receive shares that represent a stake in the mutual fund's portfolio. The mountain of funds collected from mutual fund investors is handed over to a group of professionals—either portfolio managers or analysts—who study the financial markets and determine how to make the greatest return on your money.

Mutual funds make money for you in at least three ways:

1. Your fund keeps daily tabs on how its portfolio of investments—stocks and bonds—fare. As the fund's holdings appreciate in value, so does the price of each share in the fund. Conversely when stocks and bonds that the fund owns slide, the fund's share price slips as well.

2. Fundholders also reap dividends from their investments. Bonds and a good number of stocks produce a steady stream of income. Again, your mutual fund calculates the amount of yield it receives from its investments and applies that to its own share price. If the Big League fund company reaps $1.00 for every $20 share, it will list a yield of 5 percent.

3. Funds will sell the shares or bonds they hold from time to time. If the investment is worth more than when the fund originally bought it, the fund will have made a capital gain, which is typically passed on to investors in the form of a distribution.

To get in on mutual fund investing, investors need only scrape together a minimum initial investment, the lowest amount of money the fund requires of newcomers who want to get into the pool. Generally, a mutual fund will look for $2,000 or so as a starting investment, although a good many accept $1,000, $500, or even less. And, if you agree to let a fund tap a regular monthly investment (say $50), you can get started with as little as $100. It is advisable to check the policy of any fund you're thinking of investing in. Over half the 11,000 funds tracked by Morningstar allow you to stake your first claim for as little as $100, if you promise to make regular contributions; almost 40 percent of them let you in for $50. Another way to start off for a small amount is to open an IRA (individual retirement account); in that case most funds lower the minimum initial investment required to as little as $100 or $200.

Once you've filled out an application, a fund will allot you a certain number of shares for your investment and will keep track of how much your investment increases or decreases over time. You can follow the fortunes of your fund by looking up daily quotes in the newspaper or on the Internet or by calling the customer service center most funds provide (see Figure 7.2).

You'll also receive plenty of reading material, both before you invest in a fund, and regularly throughout the year once you become a fund shareholder. The Securities and Exchange Commission requires a fund to provide potential investors with a prospectus and with a shareholder report. Both are full of information you'll want to look over: an explanation of the fund's investment style; a brief bit of background on the fund's portfolio managers; figures on how well the fund has performed over time and how that stacks up against a benchmark for the market such as the S&P 500 or the Lehman Brothers Corporate Bond Index. There will also be a printout of the list of holdings including the stocks and bonds the fund held at the end of its most recent quarter or year. Typically, management will want to show you both how well the fund is doing and what they see ahead for the market as well as your investment (see Figure 7.3).

At the end of the year, usually around November 30, you'll get notification of the fund's capital gains distribution and dividends. A fund gathers up both during the course of a year as the result of its usual operations. A

Figure 7.2   Mutual Fund Listings

Here's what your daily newspaper puts out on mutual funds and fund prices.

FUND FAMILY FUND NAME	TYPE	RATING	NAV	WKLY. % RET.	YTD % RET.	1-YR. % RET.	4-WK. % RET.
Super Funds Super Super	LG	5/5	15.90	−3.6	14.0	27.0	0.9

Here's what it all means:

Fund family	Mutual fund companies often offer up a range of funds to investors. Together, that selection or portfolio of funds is called a fund family. Fund families you might already know include Fidelity or Janus.
Fund name	The name of the fund listed.
Type	Often newspapers print a code to let readers know how the fund readers are looking up invests. Many times the code or fund "type" has been determined by a company like Morningstar, which studies the fund business and categorizes funds.
Rating	Many newspapers print fund ratings. A rating is a score for a fund's overall performance as determined by a company like Morningstar, which tracks funds and their performance.
NAV	NAV (net asset value) is the worth of all the investments— stocks, bonds, and cash—that a mutual fund holds.
Wkly. % Ret.	Weekly total return is a percentage figure that tells readers how much the mutual fund's net asset value increased during the week.
YTD % Ret.	Year-to-date total return is a percentage figure that tells readers how much the mutual fund's net asset value has increased so far this year.
1-Yr. % Ret.	One-year total return is the percentage that the mutual fund's net asset value has increased over the last 52 weeks.
4-Wk. % Ret.	Four-week total return is the percentage that the mutual fund's net asset value has increased over the last month or four weeks.

In addition . . .

You might also see listings for:	52-week highs and lows for a given fund's share price Dividend rates Average annual 3-year total returns

Figure 7.3 Fund Literature

Funds supply investors with lots of informative material you can use to help pick the best investments around and learn about investing as well.

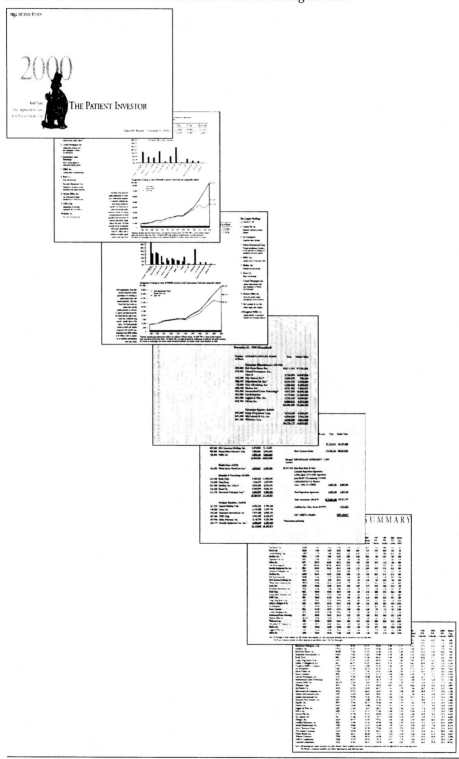

Source: Ariel Capital.

fund's portfolio manager will decide to sell stakes he or she has taken out in the stock or bond markets. If the fund realizes a profit from the sale—if the asset sold is worth more than what the portfolio manager paid—the fund logs a capital gain, which must be passed on to investors. By passing on the profits to you, mutual funds avoid paying tax on their gains. One problem: It's your tab to pay.

Additionally, stocks or bonds the fund owns pay dividends during the year. Like capital gains, dividends are passed on to investors. And like capital gains, the tax due will be your responsibility come April 15 the following year.

WHO NEEDS FUNDS?

Since mutual funds are a good anchor to any investment portfolio, consider buying into at least a couple of them.

Mutual funds are the best way for newcomers to get started. They offer instant diversification to cushion your returns from the shocks of sudden downswings, which can happen to even the best of stocks. And mutual funds not only afford you entry into the stock market, they also provide a portfolio manager to guide you along the way. On top of that, beginners can also gain a decent education in investing by merely reading and following developments that affect the fund's positions in companies and the financial markets. You'll receive literature from the fund addressing investing issues and giving you a view into how investment professionals go about their regular business.

Even if you're a wizened investor, it's advisable to use a sizable mutual fund stake as your portfolio's foundation. Handing over part of a portfolio to a professional team of investors is always a good idea. Most people can't afford the time to read up and research every bit of minutiae on their stocks and bonds, let alone a portfolio the size of a mutual fund's. Second, mutual fund holdings help cut a portfolio's overall risk.

Both reasons work to your advantage over time. Funds constantly scan the investing universe for new and intriguing opportunities, grunt work that would overburden many of us. Also, a fund checks to make sure that it has chosen the best investments.

WHAT'S IN IT FOR THEM

Suppose you're looking over two mutual funds. One has more than doubled investors' money, posting an unbelievable 130 percent for investors last year. The second, say, has stumbled, finishing the year down 5 percent. The question: Which one made more money (i.e., was more profitable)?

WEB SIGHTINGS
NAMES TO KNOW IN THE MUTUAL FUND BUSINESS

If you're looking for the lowdown on mutual funds, first, check out the Investment Company Institute (ICI), a trade organization in Washington, D.C. (202-326-5800; Web site www.ici.org) that collects data on the mutual fund industry. It also provides investors with pamphlets and brochures that explain how mutual funds work and how to get started in mutual fund investing. You'll find a list of things to look for in a fund, and explanations of how mutual funds fit into your investment plans both on the organization's Web site and in ICI pamphlets.

Another good source of information on mutual funds is some of the larger mutual fund companies. Fidelity (www.fidelity.com), Vanguard (www.vanguard.com), and T. Rowe Price (www.troweprice.com) all offer background material on investing in mutual funds, a great source of information whether you opt for their funds or not. Vanguard's plain-talk prospectuses go a long way in explaining how a mutual fund investment works, and what risk investors incur. Visit Vanguard's Web site or call the company to order a prospectus and learn more about investing.

One name you can't avoid when it comes to mutual funds is Morningstar. Based in Chicago, Morningstar has made a name for itself as a clearinghouse for all manner of statistics on funds. The company also rates funds according to its own specialized system that gauges risk and return. Morningstar may not track every fund around, but currently it follows just over 11,000 funds—and it doesn't begin covering a fund until it has been around for 3 years. You'll find Morningstar is one of the most comprehensive warehouses of fund statistics and analysis.

Morningstar research is available in a variety of forms. If your preference is no-frills print and paper, the company puts out a fund reviews and stats monthly. There in black and white is a fund's dossier including total return figures, expense ratios, contact telephone numbers, and performance compared with market benchmarks like the Standard & Poor's 500. You'll also get a glimpse of commentary written up by a Morningstar analyst who tracks the fund and its peers. Most public libraries subscribe to Morningstar "sheets." If not, a local discount brokerage like Charles Schwab should have a subscription.

The Morningstar Web site (www.morningstar.com) also is well worth a visit. It has a wealth of statistical information on practically any fund you might like to investigate. In addition there are plenty of articles everything from the basics of mutual fund investing to tax issues and analysis of trends in the fund industry.

(continued)

WEB SIGHTINGS (CONTINUED)

When it comes to gathering up mutual fund statistics, Morningstar is by no means alone. There's also Lipper Inc., a division of the news service Reuters. Lipper statistics on mutual fund gains appear in many publications. Hands down, though, Morningstar is the most accessible, most visible monitor of the fund industry around.

For the latest on the newest mutual fund Web sites around, you can check two all-purpose, Internet investment-link warehouses—Dailystocks (www.dailystocks.com) and Investorama (www.investorama.com). Both locations have stockpiled a lifetime of sites to visit and study, or at least enough to keep ordinary folks surfing for months. The two offer leads of all sorts—from mutual fund background, to results, to screens. Better yet, access to both is gratis.

Logic would seem to point to the first fund, the highflier that did so well: By bringing home the most money, it should have made the highest profit. The answer, however, just isn't necessarily that simple or that clear. Oddly enough, it wouldn't be out of the ordinary if both funds made the same profit for headquarters. The amount of money a mutual fund rakes in has little if anything to do with its returns. Instead, funds collect a list of fees from investors to pay their managers and office workers, buy office supplies, keep up with the utilities, hire lawyers, print quarterly reports, cover postage, and foot a host of other costs associated with doing business. In some cases, the fees are tied to the fund's performance, providing a prod to encourage portfolio managers to make you more money; in other cases, they don't serve as much of an incentive.

Fees come in two types. Management fees are the tab investors pay to help foot the salary of the portfolio manager overseeing your account as well as lawyers, secretaries, analysts, and the like who perform a lot of the fund's day-to-day work. Then, there are sales fees, a portion of the investment that some funds use for commissions to brokers or financial planners who steer investors into the fund.

You needn't obsess on individual management fees in and of themselves—instead, there's a figure, called an expense ratio you can use to measure how much of a fund's gains are going to pay the bills or compare one fund with another.

At the same time, you should sidestep sales fees—loads as they're commonly called in the business—altogether. The main reason is that they sap a large portion of the money your fund is earning, in return for what amounts to a commission to a broker and financial adviser who steered you into the fund. By exerting a little time and effort, you can find viable no-load substitutes that let your savings work for you instead of gilding a broker's pockets.

MANAGEMENT FEES

One of the largest sums investors cover comes under the heading "Management Fees." Essentially, they are a sort of fund "dues," the annual price you pay to have a Fidelity, Dreyfus, or Janus scout about for investments and look to increase the value of your account. In some cases, management fees are linked to the size of the mutual fund; in other cases, some portion of management fees might be tied to how well a fund does. Should a fund tear up the market, this performance fee rises; if the fund sputters, the fee also drops.

That's just the beginning of the list. Funds also charge administrative fees funds to pay for the daily operations of the fund. Then there are 12(b)-1 charges, which funds levy on investors to pay for marketing, chiefly advertising, and distribution costs for such things as brochures and mailings. (The name 12(b)-1 refers to the Securities and Exchange Commission rule that allows funds to charge the fee.)

You might not think that mutual funds make a big deal about fees. You're right—they don't. You won't receive any notice in the mail that your funds are siphoning off part of your investment to pay the rent and keep the lights on. Instead, management fees are lifted out of your return in a silent, almost imperceptible way from the balance you've invested in the fund. What's more, the total return figures reported in the newspaper or in fund literature already account for management fees—they've been calculated and subtracted from the gain or loss you see.

That's not to say that there isn't a correlation between a fund's performance and the money it makes over time. A fund that posts fabulous returns year after year is bound to stir up a buzz. And, once the word gets around that a fund manager is blazing a path to the stratosphere, new investors may flock to the fund, driving up fee revenue. However, that isn't always the case. In fact, a fund could stumble along with little to show for itself in the way of returns and still make a sizable profit.

Fund managers often have another source of ample motivation. Most portfolio managers are proud people who likely own a significant stake in the very fund they're overseeing. You might say their money is where their investing prowess, or lack thereof, is.

Although you need to consider the entire picture, by mulling over a fund, looking over returns, and checking out its fees, there's no need to get flustered. Generally, fund fees don't amount to a huge sum—say 1 percent to 1.5 percent or so of your total investment annually on average. If you comb over stats compiled by Morningstar, you'll find many funds—about 6,800 of the 11,000 funds Morningstar covers—have an expense ratio of 1 percent or more, although only 3,950 go above 1.5 percent. Around 1,640 funds charge 2 percent or more.

Such small percentages might not seem like a big deal. Watch that kind of thinking, though. No matter how tiny they seem, fees eat into your total return figure over time. Consider a $2,000 investment in a fund that averages an annual total return of 10 percent over 5 years. An annual 2 percent in fees might seem like a small figure to pay—$40 a year—while your investment is raking in $200 every 12 months. Approach the matter another way, however, and the figure doesn't seem so innocuous. That $40 lifted from your account and placed in management's hands is actually a 20 percent slice of the gains you could net and compound over time. Effectively, your investment is returning 8 percent a year instead of 10 percent. If that doesn't bother you, look at it like this: Over a 10-year period, a straight 10 percent annual gain with no fees to pay would fatten your original $2,000 investment to $5,187.48. Remove 2 percent annually and your total drops to $4,317.85. That little math exercise should prod you to look over expenses before you finally sign onto a fund (see Figure 7.4).

Load versus No Load

Management fees are one thing. Sales fees—loads as they're called in the business—are another. A load is a payment that some, but by no means all funds charge investors for the privilege to buy into a fund. Generally, as a sales fee, the load is seen as compensation for a broker or financial planner who has advised you to buy a particular fund. In other cases, it's divvied up between the fund and a broker. Either way, it works like this: If you invest $5,000 in a fund that charges a 3 percent load, $4,850 or 97 percent of the sum you're handing over will go into the fund in your name. The other 3 percent, $150 in this case, is passed on as a load.

Loads come in three varieties. There are front-end loads, which are taken from your investment, following the example in the preceding paragraph. Deferred loads nip away at your investment year after year for a set period—say 5 years. Then, there are back-end loads, which are levied on withdrawals from a fund. If you remove $1,000 from a fund with a back-end load of 4 percent, you'll receive $960; the remaining $40 will cover your load fee. By law, fund loads can't go above 8.5 percent.

According to Morningstar records early in 2000, nearly 3,200 of the 11,000 funds covered by the Chicago firm charged front-end loads; approximately

Figure 7.4   Expense Ratios

Different types of funds charge varying amounts in fees. Here's Morningstar's data on average expense ratios for a few categories.

FUND CATEGORY	AVERAGE EXPENSE RATIO
Domestic	
Large cap growth	1.46
Large cap value	1.38
Large cap blend	1.23
Small cap growth	1.69
Small cap value	1.53
Technology	1.75
International	
Foreign stock	1.71
Emerging markets	2.21
European stock	1.81
World stock	1.90
Bond	
Short-term muni	0.84
Long-term government	0.97
Intermediate-term bond	0.96
High-yield bond	1.31
Convertible bond	1.57

Source: Morningstar.

3,570 charged deferred or back-end loads. Unlike management fees, loads—front end, deferred, or back-end—aren't figured into a fund's total return figures.

In most cases, it's advisable to skip funds that charge loads, especially if you're doing the shopping yourself. Besides paying the annual expenses listed earlier, you're giving up a large slice of the returns your money would earn in a no-load fund. Assume, that the stock market averages gains of 10 percent to 12 percent a year. A 3 percent load takes a third to a fourth of that money straight off the bat. That said, if you happen to find a fund with a load that also has a track return of providing investors golden returns, you might think twice before tossing it aside.

Make no mistake. If you deal with brokers, you'll hear many reasons why load funds are a better investment for individual investors. Too often, a broker or salesperson will claim that load funds are somehow a step above or that the treatment the brokers give you somehow makes up for the load. That kind of biased advice isn't in your best interest. No studies have shown that load funds are better than their no-load counterparts. What's more, loads are pocketed by salespeople and do not go to pay for fund expenses or to compensate money managers. They are sales fees and sales fees alone.

WEB SIGHTINGS
MUTUAL FUNDS

Many mutual fund companies now sport a home page on the Net. Check by calling up a search engine (Altavista, Yahoo!, Excite) and input the name of the fund that's caught your fancy. Or, check Morningstar's Web site (www.morningstar.com), which lists contact telephone numbers for thousands of funds. And finally, you can also stop by the Internet domains of the Mutual Fund Education Alliance (www.mfea.com), Dailystocks (www.dailystocks.com) or Investorama (www.investorama.com) to find 800-numbers.

One other sales pitch you should sidestep: the claim that a broker can sell you no-load funds. The fact is that top no-load companies like Vanguard simply don't sell through brokers. How do you get around the hassle and fuss? Go directly to the fund company to make your investment. Fund companies typically have toll-free 800-numbers. Check with toll-free directory assistance (800-555-1212) to get the number.

Transaction or Redemption Fees

They don't advertise it, but fund managers would rather not see you withdraw large sums from your account because if large quantities of money flow out of the fund, management must sell holdings to cover the redemption or withdrawal. To discourage investors from running to the exits, many funds assess transaction or redemption fees on withdrawals. Don't confuse the redemption fee with a back-end load, however. Redemption fees go directly to the fund; a back-end load is paid to a salesperson, financial planner, or broker.

Low-Balance or Maintenance Fees

Often, if an account balance in a mutual fund falls below a certain floor, a fund will hit you with a low-balance or maintenance fee. Typically, it runs $10 to $50 a year.

Funds, however, overlook the fee if you set up an automatic investment program, with a fixed amount invested in the fund monthly. Otherwise,

Figure 7.5 Laying It Out

A fund's prospectus will outline how much management charges in fees.

Annual Operating Expenses
for fiscal year ended September 30, 1999

The tables below describe the Funds' fees and expenses; if you buy and hold shares in the Ariel Fund or Ariel Appreciation Fund, you bear these fees indirectly. *Both Ariel Stock Funds are "no-load" funds. You do not pay a sales charge when you buy or sell shares.*

	Ariel Fund *percentage of average daily net Fund assets*	**Ariel Appreciation** *percentage of average daily net Fund assets*
Management fees*	0.65%	0.75%
Distribution (12b-1) fees*	0.25%	0.25%
Other expenses*	0.35%	0.26%
Total annual operating expenses	1.25%	1.26%

Cost comparison examples

The examples below illustrate the expenses you would incur on a $10,000 investment in the Ariel Fund or the Ariel Appreciation Fund based on each Fund's current level of expenses. The examples assume that each Fund earned an annual return of 5% over the periods shown and that you redeem your shares at the end of each time period.

	1 year	3 years	5 years	10 years
Ariel Fund	$127	$397	$686	$1,511
Ariel Appreciation Fund	$128	$400	$692	$1,523

These examples are hypothetical and are included for the purpose of comparing the Funds' expenses with other mutual funds. They do not represent estimates of future expenses or returns, either of which may be greater or less than the amounts shown.

Source: Ariel Capital.

- **Management fees** cover the costs of overseeing the Fund's investments and the costs of administration and accounting.
- **12b-1 fees** pay for promotion and distribution of Fund shares and services provided to shareholders. Because these fees are paid from Fund assets on an ongoing basis, these fees will increase the cost of your investment and may cost you more than other types of sales charges.
- **Other expenses** include the costs of the custodian and transfer agent, accountants, attorneys and directors.

COMPOUNDING

As discussed in earlier chapters, compounding—diverting dividends and distributions back into an investment—can generate further gains for investors. The same holds true for mutual funds. Late in the year, you'll be notified of distributions and dividends the fund intends to pay out. Plow that money back into the fund, and you will reap the long-term benefits of the distribution. They might not seem like a lot any given year, but over time they add up.

Say that you invested $10,000 in the S&P 500 at the end of 1987. If you plucked away the dividends that the stocks in the index had paid over time, by the end of 1998 that sum would have grown to $44,260. Not bad, but consider this. By reinvesting the dividends, you would have had $57,969 at the end of the same period, a full 31 percent more.

---

as long-term investors, you'll probably keep your balance well above the minimum.

Sleuthing It Out

Don't worry about determining whether a fund that has caught your eye charges a load. You won't need Sherlock Holmes to figure that out. For one, the SEC now requires all funds to include in their prospectus an expense table that spells out any expenses it charges investors. There, you'll find a listing that includes sales expenses like loads. Another tip: Keep an eye open for funds with lettered shares. Typically, companies that charge loads offer fund shareholders a choice of a few "payment plans." The "A" shares might charge a front-end load, whereas "B" shares might charge back-end loads. Should any fund that you're interested in have lettered shares, you might want to take a little extra time examining its prospectus (see Figure 7.5).

A TAXING MATTER

Washington, D.C., gets you for interest you earn on your bank account. The government tags you on a profit you make from selling your home. It's only logical that the IRS would come after your mutual fund investment as well.

The problem is, however, that mutual fund investments get taxed most every year, whether you hold on to the investment or not.

Blame capital gains. Essentially, Uncle Sam goes after the profit your fund makes when it trades stocks. If it bought 1 million shares of Acme Explosives at $1 last year and now sells that stake for $1.10, it will have generated $100,000 in capital gains that someone has to pay taxes on. Don't look at the mutual funds. They're looking to sidestep the responsibility, and can by law, if they pass those gains onto you the shareholder. So, around each December, fundholders are notified how much they can expect in the way of capital gains distributions. If you are a fundholder, early the following year a 1099-DIV form will arrive in the mail. On it, the mutual fund will note how much in dividends you're being given, and how much in the way of capital gains are being distributed. You'll report each on your tax form, and likely pay 28 percent to the government.

Here's the rub. First, the capital gain doesn't do anything for the value of your shares—it's treated as an amount separate from your holding in the mutual fund. Second, you'll get the distribution whether you invested January 1 in the fund or just before the fund company makes its capital gains distribution announcement—say on December 3. That means you'll pay the same in taxes whether your fund holding benefited from the shares the fund sold or not. And you're paying taxes without cashing in on your fund holding.

What's worse, most funds trade actively—the average stock mutual fund turns over 90 percent of its portfolio, meaning it will likely sell nine tenths of the stocks in its portfolio.

There are several ways of getting around the mutual fund capital gains tax bite. If you hold mutual funds in a tax-deferred 401(k) or IRA account, you're not taxed on yearly capital gains, and only ante up on your 1040 once you begin drawing on your savings.

It's also possible to pull an end run on the capital gains distribution, by timing your mutual fund purchases carefully in mid to late December. All you need to do is call the fund to find out when the roll of investors is checked for the distribution, and when the distribution is made. By coming in after the fund has doled out its gains, you can sidestep the tax—for one year, at least.

Also if you're planning a mutual fund investment outside the tax-deferred shelter of a 401(k) or IRA, financial planners will tell you to do so early in the year. That way, your mutual fund shares will benefit from the portfolio manager's moves during the year, even if you're stuck with a capital gains distribution.

A final trick is to opt for a mutual fund with a sensitive portfolio manager. Index funds fit that bill because they tend to buy and hold the stocks and bonds they own. Since they trade infrequently, the funds tend to run up little in the way of capital gains, and therefore they incur little in the way of a tax burden to hand over to you. A number of frugal, tax-managed funds have sprung up, too—nearly 80 by Morningstar's count in early 2000. They combine the tax-minimizing qualities of index funds (low turnover) with some of the attributes of actively managed mutual funds (they trade in and out of some shares, they don't follow an index). Morningstar rates two, Vanguard Tax-Managed Growth & Income (800-662-7447) and Standish Small Cap Tax Sensitive (800-729-0066), the highest in the category as of this writing.

ONWARD

Now that you know how mutual funds work, it's time to look into ways to choose the best ones available for your portfolio. In the chapter ahead, you'll become acquainted with the enormous variety of funds out on the market today.

8

MUTUAL FUNDS—HOW TO PICK THE BEST OF THEM, AFRICAN AMERICAN FUNDS, AND MORE

Say what you will about the folks who run mutual funds across the country. They certainly seem to recognize a fortune waiting to be made when they see one. Day after day, month after month, a stampede of new funds comes to market, all to capture some slice of the billions of dollars piling up at the feet of mutual fund money managers yearly.

The new funds arrive in droves with all sorts of twists and angles on how to conquer the financial markets and deliver you the highest return possible. They come in a variety of sizes, some with their sights on companies working in cutting-edge technologies, while others opt for rust-belt favorites, big industrial concerns that still grind out steel, cars, or plastics by the ton. Some fund managers fly overseas from exotic locale to exotic locale in search of investment ideas. Still others are on the lookout for stocks that have been humdrum of late, with the hope that they'll bounce back and bag shareholders a tidy profit.

Whatever their style, whatever their affiliation, there are enough funds circulating about these days to fill several entire newspaper pages, and then some. At the current pace, you can expect to see 12,000 or more in circulation in the very near future. Intimidated? That's nothing. The scary thing is the thought of combing through a tower of prospectuses and mutual fund literature to find a fund or two worth investing in. Knowing where to start seems more a factor of blind luck than anything else.

Don't despair. This chapter helps guide you to the best mutual funds around. It includes ways to gather up ideas for the kind of mutual funds that will take your money—and you—places. You'll find the numbers you should focus on, statistics that are crucial when buying into a fund, and also will learn about the myriad groupings of mutual funds that exist on the market these days. Then you can weed the thousands of funds out there down to a short list of two or three you can invest in and live with.

STEP 1: COME UP WITH IDEAS

There's a simple starting point for investing in mutual funds, just as there is for stocks: an idea. All you need to get off and running is a handful of ideas—funds to look over, investigate, compare, and consider.

There are just a few places to start shopping for mutual funds. First, look in the financial press—investing magazines like *Black Enterprise* or *Barron's*. Financial magazines and newspapers love splashy headlines and upbeat pieces on hot mutual funds, and money managers who have Wall Street on string. What makes them a good source, too, is that many articles, no matter how compact they seem, carry enough numbers to help you get a decent impression of the fund and its advantages.

A word of caution, however. The press tends to gravitate to mutual funds with the prettiest numbers. That can be good and bad. Although managers who have a hot hand now are likely to snare good returns for a while, journalists in their rush to anoint heroes of the day can be shortsighted. Their lionized money managers sometimes are enjoying a momentary bit of good luck.

So, instead of swallowing press reports whole, use whatever list of funds you get from the newsstand as a launching point. Prepare to follow up with research of your own in sources pointed out in this chapter.

The Internet is an excellent source of ideas, too. One site that teems with mutual fund news and reports is run by Morningstar, the Chicago research firm that tracks the industry. Morningstar's site has statistics of all sorts on mutual funds, and articles that explain how the stock market ticks, and how to judge one fund alongside another.

STEP 2: DO THE RESEARCH

You can't judge a fund without the industry scorecard. In this case, that happens to be Morningstar's thorough reports. Morningstar publishes sheets that look a fund up and down, kick its tires, and do everything but take it for a test-drive. The Chicago firm looks at historical returns and matches them up against benchmarks. Morningstar analysts provide commentary after interviewing fund managers and looking over fund results. Morningstar has its own measures of a fund's risk and goes so far as to rate

---

WEB SIGHTINGS
MUTUAL FUND SCREENS

One of the best things to come investors' way—the stock screen—was discussed in Chapter 4. Contained on a Web site, easy to use, and full of data, the screen was a way to take the universe of publicly traded stocks and whittle it down to a few choice investments to mull over.

The same powerful software is now available on the Web for fund investors, too. A number of Web sites offer up fund screens that sort the market according to your specifications, allowing you to cherry-pick from hundreds of funds.

One of the best, sponsored by Quicken, the makers of financial software, and Morningstar (www.quicken.com/investments/mutualfunds/finder) lets you choose from a variety of fund categories and examine funds for total returns, expenses, and minimum initial investment amounts.

If you're hunting for fund screens, be sure to browse Morningstar's own Web site (www.morningstar.com). The leading fund research company offers a "Fund Selector," with both a choice of preset screens and a number of variables investors can plug in to research returns, expenses, and investment styles. The data is not only fresh (it comes from a company that compiles mutual fund stats by the truckload), much of it is free for the picking.

Another screen can be found at the MFEA Web site (www.mfea.org). It allows you to sort through a roster of no-load funds with 11 criteria. Afterward, you can check your results and look over the funds.

Dailystocks (www.dailystocks.com) and Investorama (www.investorama.com) also provide links to good fund screens.

---

the fund according to its own criteria. The company presents a lot of research for free on the Web. Still, your best bet is to dig up Morningstar's printed sheets (see Figure 8.1). They're often found at your local library and at brokerage offices such as Charles Schwab.

STEP 3: GET THE PROSPECTUS AND ANY OTHER LITERATURE THE FUND OFFERS

What an annual report is to a company shares, a prospectus is to a mutual fund. A fund's prospectus is essentially a long, exhaustive profile of a mutual fund. Its pages will spell out a fund manager's investment philosophies.

Figure 8.1 Morningstar

Morningstar sheets provide information on mutual funds including returns, portfolios, expenses, and turnover. The Chicago company rates funds and supplies investors with commentary as well. Morningstar sheets are available at public libraries or by subscription. Contact Morningstar at 800-735-0700.

Source: Morningstar.

There will be a discussion of some of the strategies used to invest the fund's money and very likely a list of stocks or bonds that the fund has bought. You'll find a detailed description of the fund's fees, expenses, and charges. Be prepared for a blizzard of numbers including tables and charts that provide data about the fund.

What to Get out of a Prospectus

The prospectus arrives in the mail, along with a bundle of fund literature. There are more pamphlets, it seems, than you could collect in the showroom of a new car dealership. You leaf through to see number after number, legalese atop legalese. What's an investor to do?

It can be downright difficult to dive into a prospectus. There in your hands is a 30- to 40-page document, packed with page after page of printed information. True, some of the bigger fund companies throw in pamphlets with pictures and four-color graphs. But, by and large, most funds leave most of the talking to the numbers and knotty prose (see Figure 8.2).

Don't blame the fund managers. Even financial types know the power of art and attractive presentation. Still, the average fund just doesn't have the budget to cover such luxuries. That means you'll need to sharpen your attention span and pour an extra cup of coffee to get through. It needn't be a heavy-duty chore, however. First relax; you aren't the first person who has been more than a little intimidated by the possibility of a week spent slogging through some dry reading.

That does not mean you should skip the matter altogether. It's a good thing to spend a little time checking out just where your money is going, after all. Instead, we'll provide you an abbreviated checklist that you might want to keep in mind the first time or two you glance through all the documentation:

1. *What's the fund's objective?* Here, you'll see fund investment styles put to work. Management will tell you what kinds of opportunities they look for in the market. What do the portfolio managers think about risk? Do they aim to preserve capital or angle to achieve the highest gain possible? When does the stock market look inviting, and when do the managers shut down and pray that the storm soon passes? You'll also get insight into their way of thinking. In the prospectus, they'll spell out when they like a stock and when they don't, what they pick and what they avoid. Think about this—do you agree, and does it make sense?

2. *How has the fund performed over time?* Try as the portfolio manager might to tell you in his or her own words, this is a story only the numbers can relate (see Figure 8.3). Look at total return figures, both over a stretch of time (3 years, 5 years) and for individual years.

Figure 8.2   What's It All About

A prospectus should supply information on everything from a mutual fund's address, performance, and managers to how to invest.

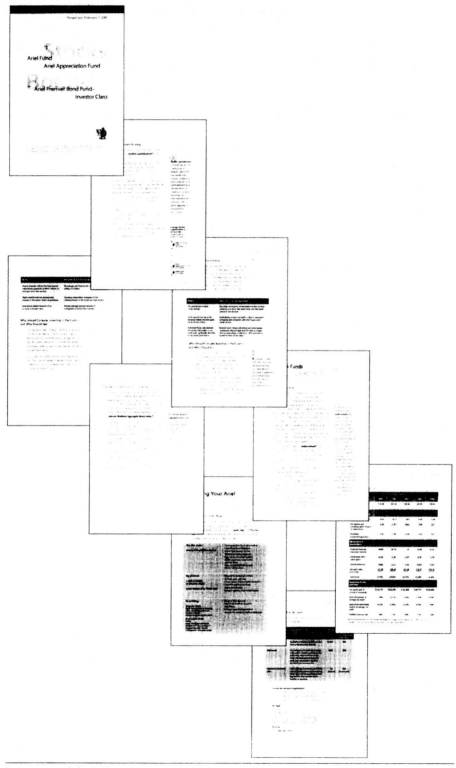

Source: Ariel Capital.

Figure 8.3 Scorecard

How's a fund doing? Its prospectus gives investors a rundown on results over time. Fund literature, too, spells out gains and total returns.

ARIEL MUTUAL FUNDS

Fund Performance as of December 31, 1999

	One Month	Quarter	Year to Date	One Year	Three Years	Five Years	Ten Years	Since Inception
					Annualized			
Ariel Appreciation Fund	3.24%	1.47%	-3.79%	-3.79%	16.63%	19.50%	13.60%	13.53%
Russell Mid Cap Index¹	8.80%	17.23%	18.23%	18.23%	18.86%	21.86%	15.92%	15.97%
Lipper Rankings² Within mid-cap value fund category	—	—	—	166/199	27/118	22/75	10/34	9/33

Average Annual Total Return does not reflect a maximum 4.75% sales load charged prior to 07/15/94. Assumes reinvestment of dividends and capital gains.

Portfolio Characteristics

Beta:	0.99
R²:	0.76
Turnover:	27.5%
Number of Issues:	37
Average Mkt Cap:	$2.7 billion

Morningstar Rating ★★★

Overall rating is based on 3,469 domestic equity funds as of 12/31/99. The fund was rated three stars among 3,469 domestic equity funds for the three-year period ended 12/31/99, three stars among 2,180 domestic equity funds for the five-year period ended 12/31/99, and three stars among 770 domestic equity funds for the ten-year period ended 12/31/99. Morningstar proprietary rankings reflect historical risk-adjusted performance as of 12/31/99. These ratings may change monthly and are calculated from the funds' three-, five- and ten-year (as applicable) average annual returns in excess of 90-day Treasury bill returns with appropriate fee adjustments and a risk factor that reflects fund performance below 90-day Treasury bill returns. The top 10% of funds in an investment category receive five stars; the next 22.5% receive four stars; the next 35% receive three stars; the next 22.5% receive two stars and the bottom 10% receive one star.

Top Ten Holdings   % of Portfolio

1. **CenturyTel, Inc.** 4.8%
   Diversified telecommunications company

2. **Lee Enterprises** 4.5%
   Diversified media company

3. **Sybron International Corp.** 4.5%
   Principal manufacturer of products for the laboratory and professional orthodontic and dental markers

4. **MBIA, Inc.** 4.4%
   Leading insurer of municipal bonds

5. **Hasbro, Inc.** 4.0%
   Prominent toy manufacturer

6. **Rouse Company** 4.0%
   Retail mall developer

7. **Central Newspapers** 3.7%
   Leading media company with daily newspapers in Phoenix and Indianapolis

8. **Herman Miller** 3.7%
   One of the country's largest manufacturers of office furniture

9. **McCormick & Company** 3.6%
   World's largest spice company

10. **Houghton Mifflin Co.** 3.6%
    Leading publisher of educational textbooks and multi-media products

% of Portfolio in Top Ten	**40.8%**

Ariel Appreciation Fund Portfolio Composition vs. Russell Mid Cap Index

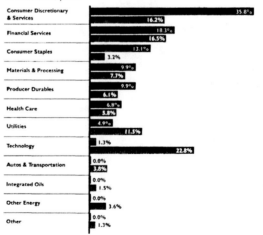

■ Ariel Appreciation Fund
■ Russell Mid Cap Index

	Ariel Appreciation Fund	Russell Mid Cap Index
Consumer Discretionary & Services	35.8%	16.2%
Financial Services	18.3%	16.5%
Consumer Staples	13.1%	3.2%
Materials & Processing	9.9%	7.7%
Producer Durables	9.9%	6.1%
Health Care	6.8%	5.8%
Utilities	4.9%	11.5%
Technology	1.3%	22.8%
Autos & Transportation	0.0%	3.8%
Integrated Oils	0.0%	1.5%
Other Energy	0.0%	3.6%
Other	0.0%	1.3%

Slow and Steady Wins the Race

Past performance does not guarantee future results. Principal value and investment returns will fluctuate so that an investor's shares, when redeemed, may be worth more or less than the original cost.

¹ The Russell Mid Cap™ Index is an unmanaged market capitalization weighted index of the 800 smallest companies of the largest 1,000 companies in the Russell 3000® Index and is adjusted for dividends. An investor cannot invest directly in an index.

² Lipper Analytical Services, Inc. is a nationally recognized organization that reports performance and calculates rankings for mutual funds. Each fund is ranked within a universe of funds with similar investment objectives. Ranking is based on total returns.

For more information about the Ariel Mutual Funds including management fees, expenses and potential risks, please see the current prospectus which must precede or accompany this material. Distributed by Ariel Distributors, Inc. 307 N. Michigan Ave., Chicago, IL 60601. 1-800-292-7435.

Source: Ariel Capital.

Figure 8.4 Getting to Know You

Want to know who's managing your mutual fund investments? Your fund provides information in its prospectus on its portfolio manager's background and experience. Look for a biography in fund literature as well.

Ariel Fund (formerly Ariel Growth Fund)   **3rd Quarter 1999**

About Ariel

Chasing the speedy or the glamorous, the trendy or hot is not the surest way to reach a goal. Just like the fabled tortoise, the symbol of our firm, we value patience and persistence over the fleeting and the flashy. Founded in 1983 by John Rogers, Jr., Ariel Capital Management emphasizes disciplined, patient investing. Today we manage over $3 billion in assets firmwide, and over $700 million in mutual funds.

Our Philosophy

We believe that the key to investment success is having a focused approach and the discipline to stick with it. We have learned that one of life's greatest lessons also holds true in investing: slow and steady wins the race.

John W. Rogers, Jr.

About the Portfolio Manager

In his role as president and co-chief investment officer of Ariel Capital Management, Inc., John manages institutional portfolios as well as the Ariel Fund. John has more than 19 years of professional experience managing portfolios and analyzing investments. Prior to founding Ariel, he worked for two and a half years at the investment banking firm of William Blair & Company, in Chicago. At Princeton University, John received a B.A. in economics and served as captain of the varsity basketball team.

Portfolio Manager Commentary

For the third quarter ending September 30, 1999 the smaller companies that comprise the Ariel Fund fell 6.52%. This result, while not pleasant, was in line with that of the small stocks of the Russell 2000 Index which lost 6.32% of their value and even the big names of the Standard & Poor's 500 Index which dropped 6.24%. Moreover, according to mutual fund tracker Morningstar, the average small cap fund gave back 7.89%.

After a brisk second quarter and its double-digit gains, the stock market carnage of the last three months was widely linked to rising interest rates and a subsequent slowdown in corporate profits—which always weakens earnings. The only issues that managed to escape the pain were those in the volatile technology sector where boom and bust cycles are so familiar. A *Fortune Magazine* headline described this narrow area of market strength as "Nothing but Net"—a clever twist on the familiar basketball saying and a clear indicator of Internet leadership.

Portfolio Comings & Goings

In the Ariel Fund, we sold out of our relatively new position in Orion Capital Corp.—a highly specialized, niche property and casualty insurer—upon the good news of its takeover by the British insurance company, Royal & Sun Alliance (U.RSA). The $50 per share takeout price represented a 23% premium over Orion's previous closing price. Additionally, we eliminated our position in long-time favorite, Ecolab, Inc., based on our belief that its shares had become fully valued. Finally, one new position was added to the Ariel Fund during the quarter. HCC Insurance Holdings, Inc. (1% of portfolio) sells property and casualty insurance, underwrites for unaffiliated insurance companies and provides related services for commercial and individual customers.

About the Fund

Investment Objective:
The fund seeks long-term capital appreciation

Investment Strategy:
The fund invests in companies with market capitalizations primarily under $1.5 billion, with an emphasis on small-cap stocks. It identifies the common stocks of undervalued companies with long-term growth potential. A stock will be held until it reaches its true value—usually three to five years. Investing in small companies may be more risky and volatile than investing in large companies.

Fund Facts

Inception:	November 6, 1986
Total Assets:	$215 Million
Expense Ratio:	1.25%
Investment Minimum:	$1,000 initial; $50 subsequent; no minimum with automatic investment program.
Sales Charge:	None
Ticker Symbol:	ARGFX
Newspaper Symbol:	Ariel

Source: Ariel Capital.

WEB SIGHTINGS
PROSPECTUS READING MADE EASY

You'll find a step-by-step guide to reading a prospectus at the ICI Web site (www.ici.com). It helps break down the job ahead into logical steps and provides just enough hand-holding to see you through, no matter how much trepidation you suffer or boredom you see ahead. It's also available from the ICI (202-326-5800).

Make sure to compare the stats with benchmarks, both the one the fund's management has picked out, and the S&P 500, which will suggest how the market has performed over the same period. Even if the portfolio managers of an equity fund are convinced they're up against another index like the Russell 2000, or the Standard & Poor's midcap 500, you should focus on how they've done vis-à-vis the broad market. After all, if they're not cutting it, you could always turn to an index fund, which will save you a tidy sum in expenses and match the stock market's advances, to boot.

3. *What is the fund manager's tenure?* There's something to be said for a stable fund whose portfolio manager has been at the controls for a while (see Figure 8.4). For one, you could reason that it's a sign that things are going reasonably well. Although there's no guarantee that a poorly run fund will chase its investment guru, a revolving door at the corner office can be an indication that things aren't ideal. A change in fund management can also be a messy time for you. When the top job turns over, a new, incoming manager may be eager to sell off his or her predecessor's picks and replace them with new stocks or bonds. That kind of portfolio churning invariably drives up capital gains and the taxes you'll have to pay on your investment.

FUND NAMES—FUND TYPES

What's in a fund name? Sometimes everything. Other times, nothing at all.

Maybe you've gazed at the paper's mutual fund listings. Or you've stumbled across ads for a mutual fund in a magazine. Either way, you've probably noticed that a lot of mutual funds, besides carrying a company name or a portfolio manager's name, also sport a label such as Growth, Value, or Growth and Income. If you know a little bit about investment styles, you could make an educated guess as to how the portfolio manager of the fund chooses investments and decides what stocks or bonds are right for the fund's goals.

You'd expect a fund called Barnburner Growth to keep to companies whose earnings or profits were increasing at a rapid rate. You'd think the portfolio manager would stock up on shares of technology companies or other companies that had shown the market that they could outdo the average firm in boosting profits year in and year out. Barnburner Value, on the other hand, would focus on companies with high dividends. You'd expect its portfolio to be full of companies that had fallen from Wall Street's graces for one reason or another, yet were poised to bounce back.

True enough, a fund's name can often help you figure out its aims and how it is run. Just as often, however, there's not much, if any correlation between its name and its investment philosophy. In a list of almost 570 large cap value funds in Morningstar's Principia database, there are more than a handful of funds carrying "Growth" as one of their names, with nothing else to qualify the label, and little else to reveal how their management intends to invest your money.

Several studies have also shown that fund names do not always accurately describe in a word or two just what's in a portfolio.

The moral? Stick to the numbers and the prospectus, and ratings companies. Total return figures go a long way in describing what a fund will do to your savings.

Endless Variety

When investing in mutual funds, it's easy to get swamped in all the choices available. There are growth funds that focus on large cap stocks—Coca-Cola, Cisco Systems, Dell Computer, and their peers. There are value funds that keep their sights fixed on smaller companies. There are bond funds. There are stock funds. There are international funds, global funds, worldwide funds, and domestic funds.

Why so many kinds? Blame old-fashioned marketplace economics. Mutual fund companies are consummate capitalists and know a diamond mine when they see one. They know that funds are popular and that individual investors are eager to rush money into portfolio managers' hands. And, most importantly, they realize that variety works wonders for any consumer product—toothpaste, automobiles, and even mutual funds.

Thus it was only a matter of time before mutual fund companies shaped, reshaped, and molded funds of every imaginable variety.

If you leaf through personal finance magazines or look at the financial pages of the paper now and then, you've certainly seen the lengths to which fund companies have taken their creativity. Some funds focus solely on Internet stocks. Others specialize in stocks of a particular country or region.

There are mutual funds that focus on large companies as well as many that limit their portfolios to smaller corporations. Some combine bonds with stocks; others stick to technology stocks.

For investors, that's both a good and bad thing. On the upside, there's practically a fund for every conceivable investment style, for every possible taste for risk, for every possible financial goal whether short- or long-term. So, if you're looking to get into the stock market, literally hundreds of funds out there can provide a good start with holdings in some of the largest corporations around—AT&T, Intel, Lucent, or Ford. If you've earmarked a certain portion of your portfolio for overseas investments, you'll find funds aplenty—646 to be exact, according to Morningstar in early 2000—that own foreign companies like Nokia, Telebras, or Sony. If you want to take a shot at smaller, technology upstarts that are relatively unknown, you might try your hand at a small company growth fund.

The downside to having so many choices? Well, endless variety makes for a lot of confusion. It's hard to figure out where to start and just what best fits your goals.

The next section provides help in sorting out which fund does what. Remember to look in the newspaper or magazines, they often have listings with a brief description of how the fund invests.

FIRST LOOK AT THE TYPE OF INVESTMENT VEHICLE THEY CHOOSE

Equity—Bond—Blended— Money Market Mutual Funds

The easiest distinction between funds is the kind of financial vehicle they invest in. There are four major categories of funds:

1. *Stock, or equity, funds.* This is the subset discussed in this chapter. Equity funds focus on the stock market although sometimes they dabble in a few bond holdings. Stock fund portfolio managers research companies, analyze their stocks, and buy and sell shares over time.
2. *Bond funds.* These funds keep to the public and private debt markets, where bonds are bought and sold. They are discussed later in this chapter.
3. *Blended, or balanced, funds.* Blended funds mix both stocks and bonds to narrow risk and cushion the fund from rough going in either the stock or bond markets.
4. *Money market funds.* This type of mutual fund functions a lot like a high-octane bank account (see Chapter 1). Money market mutual

funds invest in short-term debt and bonds. Unlike other types of mutual funds, they protect your invested principal from loss and pay interest on your investment.

Breaking It Down Further—What Kind of Stocks

Even funds that scout out the same type of investment differ. Some equity funds focus on overseas investments exclusively. They might hold shares to a bank in Indonesia, and avoid Bank of America or Chase Manhattan altogether. Others stick to U.S. companies alone.

Then, a good many funds decide to fix their sights on companies of a particular size. Some stick to the mammoths that make up the Dow Jones Industrials or the Standard & Poor's 500. Others look for smaller companies that don't attract a lot of attention in the hope of finding a jackpot before the rest of the stock market makes the same discovery.

If that wasn't enough, there are investment styles to consider. Most mutual fund portfolio managers subscribe to a certain investment style or a certain school of investing. That, in turn, helps to determine which stocks are included in a mutual fund's portfolio and which aren't.

Growth managers angle for companies that are onto a product or service that is seeing its profits or earnings increase faster than the broad market. They reason that the market loves companies like Microsoft, Sun Microsystems, or even General Electric, which have earned a reputation for delivering big earnings gains over time.

Value investing, the other camp, concentrates on stocks that seem undervalued, in other words, shares that sell at a price-to-earnings ratio (P/E) below that of the market. The value gurus out there will tell you that every stock eventually has its time to shine; so by getting to the bargains first, value stands a better chance of buying cheap and selling dear.

Value and growth styles shed a slender ray of light on how a portfolio manager might invest your mutual fund money. That knowledge doesn't necessarily tell you just what stocks he or she is going to choose, however. A value manager might stick to international stocks alone or might decide that the U.S. market is better, instead.

Size Matters—Funds That Take Their Measure of the Market

As mentioned, size often matters when it comes to the stock market. The big, well-known companies—IBM, Wal-Mart, Time Warner—attract a lot of investors. That means they offer a buffer against the volatility an upstart company's shares might weather. In the last years of the 1990s, you know that large cap stocks have enjoyed a fabulous run leading up to the year 2000. In fact, the group has averaged a total return of 28.54 percent annually over the period from 1995 to 2000, and 18.20 percent in the 10-year period ending on December 31, 1999, using the S&P 500 as a benchmark.

Then there are midlevel companies. They are large by many standards, but are not always household names. Their ranks, however, aren't limited to complete unknowns. Depending on the mutual fund manager's definition, the list of midcaps could well include companies such as ShopKo, Northrop Grumman, and Georgia-Pacific.

In recent years, with large cap stocks capturing all the glory, midcaps have been treated as also-rans. They've had some meager recognition, but few folks have really taken notice. That's a shame, because the midcap benchmark of choice, the S&P Midcap 400, has held its own admirably. It's averaged an annual total return of 23.04 percent over the past 5 years, 17.31 percent if you look out over a 10-year period.

The spunkiest shares are often the smallest around. They're the stocks of go-go companies like newborn technology firms or fledgling businesses that have the most to gain once they've begun to trade shares on the market. Over time, small cap stocks have outperformed their bigger peers. They haven't kept up to historical precedent the past 10 years, but if you look over the group's benchmark index, the Russell 2000, they have averaged an annual total return of 16.70 percent between 1995 and 2000, and 13.40 percent in the 10 years ending December 31, 1999.

Figure 8.5 shows average fund returns by category.

Figure 8.5   Average Fund Returns by Category

How do mutual funds you're looking up stack up against the competition? Here are averages for various fund categories provided by Lipper Inc. Data is for periods ending 12/31/99.

FUND CATEGORY	1 YEAR (%)	5 YEARS (%)	10 YEARS (%)
Large cap growth fund	40.37	29.35	18.84
Small cap growth fund	60.90	22.51	17.55
International equity funds	40.59	15.07	10.14
Balanced funds	8.78	16.29	11.82
Equity income funds	3.58	17.56	12.53
Corporate bond funds	−2.22	7.21	7.54
General U.S. government bond funds	−3.03	6.51	6.60
General municipal debt funds	−4.59	5.77	6.20

Source: Lipper, Inc.

SPECIALTIES

Specialized funds make sense for investors who are looking to diversify their portfolios or even get a toehold in the stock market. Some are listed in the next few pages.

Index Funds

They're the closest thing to an "un-fund" you could find. But, as quirky a beast as index funds may seem, they do particularly well alongside their cousins, the actively managed equity funds out there. So well in fact, that index funds returns regularly leave the competition in the dust.

Over the past 3 years, the Vanguard Index 500, often tagged as the standard-bearer for the group has an average total return for 1 year of 29.05 percent; 5 years, 27.78 percent; and 10 years, 18.61 percent.

Index funds have little in common with actively managed equity funds. The average fund buys and sells stocks. Its portfolio manager combs the market and selects holdings he or she thinks have the best chance of making you money. And its portfolio managers tend to shuffle their portfolios a great deal.

Index funds don't go about the business of investing your money in quite the same manner. Instead, the folks calling the shots at an index fund buy up all the stocks that make up one of the indexes that track a market—most out there home in on the Standard & Poor's 500. After that, there's not much activity. The index fund will follow the ups and downs of a market index like the S&P 500, and stay anchored on a portfolio of stocks that mirrors the index they follow. So while most equity funds shuffle their portfolio a great deal, index funds don't.

Because they don't often trade in and out of investments, index funds spend less of your hard-earned money on operations. A well-run index racks up expenses amounting to no more than 0.2 percent of its assets, compared with an average 1.5 percent for equity mutual funds. "Indexing is one way to play the market and minimize risk," says Sam Weiser, national director of Ernst & Young's Investment Advisory Services. "And in terms of costs, the funds are far cheaper than actively managed ones."

There's a hidden benefit to the index fund's buy-and-hold philosophy come tax time. Remember, the typical equity fund will generate a sizable sum of capital returns, which are passed on to you as a tax burden toward year end. Index funds sit on essentially the same portfolio all year long, with a bare minimum of change. Little trading makes for little in the way of capital gains. Small capital gains save you a tidy sum come April 15.

For all that's good about index funds, be aware that they have their peaks and troughs like any other investment. They stand a good chance of beating out actively managed stock funds in periods when investors flock to the largest, most visible corporations as a hedge against market volatility. That's what propelled the S&P 500 in 1996, 1997, and 1998. Any time investors seem nervous about the market and unsure which stocks should go up, they gravitate toward the largest companies with an established record of dependable earnings and stability.

There's another plus to investing in index funds in the year 2000. The same large companies in the S&P 500 whose stocks have done well are using their shares in a shopping spree of acquisitions. And, what better targets than other large companies says Standard & Poor's economist David Blitzer. "We've seen that a number of the companies in the index have been takeout targets over the last couple of years, and, of course, that only helps the index."

Does that mean index funds are infallible? Not quite. They could end up trailing actively managed mutual funds if stocks slide. The reason: Index funds must invest every cent of their money and aren't allowed to hold a cash position no matter what's taking place in the market including times when stocks slump.

Shopping for an index fund boils down to two things. First, you should decide what market it is you want to track. An S&P 500 fund is a good first step into the market, or simply a firm ballast for your portfolio should the financial markets suffer turbulence.

Second, you'll want to pinpoint the index fund in the category that runs a frugal, penny-pinching operation that won't eat into your returns with unnecessary expenses. Fund industry experts say the most efficient operator out there is Vanguard, the company that invented index funds. And the same pros will tell you that the investment of choice is the Vanguard Equity 500 (800-662-7447), a fund designed to track the S&P 500 at the lowest cost possible.

International Funds

Think about what you hire a fund to do. It's typically the dirty work—hunting up investments, buying and selling them, researching all the complicated market gyrations you'd really rather leave to someone else. It only makes sense, then, that mutual funds look like a good choice for investors who want some exposure to overseas markets but don't know where to start.

To slightly recast a public service announcement of the early 1970s (with apologies to the State Department): When you invest overseas you're often in for the hassle of your life. First, you've got to keep on top of politics.

As mentioned, overseas markets have gone through some rough periods. Then there are currency issues. How many yen the dollar fetches tomorrow is more likely than not going to change by next week, let alone a month from now. That fluctuation affects the value of your overseas investment. If you're not reeling in confusion by now, consider that accounting standards differ greatly from nation to nation. Often what is entered one way in the ledger books in the Netherlands isn't going to be categorized the same way in South Africa. And, different stock markets in different lands don't trade quite the same way nor do they carry the same valuation as the U.S. stock market. Sounds like a job you'd want a portfolio manager to handle, no?

Trust the fund industry to be one step ahead of you. Today, dozens of international and global funds span the globe, from Scandanavia to the Seychelles looking for investments. Some overseas funds concentrate on specific regions or nations. There are funds that focus on Africa; others keep to Japan, Europe, or Latin America. Some funds train their sights on emerging markets, a band of up-and-coming nations whose economic gains look to make impressive gains for investors. Finally, for those who feel timid about investments away from American shores, there are global funds that mix and match a portfolio of U.S. and foreign securities.

Covering the world costs money, though. And, international funds tend to pile up more in the way of expenses than their domestic equity counterparts, according to Lipper Inc., a New York firm that compiles statistics on mutual funds. While funds that stick close to home have average expense ratios close to 1.4 percent, international funds tend to range higher in the neighborhood of 1.8 percent.

The Black Market: Investing in Africa— Risks Aplenty, Some Gain

Africa has all the makings of a treasure chest full of great investments. It's a continent steeped in natural resources. Some of its nations have made great strides opening markets and establishing sound democracies. In addition, much of the region is just beginning to realize its economic power, creating a harvest of bargains from the Mediterranean on south to the Cape of Good Hope (see Figure 8.6).

Africa, though, has been a big, rocky riddle for individual investors. True, some of its burgeoning stock markets—Zimbabwe to name one—did so well in recent years that they seem like jackpots. South Africa has turned away apartheid and begun to attract investors anew. Botswana has quickly become a model of efficiency praised by economists the world over.

It's nonetheless been exceedingly difficult for investors stateside to get in on the profits. According to the International Finance Corporation, which

Figure 8.6   Investing in Africa

Because investing in Africa can carry a high risk, consider using mutual funds—
that way, your money will be spread across a number of holdings and sheltered
from big swings in value. Here is a list of closed and open-ended mutual funds
investing in Africa and their performance over the past few years.

			TOTAL RETURN				
FUND NAME	TYPE	TICKER: EXCHANGE	1995	1996	1997	1998	1999
Morgan Stanley Africa Investment	Closed	AFF: NYSE	20.8	16.3	1.1	−20.6	26.7
Southern Africa	Closed	SOA: NYSE	27.1	5.5	8.0	−23.8	59.9
Calvert New Africa	Open	CNAFX	n/a	−11.6	4.7	−11.6	−19.4

Source: Morningstar

tracks the performance of global stock exchanges, in recent years a select
group of African stock markets routinely rank among the top 10 markets in
the world each year. Yet, of the U.S. mutual funds that focus on Africa, results have been irregular; the three we list in Figure 8.6 have shown choppy
results since 1996.

Several factors are to blame. Political upheaval has beset countries
like Zaire, Rwanda, and even Nigeria. Stock markets in nations like Ghana
or Egypt are fledgling enterprises that are nowhere as efficient as the New
York Stock Exchange or Nasdaq. They trade a small number of shares. They
can go up or down in value very sharply and with little if any warning. So
to date, Africa has been nothing more than the playground of big institutional investors who have the girth to come in, take big stakes, and walk
away winners.

Individual investors have choices, but must proceed with care. Investing in Africa is no indulgence for the meek; as with any frontier, there's potential for breathtaking gains as well as blockbuster losses.

If you're still feeling up to the challenge, get a solid footing at home before setting off for Africa. As a slice of your overall portfolio, money managers
say international stocks should make up 10 percent to 40 percent of your investments, according to your temperament for risk. As tempting as Africa
might seem, it's advisable to place no more than 10 percent of your portfolio
overall in investments there. Also, get ready to do some serious homework.
While information on companies that trade in the United States is readily
available, you'll find statistics on African markets and companies relatively
difficult to come by, even when you're working through a broker. Second,
your research should cover country economies as well as stocks and mutual
funds. Overseas stocks often rise and fall in lockstep with the local economy.

If things are going great at home, and the domestic currency seems in order, chances are a company's shares will withstand any amount of jostling.

One Giant, Many Siblings

So how does Africa shape up as a continent of stock market opportunities? Well, in terms of size, there's South Africa and then there's everyone else. With $246 billion in market capitalization, the Johannesburg Stock Exchange (JSE) is the tenth largest stock market in the world. It is roughly six times the size of all the other stock markets in both North and sub-Saharan Africa combined. Bigger hasn't proven to be necessarily better: In 1996, the South African market declined some 24 percent in dollar terms from January 1996 to January 1997 because of a devaluation of the local currency, the rand. Meanwhile, some other African countries racked up impressive gains: Egypt up 87 percent; Zimbabwe rising over 70 percent; Morocco increasing 49 percent; and Nigeria up some 56 percent.

Your Choices

As far as investments go, first look at closed-end mutual funds, explained further in Chapter 8. Closed ends hold a portfolio of investments and rise and fall according to market conditions. They have a limited number of shares, and trade like stocks on the New York Stock Exchange. Often enough, closed-end funds trade at a premium or discount to their portfolio's value, measured by the fund's NAV or net asset value. Their cousins, the open-end funds, meanwhile have an unlimited number of shares, priced according to the value of the fund.

Closed-end funds are something of a safer bet in uncertain markets like Africa, simply because a change in investor sentiment doesn't necessarily force the fund's portfolio manager to dump his holdings. In Africa, where some stock markets operate for only a few hours a day, or even a couple days a week, that's important, because sales of large stakes could ultimately shake things up and push prices through the floor.

Your other choice, which is far less diversified and therefore far more risky, is picking up shares of a company, traded as ADRs in the United States. Most ADRs are sponsored, meaning that they provide U.S. investors with reports and information much as domestic companies would.

The Funds

The picture for mutual funds investing in Africa hasn't been a pretty one. Currently, two closed-end mutual funds in the United States that specialize in Africa are listed on the New York Stock Exchange: the Morgan Stanley Dean Witter Africa Fund (up only 3 percent between 1997 and the end of 1999) and the Southern Africa Fund (which managed to rise 31.4 percent in the period between 1997 and the end of 1999).

The Calvert New Africa is the sole open-end fund that targets African investments uniquely. Like its closed-end sisters, the Calvert New Africa Fund posted disappointing returns in 1996 largely because all of these funds put the majority of their capital in South Africa. Clifford Mpare, the Executive Vice President and Chief Investment Officer for New Africa Advisors, explains that larger funds that target Africa cannot ignore South Africa if they want to be fully invested and position themselves for the eventual turnaround in the South African economy.

Balanced Funds

Take the growth of stocks. Combine the shelter of bonds. Mix together into a fund. Do you gain the best of both worlds?

Yes and no. There's a logical impulse behind balanced mutual funds. Stocks rise quickly, but are volatile; bonds aren't going to make the gains stocks do, but retain better value during periods when the stock market goes through a rough patch.

By and large, by straddling both financial tools, balanced funds provide the best of each: a stock portfolio to motor growth and a 30 percent to 40 percent mix of bonds as a hedge when stocks are in trouble. In practice, it seems to work, too. Take the years 1990 and 1994, when the stock market lost 3 percent and gained a meager 1 percent. According to Morningstar's Principia database, balanced funds came out better; they lost an average 0.18 percent in 1990 and rose almost 12 percent in 1994.

Still, you should be ready to part with some of the gains you'd make with a well-run equity fund. Morningstar's figures show balanced funds logged an average annual 15 percent for 5 years up to 1999, while large cap growth funds tallied up an average 25 percent yearly.

Socially Responsible Funds

Call them the goody-two-shoes funds. Socially responsible funds are out to prove that you can let your conscience rest while reaping the highest gains possible.

Put into practice, that entails a two-part process. First, a fund has to define what it thinks are "good" companies, and which ones don't qualify. Then, comes the old-fashioned number crunching and analysis most actively managed funds perform when choosing stocks or other investments.

Coming up with a set of social criteria sounds easy enough, but in real life those standards can vary quite a bit. Many socially responsible funds steer clear of companies in "harmful" industries such as tobacco, alcohol, defense, or casinos. Some funds look closely at a company's affirmative action record or at employee relations. Some ferret out polluters or companies with shoddy environmental records.

That's enough to keep a portfolio manager busy, says Bill Thomason, director of portfolio management for Parnassus Investments, a socially responsible firm in San Francisco. Thomason says he spends 80 percent of his time examining companies and going over the numbers. The remaining 20 percent goes toward judging a company's record in community relations, labor relations, efforts to staff a diverse workforce, and a host of other criteria. And, when he interviews management before committing the fund's money to a stock, he grills them on social issues in addition to how well they attend to the bottom line.

Yet, while most socially responsible funds perform the two-part analysis, you'd be surprised at their diverse approaches to investing. The 80 socially conscious funds Morningstar listed at the beginning of 2000 come in a wide variety, each approaching market performance and corporate responsibility slightly differently.

As value funds, the Ariel Appreciation Fund and the Ariel Fund, run by John Rogers, focus on small and mid-sized companies that have been undervalued by the stock market. Parnassus, meanwhile, is on the lookout for contrarian picks, stocks that most of the market avoids, yet seem on the verge of a major turnaround. Dreyfus Third Century, managed by Maceo K. Sloan of NCM Capital Management, and Domini Social Equity funds concentrate on large cap stocks, investing in some of the biggest corporations around.

What actually makes the socially conscious funds' short list? These days, it tends to be companies in newer industries—technology, Internet, healthcare, and software firms. Still, you'll find a good many of the old standbys as well. The Domini Social Equity Fund, one of the prominent socially conscious funds around has holdings in companies like Wal-Mart, Coca-Cola, AT&T, Procter & Gamble, and Fannie Mae.

Convertible Bond Funds

Maybe you suffered a touch of acrophobia—fear of heights—once the Dow hit 10,000. It could be that you're cautious about planting cash in the stock market after such a long bull run. Or perhaps you're just looking for a relatively conservative place for the next sum you invest. Whatever the reason, convertible bond funds are worth considering.

Convertible bonds, true to the name, are something of a hybrid investment combining the steady yield of bonds and the capital appreciation possibilities of stocks. Companies that issue convertibles promise to pay holders a fixed yield, but allow investors the option to exchange the bonds for a set number of shares. The two qualities—bondlike steady income payments and a stocklike chance to see your underlying investment grow—provide investors a good hedge when stocks might seem expensive or the direction of interest rates might be uncertain. "Since convertibles capture the best of both bonds and stocks, they're a sound conservative investment," says Matthew Muehlbauer, an analyst at Value Line who tracks convertible bond funds. "They won't get every bit of capital appreciation of a stock, and not all the income a bond will, but they come very close, and won't be as risky, either."

Why? Let's say Acme Corp. issues convertibles yielding 10 percent annually. If Acme shares begin to zoom on the stock exchange, you simply convert your bond into shares. If Acme stock seems lethargic at best, you can simply stick out your bond investment and see a regular 10 percent payment on your money.

A mutual fund is perhaps the easiest way to tap into the convertible market. As in stock investing, mutual funds offer investors benefits such as a diversified portfolio that limits their exposure to any one investment. Also, since volume in the convertible market is thin and since convertibles' value depends on complicated calculations of yield and conversion value, they can be difficult for individual investors to trade profitably.

Convertible funds, nevertheless, have compiled an impressive record, by any stockpicker's standards. According to a mutual fund survey by Value Line, convertible bond funds have averaged a 12.0 percent total return the past 5 years on an annualized basis, compared with 13.4 percent for growth and growth-income funds, 12.4 percent for income funds and 15.3 percent for the S&P 500. As far as bond funds go, convertibles well outlegged the competition—corporate high yield, international, even government bond funds.

Sector Funds

There are funds that carve the world up into regions. There are funds that stick to stocks or limit their portfolios to bonds. There are funds that focus entirely on big companies or small ones. It only seems natural, then, that the mutual fund business would have thought up funds that invest in one industry and one industry alone.

They have indeed. Sector funds, as they're called, limit their bets on the stock market to a group of stocks in one business or industry. Some invest in computer stocks, others healthcare or biotechnology companies. There are sector funds for the financial service, automobile, defense, construction, airline, and consumer products industries.

Sector funds, though, seem to have great years or lousy years, but never post results in between the two extremes. Look at financial magazines' tallies of the best and worst mutual funds. You'll likely find the top and bottom lists filled with sector funds.

The reason is simple. There are times during economic cycles, or even years when certain industries do well and others get battered. Then, there are market cycles that affect stocks in an industry. Suddenly semiconductor stocks get hot and tear off to new highs for four months. Just as quickly, investors begin to feel that the group's shares are overpriced and computer chip makers find their shares slumping.

All of which points out one of the weaknesses of sector funds. As much as they might spread investors' money around by holding the shares of often dozens of companies, sector funds aren't particularly diversified. They can do exceedingly well when the industry they invest in is coasting. They will tank whenever that same group of companies slows down.

If you're starting out, stick to funds that hold companies in many sectors. A portfolio composed of stocks across many industry groups withstands shifts guaranteed to occur in the economy or stock market.

BOND FUNDS

Beware of the bond fund. It's not quite the friendly, risk-free investment it's cousin the stock or equity mutual fund is.

Yes, there are times when a bond fund is a great investment and makes wonderful sense for all sorts of investors. However, several of the reasons for choosing an equity mutual fund as a substitute for stocks don't hold for bond funds in relation to bonds.

First, recall why stock or equity mutual funds make sense for individual investors. While stocks are a wonderful way to grow your savings for retirement, college tuition, or other goals you might have, they carry a certain risk. One day, any day, management might suddenly report that prospects for the current year have come up short. Sales are faltering. Earnings are withering. What happens to your stock? Its price drops like a rock.

A stock mutual fund as your toehold in the market, however, counters the risk of owning any one stock by dividing the money you invest over a portfolio of 20, 30, even 40 stocks. If a stock holding goes down, the portfolio's other positions are there to absorb the blow and more often than not will protect your investment from a steep swoon should one company come across a rough patch.

Now turn to bonds and bond funds. Bonds have a built-in security blanket—the fact that they mature. Say you buy a 10-year bond. During the course of the next decade, your investment's value on the open market might rise and fall due to any number of factors. A sudden conflict overseas might spike up inflation. Oil prices might zoom upward. The economy might stall. And, all those changes can toss your bond's price up and down.

Fortunately, investors can revert to a couple of safety nets that bonds provide in times of uncertainty. For starters, there's a steady stream of income you'll receive through thick and thin, particularly if you hold a high-quality issue like a Treasury. Second, once your bond matures, you get your original investment back in full. So, you could very well tune out the turmoil of the outside world, sit back, and collect interest payments twice a year on your holding, calmed by the knowledge that your investment will generate a sure, predetermined return for a certain period of time and then return your principal in full.

Bond funds don't work quite the same way, however. True, they spread your investment across a portfolio of dozens of bonds of various durations and with a variety of interest rates. True, too, you'll get a slice of the interest income generated by the portfolio. Even so, a bond fund never matures. What's more, portfolio managers of bond funds don't always hold their stakes until they mature. Instead, the bonds in a fund's deck are constantly undergoing changes and some bonds are sold far in advance of maturity. At the same time, bond fund portfolios rise and fall with the myriad changes in the economy. In short, bond fund holders are open to a lot more variation—read: risk—than investors in individual bonds. And by trading in and out of bond holdings, a bond fund manager basically does away with the ever-so reliable fallback of bonds—holding them until maturity and getting invested money back in full. Bond funds can rack up impressive gains, but can lose money as well.

Still, in some circumstances bond funds make sense. Trading in bonds outside the market for U.S. Treasuries can be a tricky affair, where broker markups vary greatly. Also, it's very difficult for individual investors to gauge rating agency marks or the creditworthiness of corporate or municipal bond issuers. That work is better left to professionals to sort out.

Perhaps you don't have a large sum of cash to ante up. In some cases, a medium-term Treasury could run you $5,000. A bond fund investing in U.S. Treasuries with a short duration might well require a minimum initial investment of $1,000 to $2,500.

Finally, you might not be sure when you need to tap into your investment. Again, the market for bonds sold or bought before their maturity is a tricky one where individual investors stand to get burned badly on spreads. So, if you'd like to opt away from the risks of the stock market, yet don't know when you'd have to withdraw funds, a bond fund could make sense for you, provided it doesn't charge a load fee whenever you take money out (see Figure 8.7).

One Category, Many Choices

Just as equity mutual funds come in many varieties, as well as different investment styles, there seem to be an infinite array of bond funds. There are government bond funds, which focus on U.S. Treasuries and U.S. agency

Figure 8.7   Bond Mutual Funds Work for You If . . .

- You're not quite sure when you'll need to tap the money you've set aside.
- You're willing to take on a bit more risk than Treasury bonds.
- You have a short-term goal and are willing to take on an investment with higher risk/return prospects than a money market mutual fund.
- You're interested in tapping the municipal or corporate bond markets and prefer to have a professional make investment decisions for you.

---

debt. Municipal bond funds flourish for almost any state you could name. Junk bond funds, emerging market debt funds, are out there for the taking. And the list goes on.

Another distinguishing trait you'll want to note is the fund's average maturity. Often enough, you'll find a hint of what duration of bond a portfolio manager is investing in from the fund's name. Reason stands that the Thunderclap Short Duration Agency Bond fund will key in on U.S. agency debt with a average maturity of 2 years or so. Still, you should dig up an accurate figure either from fund literature, by calling up a fund's 800-number, or by checking Morningstar sheets on the fund.

The longer a bond's maturity, the more volatile a holding it is. So it follows that the longer the average maturity of a bond fund's portfolio, the greater its volatility, too. Short-term funds are those with average maturities of 2 to 3 years. Intermediate durations cover funds with maturities in the 4- to 7-year ranges. Long-term bond funds have maturities of 10 years or more.

NUMEROLOGY

With so many stock and bond funds out there, you'll need to go over a few numbers to settle on the winners and to weed out the many that just won't do. To sift through the bunch, you need to cover a few of the following stats.

Total Return (Important)

This is a gauge of how well a mutual fund has done with your money. Total return is expressed as a percentage gain or loss over a set period—say 1, 3, or 5 years. You can find total return figures in pamphlets put out by a mutual fund, the daily paper, or financial newspapers and magazines, or by calling the fund's customer service number. Morningstar is also a good source of total return figures.

BEGINNERS' LUCK

If you're intimidated by the $1,000 to $2,500 minimum initial invest-ment required by many mutual funds, take heart. There's a cheaper way to get started through automatic investment programs (AIPs).

AIPs are similar to the direct investment plans offered by many companies who want to sell their shares directly to the public. And like their stock relatives, AIPs require a minimal initial investment as long as you agree to have a set amount withdrawn from your checking or savings account. An AIP is simple to set up; you merely agree to let a fund tap a savings or checking account regularly (e.g., the fifteenth of every month) for a set amount—say $50. Keep in mind, though, that just how much or how little you can invest depends on the fund itself, and should be spelled out in the prospectus or in literature you receive.

AIPs are a good idea even if you're not strapped for a large lump-sum initial investment. For one, they ensure that you keep investing regularly, a great way to build up a large portfolio practically pain-lessly. Also, by investing regularly, you're sure to put your money to work both when the market is cheap and your potential for apprecia-tion is great, and during periods when stocks are expensive. That way, your investments average out over time; you've neither pur-chased the fund when it was too pricey or when its assets were prac-tically on sale.

Choices? Literally thousands of funds offer a low minimum initial investment to open up an automatic withdrawal plan. If you can start with $500 or less and agree to invest a regular sum monthly, there are over 2,142 funds to accommodate you, according to data compiled early in 2000 by Morningstar, the Chicago firm that tracks mutual funds; at an opening investment of $250, there are nearly 1,120; at $100, the list is still some 720; $50 narrows the list to 642; and no money down still gets you a selection of 452 funds. That's compared to the usual minimum initial investment of $1,000 to $2,500 many funds require. In addition, many funds lower the entry investment for an IRA to $100.

If there's just one number you absolutely should check before investing in a mutual fund, it's the total return the portfolio managers have brought investors over time. Think of total return as the scorecard on any fund, the final tally on how well investors' money would have performed.

Total return figures cover the gamut of gains or losses a fund might have made. If stocks in a fund's portfolio have appreciated in value, they'll push the fund's total return upward. If the shares owned by the fund fall, so, too, will the total return. If the fund owns shares of companies that pay out dividends, the total return will rise. If bonds the fund holds rise, they will help lift the fund's return.

Additionally, total return figures also reflect any expenses racked up by the fund. As pointed out earlier in this chapter, funds make money by charging fees on the amount you've invested. Unless you whip out a calculator and do the math yourself, you'll never see the money disappear. Instead, a fund deducts its expenses from its total return.

Typically, you'll see total return figures expressed over a period of time, say 1 year, 3 years, 5 years, or 10 years. Also, you'll often spot the 3- and 5-year figures broken down to average annual numbers, which makes it easier to compare a group of mutual funds or to compare funds with the market as a whole.

Whenever looking over fund numbers, always look for the average annual figure. Mutual fund advertisements often point to mammoth percentage figures covering a period stretching over a number of years. While 300, 400, or 900 percent gains no doubt sound impressive, they don't do much to help investors gauge just how well a fund has done year after year. A fund that's up 400 percent since inception sounds like gold mine. If it has taken 20 years to do so, posting an average annual total return of 8.4 percent, it has actually trailed the market's average 11 percent gain over time.

A 3- or 5-year average annual figure is as good a starting point as any. For one, it will shed light on how well a portfolio manager or team of managers have guided a fund, and earned money for investors over time. That's good to know, considering that the financial markets crest and fall over the course of their many cycles. Five-year figures show how the pros you've entrusted with your savings weather those constant changes. It's also worthwhile to take a peek or two over shorter periods—say the total return figure for a year like 1997 or 1998. Breaking a fund's investment record down to smaller increments will help you determine how a fund has fared during specific periods when the financials markets have done better or worse than their historic averages.

In making an investment choice, compare the total return figures of one fund with others that you're considering and set any total returns you look at alongside a benchmark figure, preferably an index that charts how well the market has done or how much comparable investments have risen or fallen over the same period (see Chapter 2, Benchmarks). Remember, you're paying a fund's management part of your hard-earned savings to pick a selection of stocks and bonds. It only follows that you want to hire equity portfolio managers who put together a winning roster that outperforms an index fund, which requires almost no tinkering by a portfolio manager. Otherwise, you might start thinking that you're paying management fees for no reason, other than to keep a fund manager in fine suits and new cars.

Expense Ratio (Important)

Fund fees can pile up, but taking a microscope to individual fund fees isn't a great idea. Examining fund fees one by one can be confusing, and get into picayune points that are frankly a waste of time for individual investors. Still, if you were to shop around for a new car, you'd want to compare charges one dealership might stack onto the sticker price, with the amount a competitor might charge. Needless to say, the same holds true for mutual funds.

Well, as luck would have it, there's an easy way to compare how lean a fund is run—its expense ratio. Expressed in the form of a percentage, an expense ratio is calculated by dividing how much a fund is taking out of your gains to run the shop—its expenses—by its total assets, or the money it has collected from investors.

As a rule of thumb, most experts will tell you to look for funds with an expense ratio of 1 percent or less. That's a good start, and a logical cutoff point to keep in mind. But remember, different kinds of funds run up different expenses. An index fund seldom, if ever, shuffles its portfolio. It doesn't require much in the way of research, either. As a consequence, index funds tend to be quite economical, as we've pointed out and generally have low expense ratios. Because it's difficult to research overseas stocks and often expensive to trade in stock markets abroad or even to covert currencies, it goes without saying that international funds run up quite a tab; their expense ratios, therefore tend to drift a good deal higher than domestic equity funds.

Be sure to look closely at what the fund's peers or rivals charge as a second criterion. Why? Fund expenses vary differently according to how a manager operates. Some are frugal, and some aren't.

Net Asset Value or NAV (Minimum Importance)

Net Asset Value is your fund's share price. It has a certain importance, but it is better to concentrate instead on how much your fund returns over time. You'll find NAV in pamphlets put out by a mutual fund, the daily paper, or financial newspapers and magazines, or by calling the fund's customer service number.

As a calculation of your mutual fund's share price, net asset value (NAV) certainly sounds like an important figure. Not only that, but you'll also often see NAVs of many of the biggest mutual funds around quoted in the financial section of your local paper or in daily or weekly financial publications alongside the endless list of stock and bond prices. Indeed, you might be tempted to think it is of the utmost importance to keep up with NAV day in and day out. Not so.

No matter what a fund's NAV is, your primary concern should be the percentage that figure increases year after year coupled with just how much money your fund makes year in, year out (i.e., its total return). For proof that NAV isn't crucial, look through a magazine, read a newspaper interview with a fund manager, or listen to one closely on a show like PBS's *Wall Street Week* with Louis Rukeyser. They'll almost always want to crow about their total return or at least touch on how well the fund is doing—what percentage it's up or down that year, or over time. On the other hand, you'll have better luck catching a lightning bug in Alaska on December 15 than hearing fund managers quote an NAV. The fact is, they're too busy obsessing on their return figures; many just don't keep up with NAV on a daily basis. On the other hand, portfolio managers can't seem to step out of the office for more than a minute without checking their total return figures.

Still, it's good to know how your fund comes up with the figure. NAV is figured out by dividing the value of a mutual fund's investments by the number of shares it has sold. For example, if Fidelity Magellan has $8 billion in assets and 80 million shares, its NAV is $100 a share. Then if the stock market makes a strong climb, and Magellan's assets rise to $16 billion, the same 80 million shares will have a NAV of $200 a share.

Dividend—Yield (Somewhat Important)

It's not the flashiest component of total return. Still, if a fund is in line to collect dividends from the stocks or bonds it owns, it, in turn, passes that flow of income onto you the investor. It's also calculated as part of your total return. If you're curious how much dividend income, your fund is bringing in, check its yield, calculated by taking its average yearly dividend per share and dividing that figure by its NAV.

When it comes to equity funds, yield figures are good to know, but nothing to really meditate on. They come in handy, if you're a conservative investor who is angling for a fund that has the sturdy anchor of good, high-yielding stocks. Otherwise, we'd advise you to focus on total return.

Turnover (Important)

Mutual funds save a lot by running an investment portfolio over a very large base—its collected assets, to be exact. That's especially useful when it comes to the fund's trading costs, commissions paid to buy and sell shares. From the looks of it, that savings isn't likely to go unappreciated anytime soon. Mutual funds love to trade, to shuffle portfolios.

There are several reasons you might want to keep up with turnover. For one, funds that shuffle their portfolio constantly are going to run up

CLOSED-END FUNDS

After a while, you're bound to come across the divide between open-end and closed-end mutual funds. There's a big difference between the two that you should understand.

Open-ended funds are mutual fund investments that create as many shares as possible of their portfolio in exchange for investors' savings. If, say, you decide to put $2,000 into a fund for shares that are priced at an NAV of $15.22 each, you'll receive 131.40604 shares of the fund, a figure derived from dividing 2,000 by 15.22. Then, if you come back in 2 months with $3,000 to invest, and the fund's NAV is $17.33, you'll get 173.11021 additional shares, that is 3,000 divided by 17.33. There's no limit on the amount of shares you can buy, and the fund is more than willing to issue fractional shares to your account. Then, the day you close your account, you'll cash your total of 304.51625 shares at the fund's current NAV.

Closed-end funds don't operate quite the same way. Yes, they hold investment portfolios, just like their open-end cousins. Yes, they also issue shares for investors to acquire and hold. There are even a variety of closed-end funds, just like open-end funds. Some, like Bergstrom Capital or H&Q Life Sciences Investors invest mostly in U.S. stocks; others focus on stocks of one particular nation like Brazil, the Philippines, or Japan; still others keep to a set group of bonds.

That's where the similarities end. Unlike open-end funds, which issue out shares whenever money comes in, closed-end funds have a finite number of shares that trade. Another big difference is that closed-end funds are listed on an exchange and trade like stocks. Some closed-end funds are listed on the New York Stock Exchange, and others trade on the Nasdaq.

Closed-end funds are also valued differently from open-end funds. At the end of any trading day on the market, open-end funds essentially take the value of their portfolio and divide it by the number of shares they have outstanding. Closed-end funds, on the other hand, list a price per share based on how the stock market has valued their portfolio. Prices are listed in increments no smaller than $\frac{1}{16}$ of a dollar or 6.25 cents, the smallest unit listed for stocks. And investors can only buy set share amounts without the fractional shares open-end funds offer.

A quirky thing happens to closed-end funds out on the market. Their portfolios never trade at the value of their investments. Instead, closed-ends sometime trade at a price set by the stock market at a discount or below the portfolio's NAV, its portfolio's NAV, or share price based on its holdings. Other times, a closed-end will trade at a premium or at a price higher than the value of its portfolio.

(continued)

225

CLOSED-END FUNDS (CONTINUED)

Keep in mind another fundamental difference. When you buy and when you cash in your closed-end shares, you'll pay a commission to a stockbroker or discount broker. On top of that, you'll pay the same management fees that an open-end fund is assessed. Remember, no-load, open-end mutual funds do not charge money to invest or to cash out of your investment, although they, too, will assess management fees on your stake.

All told, if you have a choice between a closed-end and open-end fund (there are often open-ends available that invest in the same types of stocks or bonds), we advise you to steer your money toward an open-end fund. You'll have fewer hassles buying and selling shares and will profit from the value of the mutual fund's instead of the market's slant on the portfolio's worth.

---

substantial capital gains. At the end of the year, those gains are passed onto you, and your April 15 tax bill.

A high turnover can also indicate that a fund is undergoing either management changes or some sort of upheaval. New portfolio managers have egos and want to see their special stocks instead of someone else bringing in the returns. They are therefore likely to sell their predecessor's holdings and buy new ones of their own.

Turnover figures appear as a percentage representing the portion of a fund's holdings that was liquidated and replaced. The industry's average is rather high—90 percent—although index funds and bond funds are far more patient.

Ticker (Not Important)

If you've looked up stocks in the paper before or on an online sight, you've often seen companies listed by a three- or four-letter symbol, called a "ticker." McDonald's shares are listed by "MCD," Intel by "INTC," and General Electric by "GE." Brokerage firms and financial planners feel that shorthand helps them differentiate between the over 9,000 stocks out there.

Many mutual funds are assigned five-letter tickers, for identification. Knowing a fund's ticker doesn't necessarily win you points when you call a discount- or full-service broker to buy into it, but it can help clear matters up when there's a possible question—say the difference between the 164 Fidelity funds listed on Morningstar.

Minimum Initial Investment (Important)

It goes without saying that you'll want to know how much to ante up when investing in a fund. Funds can require a wide range of amounts for a first investment. In some cases it's as low as $50, if you enroll in an AIP. In other cases, it can rise as high as $5,000 or $10,000 outside an IRA.

THE BLACK MARKET: AFRICAN AMERICAN MUTUAL FUNDS

Chalk it up to the anti-apartheid movement or credit municipalities and state governments that have earmarked a portion of their huge pension funds for minority money managers. For one reason or the other—probably both—there's been a veritable boom in African American owned mutual funds.

It started in the late 1980s, when John Rogers, head of Ariel Capital Management, set out on the market with his own Ariel Growth. Now, the list of black funds has mushroomed to 17, and counting.

African Americans didn't get this far by tiptoeing. In fact, the bumper crop of new funds represents the culmination of strides blacks have made in the world of money management the past 30 years. Managers such as Rogers, Lou Holland, Eddie Brown, and Maceo Sloan got their starts in the late 1970s and early 1980s, often when government or private institutions moved to get their money out of apartheid South Africa. From there, they worked hard to drum up business, and win over large institutional investors. And after years of stumping, glad handing, sales pitches, and layovers in airports from Columbus to Phoenix, some are even hitting paydirt—$1 billion in assets.

Money managers will tell you that the logical next step in their business is the "retail" or mutual fund market, the part of the industry that caters to individual investors. As a result, African Americans now offer funds that span the investment spectrum. Ariel Capital's Ariel and Ariel Appreciation Funds specialize in midcap stocks, the kind Wall Street doesn't keep the closest of tabs on. Lou Holland's Holland Growth Fund focuses on growth stocks, but only if they're reasonably priced. The Edgar Lomax Value Fund, run by money manager Randall Eley, sticks to large cap stocks that sell at a discount to the broad market.

It doesn't hurt that the pool of black talent issuing orders to buy and sell stocks has some substantial experience in the investment industry and in some cases ranks among the best in the financial world. Barbara Bowles of the Kenwood Growth and Income Fund, John Rogers, and Eddie Brown boast 10 years or more of experience overseeing pension fund money for corporations and local governments. Randall Eley, the money manager at the helm of the Edgar Lomax Value Fund was dubbed by *Wall Street Week* host Louis Rukeyser as "perhaps the best money manager you've never heard of."

Still, most black funds, outside of the Ariel and Brown offerings, are start-ups and small compared with the competition. That has its advantages and disadvantages. On the upside, it's given several of the funds a folksy, almost grassroots appeal. It's not uncommon to spot Bowles or Eugene Profit of the Profit Value Fund canvassing a church convention or a gathering of Linx members like a Baptist preacher combing through a revival. "You get to know your first investors very well because many of them are friends and family," says Bowles. Profit, meanwhile, has put thousands of miles on his odometer the past few years driving about every weekend to drum up new business. "There are lots of car trips to social organizations and churches," he says. "When you're signing the check, you realize you just don't always have the money for direct mailings and the various types of literature you might get from a Fidelity or Vanguard." That homespun, personalized approach is also reassuring. Face-to-face contact is important for African Americans who haven't gotten much one-on-one time with the investment world.

The upstarts have their work cut out for them. The annual expenses for a new fund often add up to $150,000 or more a year, including filing paperwork in all 50 states and with the Securities and Exchange Commission as well. Important jobs like picking up on investor calls and answering inquiries have to be outsourced, another bill to pay. And, in the very beginning, some of the new African American funds simply have to operate in the red until they reach critical mass. Experts say that a mutual fund needs $10 million or more in assets to run at its most profitable level. Before that, money managers are basically subsidizing the fund's start. "I'd say the toughest thing for us was getting the $30 million in assets or 1,000 shareholders you need to break into the financial section of the newspaper," says Rogers.

There are other sources of publicity that most African American funds are still not large enough to tap. One is Morningstar, which tabulates tomes of statistics and investor-friendly reviews that many financial planners and do-it-yourself investors swear by. Morningstar doesn't weigh in with a review of a fund until it's been around for three years or more, a hurdle that still excludes the latest crop of African American funds.

Safeguards

All the talk of new, fledgling African American funds might leave you a little wary. Just what safeguards do you have as an investor?

Rest assured: The SEC and state regulatory agencies team to monitor funds on a federal and state level. Funds are required to file paperwork regularly, and must follow guidelines on everything from prospectuses to reporting results.

All the same, a little homework on your part doesn't hurt. Go over a fund's prospectus and the fund manager's track record closely. Also find out whether the fund manager you're betting on has a solid institutional investing business going already—say $100 million or more under management for pension funds and the like. That way, the manager will generate enough money to keep the fund going in those first lean years.

Don't cry for the little guys. Retirement money keeps pouring into mutual funds by the truckload. That's why Morningstar's head, Don Phillips estimates that most funds, whether long-established or newly minted stand about a 90 percent chance of surviving.

The Funds

The following list provides brief descriptions of African American mutual funds along with contact numbers (see Figure 8.8).

Ariel
Ariel Appreciation
Ariel Premier Bond
800-292-7435

Ariel's got to be the youngest grandfather you'd ever want to meet. A graybeard among its upstart peers, the first Ariel fund was founded by John W. Rogers in 1986. Both Rogers, who supervises the Ariel Fund, and his cohort Eric McKissack, who oversees the Ariel Appreciation Fund, don't waiver from their value investing roots. They run funds that look for small and mid-sized stocks. Both look for companies that are undervalued by the market in the hope that the shares will be noticed and regain favor. More importantly, both avoid technology shares, opting instead for low-risk consumer goods companies like toymaker Hasbro or Specialty Equipment, a company that manufactures grills and ice cream makers for restaurant chains such as McDonald's. The strategy helped Rogers bypass his peers during the fund's first three years, but later came under question when Ariel missed out on the gains many tech shares enjoyed in the early and late 1990s. The fund has also had stakes in Rouse, a shopping mall developer, and International Game Technologies, which manufactures electronic slot machines.

Although Ariel Appreciation is a variation on Rogers' old theme, it also buys into large cap stocks. Manager Eric McKissack keeps to the same Ariel value-oriented formula, and likes stocks trading at a 80 percent discount to the market's price-to-earnings ratio (P/E). Like Rogers, he favors companies with a strong consumer franchise when possible. The fund's largest holdings include Hasbro, Carnival Cruises, and Clorox.

Figure 8.8   African American Mutual Funds

FUND NAME (TICKER) WEB ADDRESS	1-YEAR AVERAGE ANNUALIZED TOTAL RETURN	3-YEAR AVERAGE ANNUALIZED TOTAL RETURN	5-YEAR AVERAGE ANNUALIZED TOTAL RETURN
Ariel Appreciation (CAAPX) www.arielfunds.com	–3.79	16.63	19.50
Ariel (ARGFX) www.arielfunds.com	–5.76	12.21	15.64
Ariel Premier Bond (APBFX)	–0.55	5.33	n/a
Brown Capital Management Balanced (BCBIX) www.browncapital.com	5.21	16.57	18.54
Brown Capital Management Equity (BCEIX)	7.79	19.52	21.90
Brown Capital Management Small Company (BCSIX)	25.44	43.98	25.35
Edgar Lomax Value Fund (n/a)	5.01	n/a	n/a
Kenwood Growth & Income (KNWDX)	3.04	9.70	n/a
Lou Holland Growth (LHGFX)	9.01	23.71	n/a
MDL Broad Fixed Income (MBMFX)	9.33	n/a	n/a
MDL Large Growth Equity Fund (MLGEX)	28.23	n/a	n/a
Profit Value (PVALX) www.profitfunds.com	27.62	n/a	n/a
Unity Fund	5.01	n/a	n/a
Victory Lakefront (n/a) www.victoryfunds.com	13.86	n/a	n/a
Subadvised Funds			
Calvert New Africa (CNAFX) www.calvertgroup.com	–19.42	–9.32	n/a
Dreyfus Premier Third Century (DRTHX) www.dreyfus.com	29.90	30.16	29.92
Noteworthy Funds with African American Managers			
American Century Growth Investors (TWCGX) www.americancentury.com	34.68	33.55	26.95
Globalt Growth (GROWX)	27.28	27.22	n/a
Seligman Common Stock (SCSFX) www.seligman.com	3.81	14.63	17.38

Note. Data as of 1/25/00.
*Includes minimum initial investment amounts for IRAs and Automatic Purchase Plans as well.
Sources: Morningstar, Mutual Fund Education Alliance, fund literature.

Figure 8.8 (*continued*)

EXPENSE RATIO %	MINIMUM INITIAL INVESTMENT*	TELEPHONE NUMBER
1.26	$1,000 ($250 IRA; $50 Auto)	800-292-7435
1.21	$1,000 ($250 IRA; $50 Auto)	800-292-7435
0.45	$1,000,000	800-292-7435
1.20	$10,000 ($2,000 IRA; $10,000 Auto)	800-525-3863
1.20	$10,000 ($2,000 IRA; $10,000 Auto)	800-525-3863
1.50	$10,000 ($2,000 IRA; $10,000 Auto)	800-525-3863
1.75	$2,500 ($1,000 IRA; $1,000 Auto)	888-263-6438
0.99	$2,000 ($250 IRA)	888-536-3863
1.35	$2,000	800-295-9779
0.90	$500	800-932-7781
1.26	$500	800-932-7781
1.95	$2,500 ($1,000 IRA; $500)	888-744-2337
1.75	$1,000 ($250 IRA; $100 Auto)	800-385-7003
0.32	$500 ($100 IRA; $500 Auto)	800-539-3863
3.25	$2,000	800-368-2748
0.96	$1,000 ($750 IRA; $100 Auto)	800-373-9387
1.00	$2,500 ($1,000 IRA)	800-345-2021
1.17	$25,000	877-289-4769
1.11	$1,000 ($100 Auto)	800-221-2783

Ariel Premier Bond has been around since 1997. It invests in corporate and government paper and keeps its exposure to junk bonds to a minimum.

Brown Equity
Brown Balanced
Brown Small Company
800-525-3863

Not long ago, you needed at least $5 million to hire Eddie Brown as your stock picker. That high price of admission reserved his expertise almost exclusively to pension funds. These days, Brown's turning more of his attention toward individual investors. He's lowered the minimum initial investment required for his funds to $10,000.

Brown's forte has been midcap to large cap stocks, as well as small companies. He looks for corporations with good earnings increases that carry a P/E ratio not too far from the market's average. Brown's large company favorites have included Cisco Systems, Chase Manhattan, and Home Depot. The small company fund, meanwhile has stocked up on companies such as BMC Software and fellow Baltimore mutual fund manager T. Rowe Price. Brown's balanced fund adds a dash of bonds to the mix.

Chapman Institutional Cash Management Fund
Chapman U.S. Treasury Money Fund
410-625-9656

You'll probably not see much about Nathan Chapman's funds in personal finance magazines, since their minimum initial investment of $1 million narrows the market to institutions and high net worth clientele. Chapman, who arguably has bragging rights to being the first African American to establish a fund from the ground up, has won over business from corporations like Texaco and the City of Baltimore by running a lean shop to keep expenses to a minimum.

Edgar Lomax Value Fund
888-263-6438
Unity Fund
800-385-7003

As a large cap value manager, Randall Eley approaches the stock market's biggest companies looking for bargains. The proof is in his portfolio: It's typically filled with stocks carrying price-to-earnings multiples 20 percent or so below that of the S&P 500. Eley's also a stickler for dividends, and the Edgar Lomax fund often offers a yield is that is 50 percent higher than that of the S&P 500. Looking for a combination of high yield and low price,

Eley has gravitated to stocks like Chevron, Exxon, 3M, the Limited, Du Pont, and International Paper.

Eley also manages the Unity Fund for the Liberty Bank and Trust Co. of New Orleans. Unity's portfolio is exactly the same as the Edgar Lomax Value Fund.

Kenwood Growth & Income
888-536-3863

Chicago-based Fund manager Barbara Bowles is a value investor who sticks to companies that have often fallen out of favor with the market. She has an eye for cheap companies, provided they hold some undiscovered or overlooked value. Bowles keeps to the market's midrange, that is S&P Mid-cap 400, a benchmark of medium-sized companies nestled between the Goliaths and the small fry. Bowles' portfolio has included companies like Tenneco, Bergen Brunswig, and Kmart.

Lou Holland Growth Fund
800-295-9779

Chicago money manager Lou Holland steers his fund toward growth stocks—often technology or telecommunications picks that look to be boosting profits quickly. All the same, Holland doesn't like to overpay for his favorites. That keeps Holland's picks pretty close to S&P 500 P/E of 20. Holland's criteria zeroed in on companies like Microsoft, Lucent Technologies, AT&T, and Cisco Systems.

MDL Broad Market Fixed Income Fund
MDL Large Cap Growth Equity Fund
800-932-7781

Pittsburgh fund manager Mark Lay likes to keep his bond fund as risk-free as possible. And to safeguard investors' principal, he sticks predominately to Treasury bonds and government agency debt, shuffling his portfolio from time to time to angle for better returns in the fixed income market. The MDL Large Cap Growth looks for companies whose earnings are on the rise, provided their stock market valuations aren't too dear. MDL manager Steven L. Sanders' portfolio has included names such as Wal-Mart, Intel, Applied Materials, Pfizer, Oracle, and Citigroup.

Profit Value
888-744-2337

Eugene Profit will say that, at its core, his fund is a value portfolio. He wants his stocks at a cheap price and ready to go higher. Still, Profit has an interesting spin on value-investing principles. He likes to gauge the entire market and include a lot of technology shares that he feels offer good growth at relatively low prices. That's why Profit has gravitated to stocks like Cisco, Wal-Mart, MCI WorldCom, and Sun Microsystems in the past.

Victory Lakefront
800-539-3863

Big stocks due for a comeback fill Nathaniel Carter's Victory Lakefront fund including names like Chase Manhattan, IBM, and Texas Instruments. Carter's penchant is for cheap, large cap stocks whose price-to-earnings ratio trails the overall market's. The companies that get his money though are the ones that look to snap back quite soon. Carter runs the fund from his offices in Cleveland.

Subadvised Funds
In the world of mutual funds, there are times when big fund companies hire out money managers to select portfolio and keep an eye on the day-to-day well-being of the fund's assets. The money manager under contract is often called a subadviser.

Maceo Sloan's money management firm, NCM Management, handles those matters for two funds—the Calvert New Africa Fund and the Dreyfus Premier Third Century Fund.

Calvert New Africa Fund
800-368-2748

Calvert's New Africa Fund invests almost exclusively in African companies from the Cape of Good Hope on to the Straits of Gibraltar. The fund's fortunes have mirrored those of the continent whose markets went through some rough trekking in the latter half of the 1990s.

Dreyfus Premier Third Century Fund
800-645-6561

As a large cap growth fund, Third Century shops for big names with a little spice—earnings momentum. Sloan aims to have a portfolio of socially conscious companies as well. So, companies that make Sloan's portfolio have to not only pass muster as investment opportunities, they must get through Sloan's social screens for hiring practices, environmental safety, and consumer protection issues, too. The list that passes Sloan's tests includes names such as Merck, Oracle, Lucent Technologies, IBM, and Microsoft.

African American Fund Managers
African American mutual funds don't have a corner on the market for black money managers. There are also some very good funds whose portfolio managers happen to be African American, too.

Start with the American Century Growth Investors, which boasts C. Kim Goodwin as one its comanagers. The American Century fund has regularly kept ahead of its growth fund competition with investments in stocks like General Electric, Cisco Systems, Vodafone Airtouch, and Wal-Mart.

A second choice is the Seligman Common Stock, where Rodney Collins is a comanager. Seligman's fund concentrates primarily on large cap stocks such as United Technologies, Citigroup, General Electric, and Microsoft. Finally there's the Globalt International Fund, run by Bill Roach, a selection that aims for domestic companies that derive 20 percent of their revenues from overseas sales.

ONWARD

You now have a grasp of stocks, bonds, and mutual funds. It's time to look into shaping them all into a coherent financial plan and to go shopping. In Chapter 9 you'll learn about some of the folks who can help you out, if you need it, and some of the ways you can buy investments and put them together in a portfolio.

9

ASSET ALLOCATION

How to Minimize Risk through a Diversified Portfolio

There's one thing books like this, financial magazines, and investment newsletters are all guilty of: an overabundance of numbers. Facts and figures are piled high in all sorts of publications in the hope of getting your attention. There are magazine covers hawking, "5 Great Stocks to Devour Now," or "10 Mutual Funds You'll Never Regret Owning." You can read article after article about hot technology plays or stocks slated for a boom. Analysts dissect the wonderful results of Company A, the magical comeback of Company B, and so on. You'd have to wonder why investors would ever need anything else in the way of bonds or cash. Get one thing straight, though. Stocks, bonds, or cash alone aren't going to build wealth over the long haul. For that, you'll need to strike a balance between all three.

History seems to point the way to average annual gains of 10 percent in the stock market, and bonds through the years have brought 5 percent even 6 percent. But along the way, many factors can swoop down and send stocks hurtling earthward. Investments like stocks and bonds are resilient, but there have been drops in the past, and most likely some will occur in the future, too. The mouthwatering stats in this book have served to get your pulse up, to get your investment juices flowing. Now the time has come to talk about risk, about possible losses, about defending your money against those losses by spreading your money out in several assets—stocks, bonds, and cash. It's time to adopt a portfolio strategy.

Face it. No matter how carefully you choose stock and mutual funds, your investment portfolio can quickly become vulnerable. Stack too much of your money on that awe-inspiring Internet stock, and you might see much of it disappear one day. Play it too safe—say pile all of your kid's college funds in safe and snug bonds, and you'll probably end up needing to send your kid to the cheapest community college around. Translation: You'll need bonds to help lock in the gains you've made in the stock market.

Striking a balance between growth and preservation isn't necessarily complicated, but it's important and it's what asset allocation is all about. Another one of Wall Street's unwieldy terms, asset allocation is a label tacked on to a relatively routine procedure carried out by professional money managers again and again, sometimes daily, weekly, or even once a year. It's a three-step process:

1. Draw up a timetable for your investments. When do you plan to use them? When do you need them?
2. Think about how nervous you get about your savings. Do you switch on the financial news network 12 times a day to see how many sixteenths of a dollar your stocks have inched up? Or can you keep your cool even when panic breaks out? Your risk tolerance will have a lot to do with finding investments that make you comfortable.
3. From time to time, look over your game plan. At times, it will make sense to alter it according to changes in your life or new responsibilities. Under other circumstances, a rise or fall in the value of your investments will alter your portfolio and drag your money away from your blueprints. In those instances, you'll probably want to reshuffle your money and set it back on course.

This chapter covers the ins and outs of asset planning, as well as how to tailor a portfolio that accounts for factors such as your age, the length of time the money can stay in the account, and the degree of risk you are willing to take on. The result: You'll have a portfolio you have shaped to fit your specific needs and goals.

THREE-PART PORTFOLIOS

You could easily divide the whole process of investing into three parts. First, there are stocks, the rocket fuel you need to stretch regular savings out to meet your hefty financial goals (e.g., retirement or college tuition). Next, there are bonds, the great way to secure some of your gains and still get a sizable return on your money. And there's cash, liquid funds stored in a money market mutual fund where they're accessible in a pinch (see Figure 9.1).

But, while you've been reading this book, a question has most likely cropped up in your head. It seems that stocks are the best thing around at growing wealth. They make you 11 percent or more a year on average. So why even bother with anything else? Why allocate funds in a portfolio

Figure 9.1   Asset Allocation Works For You If . . .

- You're looking to make big gains in the market.
- You want to protect the money you make and your savings from a sudden drop in value.
- You're a daredevil who wants your portfolio to take on more risk in the hope of maximizing the money you make investing.
- You're jittery any time you hear the market's down. You know you have to take on some risk to be a successful investor, yet want to be as conservative as possible.
- You need a set amount of money at the end of a time period, and you can't afford to see any large portion of your savings disappear in a sudden market downturn.

---

between bonds, stocks, and cash? Why not lean on a few good stocks to conquer the world?

Well, in a perfect world without up and down cycles, there would be no need for asset allocation. There would be a steady stock market, a dependable place where your money would earn a good chunk every year, year-in and year-out. You'd merely have to set enough money aside, harness it to a few stocks, and count your savings as they increased over time.

Everyone knows that's not the case. The market has a funny way of heading upward, sometimes quickly, and other times at a slower, steadier trek. And every once in a while, a period comes along when stocks—either certain company shares or the entire market—go into a tailspin. Thank goodness that doesn't occur too often, or else investing would resemble betting on the horses. Still, it's a factor that should be on every investor's mind.

That kind of uncertainty is defined as risk. There's a chance that stocks or other investments might go down or lose value. Worse yet, you don't know when the market is going down. Not even psychics have an idea when certain stocks or mutual funds you hold are going to take a snooze, let alone which ones will tank and which will come through with no problem.

Plain, simple mathematics tells us that over a long period, though, those occasional bumps the market hits, those jolts share prices take from time to time are smoothed over. Every so often, nonetheless, there will be some turbulence, or volatility, as the pros call it.

So the question really isn't whether the stock market will come through. It has, and in all likelihood, it will continue to do so. The conundrum investors face is this: Can you afford to wait out periods when the market isn't behaving up to historic averages.

Those are the times when cooking up an investment mix makes the most sense. Eventually, you'll need to draw on the money you've put aside. If you're saving for your daughter's college tuition, that's a period of anywhere from a year to 18 years. You could well have 30 years to build a retirement portfolio; you might have just 15. Or, if you've set your sights on getting together a down payment on a new home, you might have just 3 years to secure the money you'll need.

Now factor in the amount of risk you're willing to take on when you put your money to work either in the stock market or with bonds. Can you live with losing money? And just how much could you see vanish and still not regret too much? Are you comfortable putting your money behind financial instruments that can sometimes go down? And how much are you willing to stake on volatile investments?

As you're now starting to see, your portfolio is also a personal approach to the market, something akin to your fingerprint or the way you've furnished your home. When it comes to investing, your personality plays an important role. Are you a thrill-seeker, a daredevil who likes to take chances in the hope of securing the greatest possible reward? Then you'll probably gravitate toward volatile investments that have a higher risk but most probably will pay investors a greater reward. That means you'll opt for stocks over bonds; for growth stocks or small company shares over blue chips or corporations that pay high dividends. On the other hand, if you're a nail-biter, whose hair turns gray whenever the unexpected crops up, you'll go heavier on the bonds in your portfolio and probably lean toward safer big company shares instead of taking a chance on start-ups.

Grouping, Regrouping, and Grouping Again

Whenever professionals talk of asset allocation, they divide the world of finance up into three categories: stocks, bonds, and cash. In one article a money manager might recommend that investors opt for a portfolio that is 60 percent stocks, 30 percent bonds, and 10 percent cash. In another, a famed financial guru will say that it is best to allocate 70 percent of your funds in stocks, 25 percent in bonds, and the remaining 5 percent in cash. What do they mean? Well, in simple terms, a $10,000 portfolio that is 60 percent stocks, 30 percent bonds, and 10 percent cash will have $6,000, or 60 percent of its value, tied up in the stock market in company shares. Another $3,000, or 30 percent of its value, will be in bonds; the remaining 10 percent, or $1,000, will be held in cash, most often in a bank account or money market mutual fund as recommended earlier.

Those numbers are straightforward. Still, a couple of things might leave you scratching your head and looking over your brokerage statements. For one, there is that quirky little investment called the mutual fund. But that problem is easily solved. Funds tend to focus on one type of investment or another—a stock fund puts most of its money to work in the equity or stock market. Therefore, think of it as part of the stock portion of your portfolio. A municipal bond fund will channel most of investors' money into the bond market. Think of it as making up part of your bond portfolio. Cash? Well, you should think of cash as money that's waiting to go into the market, *aside* from the emergency fund discussed in Chapter 1.

It's easy to get mixed up on another aspect of asset allocation: the constantly changing value of your investments. Fifty shares of AT&T may be worth $2,500, or $50 a share one hour of one day, and 5,000 or $100 a share a few weeks later. Consequently, the portion of your portfolio anchored in stocks might slide up or down over time; your bond weighting, as professionals call the amount of an investor's holdings put into one type of investment, will also fluctuate up and down, day in and day out.

As much as your investments head up and down, rise and fall, you needn't get too upset—that's just part of how the markets work. Nevertheless, it's still a good idea to look over your portfolio from time to time—maybe every 6 months, even once a year. That's because over long periods portfolios have a way of getting skewed. A portfolio that is 80 percent stock and 20 percent bonds might shift in value as the stock market rises in value more quickly than the bond market. Under that kind of a scenario, in 6 months' time, you could find that 95 percent of your holdings are in stocks (i.e., 95 percent of your portfolio is now in company shares or stock mutual funds). The bond slice, meanwhile, might have shrunk to 5 percent or so. If you're aiming to have a 80/20 mix, you might funnel more cash into bonds to even things up. You might sell some stock and purchase bonds, too.

Either way, asset allocation is an ongoing project. Your portfolio is constantly changing. Your needs often shift, too. So, set aside an hour or two every so often and review things.

Time as a Factor

Time has a way of smoothing things out. Relationships gone sour can often start anew after a few years have taken the sting out of differences we have with a loved one. Come back to a town wrecked by a hurricane. After a few years, there will be few signs of the disaster, maybe no trace at all.

Time's healing properties hold true in investing as well. Days the market implodes and stocks lose their value are often forgotten after a matter of years, months, sometimes even weeks. For a fitting example, look at what happened after the market crashes in 1929 and 1987. In both cases, the market took some time, set itself straight, and bounced back. After 1929, with the Great Depression looming over the nation at large, stocks stumbled for a few years. By 1933, though stocks were back on track and posted a 54 percent gain, according to the S&P 500 index. In 1987, it was a matter of weeks before the market had righted its course; stocks actually finished up for the year and provided investors with a total return of 5 percent. The next two years practically wiped the disaster from memory; the S&P 500 in 1988 delivered a total return of 17 percent, followed by 31 percent in 1989.

What accounts for the resiliency of the market? You could say it's the law of averages. Stocks have returned investors a little over 10 percent yearly. That's plenty of reassurance for investors willing to wait out rough patches when the market can't hold to its historic levels. Over time, the market has plowed through the troubles and continued on its winning way. And, as a result, patient investors are rewarded, and many folks trust that their investments in the stock market will increase in value, if only they wait out the storm. The more years you're willing to stick it out, the greater the chance that things will go well for stocks.

There's another lesson to be gained from the effects of time. Because time often repairs whatever damage a drop in the market might do, the longer you can keep your money invested, the riskier your investment mix may become. Put into practice that means the longer you are willing to keep your money invested, the more you can lean on slightly riskier holdings like stocks to give your portfolio a greater kick. The closer you are to a time when you'll have to rely on those same funds, the more you'll want to choose safer investments that fluctuate less in value such as bonds or money market mutual funds.

Consider a short-term goal, such as the money for a new automobile or the down payment for a house. You'll probably tap funds you set aside for those goals in a couple of years, maybe 5 years at most. True, if the market holds to historical averages or even blazes forward, you're in luck and you'll have more cash at your disposal. But, chances are you'll not want to risk the money you've stockpiled. Imagine that just 6 months before you tap the $10,000 you've carefully salted away for a new house, the market loses 10 percent. Swiftly, with no warning at all, you're in the hole for $1,000. Not a pleasant thought. Under that kind of scenario, short-duration bonds or a money market account can keep much of your money intact and still secure a decent return on your savings. You'll also sidestep any damage in the event of a short- or long-term bear market.

Now look at a target that's further off in the future, say your retirement 30 or 40 years ahead. The time when you'll need to tap your savings is far away. You'll also have to hoard quite a sum to make your days comfortable. Combined, those two considerations might prod you to put more money into the stock market, where stocks' long-term average gains will help grow your savings.

You'll get a good idea of just how much risk you're willing to take on by asking, "what if." What if the money you'd invested for a new car was tied up in the market and stocks slumped? What if your daughter was starting college next year, and the sum you had set aside were to lose some 15 percent of its value?

Managing Risk

Time is just half of the asset allocation equation. The other 50 percent is more personal, more malleable, and more a result of your personality or temperament. It's what the professionals label your risk tolerance. Think of your risk tolerance as the answer to that list of "what ifs" we just mentioned. Here are some more. What if you saw the worth of an account cut in half? What if you could avoid any sort of roil and rumble in the financial markets? What if you could lock in bigger gains by being patient when your investments rose and fell during a short period of time? Maybe you'd shrug it off, confident that things would eventually turn for the better. Maybe you'd panic. Either way, thinking over possible scenarios helps investors take steps to construct an appropriate portfolio.

In each case, you're not only determining how much risk you can withstand, you're essentially figuring out how much stress you'll take on with different investment portfolios and how well you can deal with it.

Break risk tolerance down to real-life circumstances; you're tailoring a portfolio of mutual funds, stocks, and bonds that holds true to your makeup. If you're a skittish type whose pulse races with every rise and fall of the market, you might opt for more in bonds to provide ballast for your account, and more comfort for your soul. If you're more daring, you might look for additional punch in your portfolio in the form of stocks.

The Trade-Off

To get an idea of just how different recipes of stocks and bonds affect a portfolio over time, look at some figures put together by the Baltimore mutual fund company T. Rowe Price. Experts at T. Rowe culled data on the financial markets and examined a variety of portfolios, some composed primarily of stocks with a smattering of bonds and cash, others made up of equal stakes of bonds and stocks. They tracked the performance of each from 1955 to 1998, including the best and worst years for each.

Here are charts and a brief analysis of the five T. Rowe Price portfolios from most conservative and risk-adverse to the most daring and potentially more volatile.

Conservative: 25 Percent Stocks, 40 Percent Bonds, 35 Percent Cash

Anchor a portfolio with bonds, and you'll have a low-risk asset mix that even in the worst of years probably won't lose much of its value. At the same time, however, you'll give up some of the punch possible with a heavier weighting in stocks. Thanks to its 75 percent position in bonds and cash, this conservative mix successfully muted any of the topsy-turvy tumble of the stock market.

That would definitely tailor this kind of strategy to short-term holdings—the down payment for a house, for instance, or the money for a new car—where you can't afford to lose much money. For a longer term, however, it's a somewhat stodgy mix. It might be too lazy for retirement funds or long-term goals that need some mustard, some more oomph from stocks (see Figure 9.2).

Moderate: 40 Percent Stocks, 40 Percent Bonds, 20 Percent Cash
Up the portion you devote to stocks, and already you can see a sizable difference. The average annual return rises to 9 percent, but you're taking on more risk, which in the short run could be costly. A heavier weighting in stocks gives this portfolio a lot more punch over the long haul (see Figure 9.3).

Balanced: 60 Percent Stocks, 30 Percent Bonds, 10 Percent Cash
If you raise the value of the stock holdings another 20 percent, that raises the average annual return to just over 10 percent, not much for a short-term investment. At the same time, you've added still more risk to the mix. Over the longer term, however, the benefits of more stock are evident (see Figure 9.4).

Growth: 80 Percent Stocks, 20 Percent Cash
Aggressive portfolios like this one gain long-term results. They're not the best for near-term outlooks, however. With an 80/20 mix, you gain a 10.9

Figure 9.2   Portfolio 1—Conservative

This very liquid, safe mix leans heavily on bonds and cash and goes light on the stock market. It works best for short-term goals of 5 years or so, but can be flat for a long-term retirement savings.

Makeup: (pie chart)   25% Stocks
                       40% Bonds
                       35% Cash

Upside: Limited but good
Average annual total return (1955–1998): 8%
Best year: 20.7%

Value of $10,000 after 10 years $26,600
Value of $10,000 after 20 years $81,400

Downside: Minimal
Down years: 3
Average loss during a down year: 0.7%
Worst year: –1.5%

Source: T. Rowe Price.

Figure 9.3 Portfolio 2—Moderate

A heavier mix of stocks—40%—gives this portfolio more spunk, while a sizable bond and cash weighting keep volatility down. It's a good consideration for intermediate term investments of 5 to 10 years when investors want to take more risk in the hope of reaping higher returns via the stock market.

Makeup: (pie chart)   40% Stocks
                            40% Bonds
                            20% Cash

Upside: Pretty good
Average annual total return (1955–1998): 9%
Best year: 22.8%

Value of $10,000 after 10 years $ 32,200
Value of $10,000 after 20 years $108,400

Downside: Minimal
Down years: 8
Average loss during a down year: 2.0%
Worst year: –6.7%

Source: T. Rowe Price.

Figure 9.4 Portfolio 3—Balanced

This portfolio lifts its reliance on stocks for a larger average annual return. At the same time, a 30% slice invested in bonds helps steady things somewhat. It makes sense for long-range goals such as retirement, although younger investors might want to lean on stocks a bit more to perk up returns over time.

Makeup: (pie chart)   60% Stocks
                            30% Bonds
                            10% Cash

Upside: Good
Average annual total return (1955–1998): 10.1%
Best year: 28.1%

Value of $10,000 after 10 years $ 39,800
Value of $10,000 after 20 years $149,700

Downside: Nothing extraordinary, but certainly worth notice
Down years: 8
Average loss during a down year: –6.7%
Worst year: –13.4%

Source: T. Rowe Price.

Figure 9.5   Portfolio 4—Growth

A portfolio that leans on the stock market boosts returns considerably. One downside: those occasional off years can hurt.

Makeup: (pie chart)   80% Stocks
                       20% Cash

Upside: Very good
Average annual total return (1955–1998): 10.9%
Best year: 35.0%

Value of $10,000 after 10 years $ 46,200
Value of $10,000 after 20 years $186,500

Downside: Considerable for short-term investors. Longer-term, the stock market's historical averages should help smooth out any bumps.
Down years: 9
Average loss during a down year: –7.1%
Worst year: –19.6%

Source: T. Rowe Price.

percent average annual return over the period from 1955 to 1998, but the risk rises appreciably, too. Longer-term results, buoyed by the market's resiliency, are impressive. A relatively aggressive portfolio like this has the kind of spunk investors need for retirement plans (see Figure 9.5).

Very Aggressive: 100 Percent Stocks

Pull out all the stops and put all your money in stocks. T. Rowe Price's numbers show that to be a risky move indeed, and jarring for short-term

Figure 9.6   Portfolio 5—Aggressive

Put it all to work in the stock market and here's what you get—more bang for your buck, but the risk of some bigger bumps along the way, too.

Makeup: (pie chart)   100% Stocks

Upside: Substantial
Average annual total return (1955–1998): 11.9%
Best year: 43.4%

Value of $10,000 after 10 years $ 57,800
Value of $10,000 after 20 years $262,400

Downside: Possibly very, very high for short-term investors. Longer-term, the stock market's historical averages should help smooth out any bumps.
Down years: 9
Average loss during a down year: –10.5%
Worst year: –26.5%

Source: T. Rowe Price.

prospects, despite its high average annual return. Stay the course for a time—10 years—and a daring strategy like this pays off (see Figure 9.6).

LONG- AND SHORT-TERM INVESTMENTS

If there's a lesson to be learned from the T. Rowe Price data, it's this: Short-term goals are best served by conservative investments. In shorter time-frames, the average annual gain by stocking up on company shares is minimal. Meanwhile, stocking up on company shares increases the chance that your portfolio could suffer a devastating loss in a down year.

Long-term investment projects are a different thing altogether. They truly benefit from the higher return of heavier stock weightings. And a longer horizon allows a portfolio more time to recover from any major downturns in the stock market.

Rules of Thumb

It's next to impossible to prescribe a set asset allocation in a book like this: Each investor must determine his or her way to get into the market, to mitigate risk, to meet future aims. A few examples, however, may help you make your asset allocation decisions.

The following sections focus on three scenarios: retirement, tuition, and short-term savings and suggest reasonable degrees of risk in each case. This should help you map out an investment strategy or asset allocation that fits your needs and outlook.

LONG-TERM SAVINGS

Name a goal way off in the future that everyone eventually has to fret over. You guessed it—retirement. No matter how you look at it, retirement's a challenge. Despite the difficulty, your task is to determine how much money you'll need to live in later years. You have to grapple with uncomfortable issues, such as how long you expect to be around and how comfortable you expect your last years to be. Retirement is also going to require a load of cash. That's to say that your investment plans are going to have to do a lot of work, and deliver consistent growth that you can rely on. That means you'll need to put your savings in stocks to build them up. As already seen, time takes some of the sting out of the stock market's volatility, and time will be on your side.

How do you approach retirement investing? How do you divvy your money up between stocks and bonds to secure the best possible return? In the not too distant past, investment pros had a simple formula. Take your age, and subtract the figure from 100. Then, looking over your portfolio, they would recommend that you invest a percentage equal to your age in bonds. The remainder, they said, would be earmarked for the stock market.

There's just one glitch, however. Thanks to better food, stronger medicine, central heating, and the like, the life expectancy of Americans is increasing. In the United States it's as high as 76 years; on average, African American men live 66 years; African American women, 74 years.

That's the good news. The bad news is that you'll be tapping your retirement savings a long, long time. And while you may be around longer to enjoy shuffleboard and trips to National Parks in your motor home, you'll have to put together a great amount of cash to do so.

Stockpiling that extra money means only one thing: You'll need to rely on stocks longer to help beef up your retirement assets. So, instead of using 100 minus your age as a good rule of thumb, the experts have upped the ante somewhat, advising you to move up to 120 minus your age. Otherwise, the process remains the same: You devote a percentage of your portfolio equal to 120 minus your age to stocks. The remainder can well go into bond holdings.

Take as an example a 30-year-old working his or her way up the ranks. Thirty is still a far cry from 80 years or so. To come up with a good mix of stocks and bonds, he or she would take 120 and subtract 30 from the figure. The result, 90, indicates he or she should put 90 percent of the portfolio into stocks to help boost the retirement account over time. The remaining 10 percent could go into bonds, where he could preserve some of the capital.

Wondering how your risk tolerance comes into play? Well, it figures in quite simply, the truth be told. If you feel aggressive and want to put more of your money in stocks to grow your savings in the market, raise your stock allocation 10 percent. If you're feeling quite frisky, you might even move that allotment a bit further, say 20 percent, but no more than that. That way, you can adjust your portfolio to your wishes, and still not go too far overboard.

INTERMEDIATE TERM—SAVING FOR TUITION

In many ways, sculpting a portfolio for retirement is relatively easy. You have a relatively simple equation to follow as a guideline, and you needn't shift assets from stocks to bonds too often—perhaps every 5 years or so, maybe as infrequently as once every 10 years.

Tuition is a goal with a shorter time horizon. Even the most conscientious, well-organized families have only 18 years to save for their kids' college debut. That seems like a long-enough period of time to put money to work, but as any parent will surely tell you, time has a way of quietly and slowly accelerating. Look up one day, your kids are racing from door to door in diapers;

AGGRESSIVE WITHIN ASSET CLASSES

Hold it, you say. All this talk of carving up portfolios into stocks and bonds sounds great on paper. But in practice no two stocks are truly alike. Besides that, aren't there mutual funds that are far more risky and volatile than others?

You're right on both counts. You needn't look any further than a stock price chart or the stock quotes in the newspaper to know that shares of Yahoo and General Motors are two completely different beasts. Yahoo has tended to zip and zoom upward and downward, making large movements in days, and weeks. It's not uncommon to see the stock rise, or drop, $10 or more in a day. General Motors shares, on the other hand tend to move in a more determined fashion. You might see the stock go up or down 50 cents a share on any given day, maybe $1.00 on the rarest of occasions. Yahoo probably is a riskier stock, but at the same time it offers investors the potential of a higher reward or greater gains. General Motors, by contrast, is less volatile, but its rewards would probably be a good deal less than Yahoo's.

There can be a great amount of variety from one mutual fund to the next, too. A holding like the Munder Net Net fund might leap and bound in price; its portfolio is made up of Internet stocks, the kinds of shares that flit about in value. A staid fund like Vanguard Windsor, on the other hand, tends to make its way to peaks and valleys at a slower pace. The stocks it holds certainly do, and it goes without saying that whatever makes up the portfolio will have a direct effect on the fund. In other words, Munder Net Net offers investors a riskier ride, but also the potential to increase in value. In all likelihood, Vanguard Windsor will glide along more smoothly but not climb as quickly or drop as sharply as Munder.

Variation from stock to stock and from fund to fund can serve investors like yourself well, allowing you to mold a portfolio to your preferences. Feel like taking a risk? You'll opt for shares or funds with more "spice," that's to say more risk and potential reward. If you hate uncertainty or want to cushion your stock market experience as much as possible, you'll probably turn to quieter stocks and funds (see Figure 9.7).

soon they are hoarding Pokemon cards; and in a flash they're asking to borrow the car and are talking about first-choice and safety schools.

Whether you start salting away money for college early or are just now starting to save, the fact is the time you'll need to tap funds is approaching quicker than retirement. As shown by the different asset mixes earlier in

Figure 9.7 The Risk/Reward Balance of a Variety of Investments

The greater the risk, the higher the potential reward, so the old investment adage goes. Here's how a number of investments stack up.

LOWEST ──► HIGHEST

Certificates of Deposit	Municipal bonds	Large company stocks	Mid cap stocks	Small cap stocks	Junk bonds
Bank savings accounts	Corporate bonds	Foreign company stocks		
Money market accounts	Stock mutual funds			
Money market mutual funds	Bond mutual funds			
U.S. Treasury bills				

250

this chapter, that's an important point. The shorter the waiting period before you have to use the money you're saving, the less you can afford to risk your savings to short-term turbulence in the stock market. If stocks you've invested in succumb to a skid and shed $3,000 in value, you're stuck. After all, there's no time to hold off and wait for stocks to rally when the bursar at State College comes calling.

Nonetheless, to meet the high cost of school, you'll definitely need the boost stocks give a portfolio. That's especially true early on, when your child is young, and move-in day at the campus dormitory is still over a decade away.

Put two considerations like those together, and it becomes clear that you need a compromise. William Casill, a TIAA-CREF actuary who helps design asset allocations for state sponsored tuition programs run by the money management firm, says saving for tuition requires a balancing act, one that leans heavily on stocks at the beginning of a tuition investment program, while slowly sifting assets into more conservative bonds and money market funds over time. "You just can't get around the fact that your kid is bound to start college around the age of 18," he says. "That locks you into a certain set of strategies. When your child is young, you still have time to live through any sort of changes the stock market undergoes; when kids reach 10, 12, 14 years of age, however, you should be leaning more toward preserving capital."

Here's a rough outline of asset allocations Casill recommends. The following guidelines are a good approximation of how tuition money might be best divvied up over time (see Figure 9.8).

Figure 9.8 TIAA-CREF Recommended College Tuition Asset Allocation Mix

How much of your kid's college account should be in stocks, how much in bonds? The institutional investment firm TIAA-CREF recommends the following asset allocation, gauged by your son's or daughter's age.

AGE	EQUITIES (%)	FIXED INCOME (%)
1–2	75	25
3–4	65	35
5–6	60	40
7–8	55	45
9–10	45	55
11–12	40	60
13–14	30	70
15–16	20	80
17–18	10	90

Source: TIAA-CREF.

While your kid's a preschooler, Casill says your best bet is to tuck much of your tuition account into equity mutual funds or stocks to generate the growth you'll need to get off and running. A good target is between 60 and 80 percent equities or stocks; the rest set aside in bonds.

Gradually over time, shift money from stocks or equities to bonds. By the time your son or daughter reaches 8 to 10 years of age, Casill says it's a

---

TUITION

You'd think the cost of professors, chalk, seats, heat, and classroom maintenance wouldn't amount to this much. Think again. For 1999, the College Board, the Princeton, New Jersey, company that administers the SAT and helps stockpile financial aid statistics says the average price for tuition and a range of college fees stretched from $3,243 for a four-year state or public university to $14,508 for a private four-year college. Tack on another $4,530 a year for a public school's room and board, and $5,765 for the same at a private school. All told, the College Board said the entire bill including books, supplies, transportation, and the like ranged from $10,458 a year at public schools to $22,533 for private schools.

Don't gasp—yet. Depending on the estimates you see, the price of school is going up between 5 and 7 percent each year.

There is some help on the way. Recently a number of new state-sponsored plans have cropped up that not only help you salt away funds for your son's or daughter's time on campus, but also give you a tidy tax break. You might call these new programs Section 529 plans for the tax code that has helped them along.

Here's how they work. Most 529 plans allow you to make a yearly contribution up to a maximum, and to deduct whatever amount you put in from your state tax load. As of this writing, New York State, for example, allowed a yearly contribution of $5,000 or $10,000 for a couple. Those funds are then invested by a money manager that runs your state's plan. The institutional money management firm TIAA-CREF manages plans for New York, Missouri, and California and adjusts the asset allocation of your account's portfolio according to your children's ages and how soon they would expect to start college. As a kicker, your investment is allowed to grow tax free. That helps your savings compound at a far higher rate than if they were taxed yearly. In fact, no taxes are due on Section 529 plans until you withdraw funds. At that point, the withdrawals will be taxed at your young scholar's tax rate, which in all probability will be much less than your own.

WEB SIGHTINGS
COLLEGE PLANS

If you are interested in state programs such as Section 529 plans and traditional prepaid college plans, visit the Web site www.savingforcollege.com, which compiles info on offerings from coast to coast and goes so far as to rate them, too.

---

good idea to have the tuition account split 50/50 between stocks and bonds. The reason: The closer you get to the day that your kid enrolls, the safer you should play the financial markets. If you're a more aggressive investor, Casill says you can up your equity allotment by 10 percent to 15 percent; by the same token, if you feel timid, you might trim your exposure to stocks by a similar percentage.

You reach another milestone when your kid is 14 to 16 years old. Here, it's a good idea to bring as much as 70 percent to 80 percent to fixed income investments such as bonds, short-term bond funds, and money market mutual funds. Your goal is to safeguard what you have. A money market mutual fund, the same financial instrument you've used for your emergency stash of cash, works well here. Short-term Treasury bonds, too, will keep your savings intact. If you're feeling aggressive, look to a bond mutual fund, preferably with a short (3 to 5 years) average maturity. That way, should interest rates rise or the bond market pass over a rough patch, the money you have invested won't fluctuate as much as savings invested in a bond fund with intermediate or long average maturities.

SHORT TERM: SAVING FOR A CAR, A DOWN PAYMENT

Remember, as a kid, the time you had a shiny balloon in your hand. Remember how it glistened and sent off the sun's rays, how it bobbed about in the wind, how it danced on the end of a string? Now, if you dip down into your psyche, you'll probably recall how all of its beauty, its life, all came to an end the minute you lost grip of the balloon's cord in your hand, when you squeezed the balloon too tightly.

Hold onto that memory for a second longer; it will help you understand a thing or two about short-term investing. Your savings for the down payment on a home or the purchase of a car are a lot like that balloon. They're special. They're also fragile and need protection.

So, as tempting as it is to jump into the stock market's stampede ahead, remember that there were times in the past (and certainly there will be times in the future) when that precious stash of money would surely have taken a hit in the stock market. Invest your money prior to one of those instances, and you'll quickly feel that same sinking sensation in your stomach that you had when your balloon flew away. And should you suffer a loss of $2,000 or more, your plans might get derailed at the worst possible time— say that week after the realtor showed you the home of your dreams.

Take a very conservative approach to investing savings you'll have to tap sooner than later—say within a 3-year time frame. As pointed out earlier, for emergency funds the safest route is in a money market mutual fund. There are three reasons the money market fund works so perfectly in such circumstances: (1) your principal is protected; (2) you can tap your investment—it's liquid and you need only to write a check or visit an ATM location; and (3) you're earning a respectable rate of interest on your money.

There is a second choice, if you're looking to boost the interest you're getting, but want to keep risk to a minimum: a short-term bond fund with an average portfolio maturity between 1 and 3.5 years. Short-term bond mutual funds have a respectable record—Morningstar reports that the group has averaged an annual total return of 5.10 percent over the 3 years ending January 1, 2000, 6.00 percent over 5 years and 6.53 percent in the past decade. As far as safety goes, the group has fared well even when the bond market went through disturbances. In fact, 1994 was the last time Morningstar's average for the group ended the year down with a –1.02 percent total return for the year. In 1999, when bonds tossed and turned, the group averaged a total return of 2.14 percent.

ONWARD

Now that you've got a handle on mixing and matching investments to suit your needs, it's time to head to the markets with some important choices to make. How do you want to purchase stocks, mutual funds, or bonds? Do you want advice and how much are you willing to pay for it? The next chapter lists the options—from financial planners to brokers—and spells out the costs, the pros, and the cons of each choice.

10

FINANCIAL PLANNER,
FULL-SERVICE BROKER,
OR DISCOUNT BROKER

Your Choices Made Simpler

There is milk. There are sweaters, shoes, oranges, shirts, umbrellas, too. They are basic necessities. They're all easy to find, even easier to buy. All you have to do is hop in the car, step on the accelerator, gather them up, open your wallet, and make the purchase.

Try to think of stocks, bonds, mutual funds, and the like as essential needs as well. They're not quite so easy to get, though. There is a market of sorts where you can get them, yes, but often you'll need an intermediary, a broker or some other helper who's ready to take your order to buy or to sell. From there, whoever is doing your bidding will search near and far for someone to sell or buy the shares you're buying or selling. They'll negotiate a price that you can agree on. And, to cap it off, they'll take a cut of the action, their commission or fee.

The process of finding buyers and sellers comes in a variety of packages. In some instances, you can hire a professional to both trade stocks, bonds, and mutual funds and provide a lot of other financial services—coaching and comforting included—at a price. A financial planner will examine your budget, concoct an investment strategy for you, and then guide you on your way to the market. You are paying for an expert, and his or her advice on a range of matters. Full-service brokers promise to advise you on what they feel are the best investments around and then will arrange whatever deals you need to build your portfolio. Under both scenarios, you can expect to get more service than just a deal struck in the financial markets. You can expect to pay for the help too, in the form of high brokerage commissions or fees for services rendered.

Maybe you don't need all that hand-holding. Perhaps you're confident enough to manage things on your own. For you and your minimal needs, then, there are outfits that will do less and charge smaller fees or commissions. Discount brokers, for example, promise to get your orders for stocks or bonds filled with few frills.

REALITY CHECK

Sometime around July 1999, Rob Williams, an insurance executive in Indianapolis, decided to cut loose. For years, he had been a dutiful investor. He had made the biggest contribution he could to his 401(k) each year, while he and his wife had saved for a dream home just outside Indianapolis. It was time to open an online brokerage account.

"We had some extra savings—say $2,500, and saw that technology stocks were doing really well," Williams remembers. "I had taken aside a little money, studied up on stocks, read through the Motley Fool Web site, Yahoo!, and the rest . . . I felt it was time for me to try my hand at choosing stocks and do some of it myself."

Williams' first step was to surf. He logged on, spent a few hours, and gave the once-over to a dozen or so e-brokerages. He settled on E*TRADE. "My wife and I don't do a lot of trading, and we don't feel that we need an extraordinary amount of hand-holding," says Williams. "We looked around, and though E*TRADE didn't have the cheapest trades in the business, they certainly had very good research."

Williams started off by buying stock in a local favorite, the pharmaceutical company Eli Lilly. Lilly has long been a mainstay in Indianapolis, and Williams feels as if he knows the company from the chief executive down to the factory floor. "We know people who are in the company profit-sharing program, we read about the company's new pharmaceuticals," he explains. Visiting E*TRADE's Web site and other sites, Williams says he has kept up with Lilly's research spending, as well as news of new product launches. He's kept up with news on Lilly's blockbuster products such as Prozac, and was able to follow developments when Wall Street was concerned about company sales. Williams has dug up Lilly's price-to-earnings multiple, estimates of its earnings growth and even press releases the company has issued. "You can do all that now," says Williams, "It's all there in cyberspace, and most importantly, it's free."

What works best is really up to you. In deciding what fits your view of financial matters, you might want to consider a few factors. Just how much independence do you want? How confident are you about your ability to invest and understand the market? How much are you willing to pay for advice or even a shoulder to soak in tears? This chapter will help you answer those questions.

A FINANCIAL PLANNER

It's hard these days. In all the confusion of family, work, home, and finances, you might feel just too busy, too tired, or even overwhelmed to set things straight and start investing. In that case, you'd be wise to consider a financial planner.

Financial planners help you set up a budget and figure a way to get invested. They offer a service tailored to your own needs. You say you're afraid that you might botch up your finances and therefore your future? A good financial planner can take you by the hand and lead you toward success.

If you want a guru to teach you how to handle your money; a mentor to guide you through the maze of insurance policies, mutual funds, savings plans, and debt reduction schemes; a coach to cheer you on when you're doing well and make sure you don't actually fall when you make a mistake . . . then you want a financial planner (see Figure 10.1).

At the bare minimum, here are some specific activities you can expect from a financial planner. First, a planner should sit down and collect data by asking probing questions about your income, your debt, what you own, and what you've saved. The planner will take that information and line it up in columns listing your assets and liabilities. After completing that tally, he or she will tell you your net worth.

From there, it's best to keep to a simple plan. A financial planner should want to know your short- and long-term goals and when you would

Figure 10.1   A Financial Planner Is for You If . . .

- You'd rather leave all the fuss, number crunching, and some decisions to a professional.
- You'd like someone to suggest investments and guide you step by step to a portfolio that meets your needs.
- You'd like to have a tutor set up a blueprint for your finances and school you on the markets and good investing.
- You're pressed for time.
- You have a specific project—say a financial plan—that you'd like guidance in setting up.

like to make those dreams come to life. That list could include several items. A well-financed retirement could head it up, but you might also include your desire to pay for a top-tier private college for your kids. You might be angling for a larger home, or yearn for a trip to Africa.

Your planner will then point out ways for you to attain your desires, mapping out the strategies, the risks, and the time frame required. Once you've entrusted your finances to him or her, a good planner will report back to you whenever a change is necessary. Put all those pieces together, and you get a sound financial blueprint to help guide your life.

A key service the planner should provide is determining just how much risk you're able to stand. If you're a high-strung sort who's bound to fret over every move in the stock market, your nervous condition will probably necessitate a mix of investments whose volatility is minimal. If you're a daring sort with Freon in your veins, your planner might steer you toward investments with higher risk and the potential for greater rewards. After your preliminary talk of targets and timetables, you'll get—in return for your fees—a set of blueprints to help you fulfill your wishes on schedule. That entails drawing up a financial plan and then setting your finances on that same path. A planner will help hammer out a budget and recommend that you reshape your cash flow to open up as wide a current of money as you can.

Next, it's his or her job to identify the investments that will generate the wealth you need to attain your goals. That requires a balancing act: A planner wants to keep you from fretting every waking moment over losing your savings. Also, with the IRS looking over your shoulder, a planner wants to keep your tax burden in check. "Nobody has ever benefited by paying taxes," says Los Angeles financial planner Percy Bolton.

You might well bring up the topic of insurance, too. Life, disability, health, and auto insurance are all financial products designed to protect you in the case of a mishap, an emergency, or some other unexpected event that could sap your income and divert money from investments.

You should look at your planner as a teacher. He or she should tutor you on how to invest, and how the markets work. That calls for detailed explanations at each step your planner takes, as well as some sort of analysis of the recommended investments. In fact, most planners provide clients with copies of Standard & Poor's, Value Line, or Morningstar reports that detail how certain investments have done and how they are expected to do. Figure 10.2 lists the services provided by financial planners.

What They Cost

There are several ways financial planners pay their bills. Some planners make their living off of commissions. Each time they invest your money

Figure 10.2   Financial Planners

What they do:

Ask a lot of questions about your finances—what you make, what you own, what you owe.

Ask about your dreams, both your long- and short-term goals.

Ask about how much you worry and what level of risk you can tolerate with your investments.

Help you decide about insurance, savings, and debt reduction plans.

Help you keep your tax burden to a minimum.

Teach you about investing and your finances every step of the way.

What you need to find out:

How does a financial planner intend to bill you?

Does he/she make money from fees or commissions?

What is his/her experience?

Is he/she certified?

How does he/she keep up with changes in the business?

How often does he/she intend to notify you and under what circumstances?

---

with certain mutual fund companies or investment firms, they receive a kickback essentially for handing over a portion of your savings. In turn, the investment firm will typically levy a sales load on your money, a fee for using their services.

A conflict of interest? Suffice it to say that dealing with commissioned planners can be a tricky proposition. Their salary, their kids' tuition, their mortgage, and car note, all come from the investments they're selling to you. At the same time, they're steering you into the arms of investment companies that are pocketing some of your savings just for the privilege of using their services. That's a cut out of your savings and hence a slice of the gains you could be making. Remember, there are dozens of great mutual funds out there that don't charge loads and won't skim away part of your investment. Look at it this way: You can bet that when you go to a car dealership that sells the Flash 3000, you probably won't get a salesperson who will talk up the competition's new Orion model, no matter how good it is. The same holds true in financial planning. A commissioned planner is probably not going to talk up the investments of load-free firms like Vanguard or Janus, if only because he or she won't get a cut of the action.

Other financial planners work for fees. Fee-only planners bill you for the work they do, much as a mechanic, a dentist, or a music teacher would. Some charge by the hour—often at a cost of between $100 and $250, according to Percy Bolton. "It varies a lot, but you could say that it depends on the region where you are . . . clients can expect to pay more on the coasts, and in bigger cities, too," he says.

Some fee-only planners levy a charge calculated as a percentage of the assets they manage for you. Bolton says the fee can range from 0.5 percent to 1.5 percent. Planners who charge on the asset base they're managing tend to require a minimum investment—$100,000 for less established or newer planners, according to Bolton, and $1,000,000 to $2,000,000 for those who've been in the business a while.

In addition, there are fee-only planners who charge by the project. Each undertaking—a financial plan, an estate plan, and the like—carries its own separate charge. Bolton says the fees can vary, according to the complexity of the project at hand, but tend to fall between $500 and $7,000, although there are times the charges mount up to $10,000.

Whichever way they bill you for their services, fee-only planners are free to select the investments that make the most sense for you and have the best track record. Their pay isn't linked to commissions—it's essentially tied to how pleased you are with the work they do. The incentive, therefore, is to get the most for your money. After all, if you're rich and happy, you're likely to have passed the word around to friends and family. And the more clients a planner has, the more fees there are to collect.

Often, there's another plus to fee-only planners: They tend to be more experienced. Planners who are just starting out probably need all the commission income they can get to make ends meet. An established planner who has a long client list is likely to be able to make a good living by merely charging for his or her work.

Lastly, there are fee-based planners, a hybrid category that makes money off of both fees and commissions. For some projects they might charge you a fee. They might also reap commissions from the investments they pick for you. Beware. Fee-based planners, because they receive commissions, are still likely to push investments that generate income such as mutual funds that charge a load. Figure 10.3 lists fee structures for financial planners.

What to Ask of Your Planner

You're first meeting with a financial planner is an introduction, a chance for you and your planner to get to know one another and for you to find out more about the professional you're hiring. You'll learn about the services provided and can ask about the planner's experience and qualifications.

"You're hiring someone for the long haul," says Bolton. "Come prepared to talk about your strategic vision, just what you want to do and when." Another tip, offered by Bolton: Listen for ways that the planner is customizing a plan for you, and not just "pushing products," that he or she

Figure 10.3   Financial Planners and How They're Paid

Commission-paid planners	Planners who work on commission are paid a percentage of the money you invest in certain mutual funds or investments. Caution—they're likely to steer you toward investments that will help them make their paycheck.
Fee-only planners	Fee-only planners charge you for the work they do. Some are paid by the hour. Others charge a set sum for each job (e.g., drawing up a financial plan) that they perform. Still other fee-only planners charge a set yearly percentage of the total funds they manage for an investor.
Fee-based planners	Fee-based planners work for both fees and commissions. In some cases, they charge a sum for a project or a percentage of the money they manage. At other times, fee-based planners steer the investor's money to investments that help them earn a commission.

might use for anyone. And finally, meet with several planners and interview each one carefully, before making any commitments.

Certification

Lawyers have to pass a bar exam to practice; physicians must be certified by the American Medical Association and state regulators. But until a few years ago, there were no set degrees or standard affiliations for financial planners. Today, a Certified Financial Planner (CFP) designation, held by over 32,000 advisers nationwide is most widely accepted as the de facto standard. It's issued by the Financial Planning Association (800-322-4237) in Washington, D.C., and requires that planners pass rigorous testing and follow up on changes in the industry by attending seminars. Still, that's not the only professional group or affiliation around—there is the National Association of Personal Financial Advisors (NAPFA, 708-537-7722), which can also supply you with names of members in your community. Another option is the grapevine: Friends or family who are pleased with their planner are sure to want to share their name with you.

Fees, Commissions

Make sure to have all financial planners spell out how they make their money. Ask for hourly rates or service rates. Ask whether any commissions are charged for the investments you choose and how much they might be.

Keeping Up

Check to see how your planner is keeping abreast of changes in the industry. That's because tax laws, new products, and new funds crop up in bunches. Financial planner Bolton says that no one within his industry can afford to remain in a shell with changes coming often and fast in the business. His advice: See what your planner does to keep up with the world of money and finances, and ask what courses, conventions, or seminars he or she has attended.

A BROKER

Although there are plenty of ways to buy stocks, bonds, and mutual funds directly from companies, investment firms, and even the government, many people buy through a broker. Here's why: Even with direct stock purchase plans, Uncle Sam's programs that sell Treasury bonds directly to the public, and mutual funds accessible by toll-free 800-numbers, there are some investments you just can't get without a broker. A good many stocks don't have direct purchase setups. Treasury STRIPS aren't traded by the U.S. government.

Then, there's a matter of convenience. When you work through a full-service or discount broker, you're guaranteed a paper trail of monthly statements, transaction statements, and year-end summaries to help you keep track of all the investments you have bought and sold with the brokerage's help. That can be a godsend come tax time, when even well-kept records have a way of becoming disorganized.

Keep in mind, too, that a brokerage account can be a good source of both investment ideas and research information on stocks, bonds, and mutual funds. Full-service brokerages can spend upward of nine figures to staff and equip teams of analysts to cover the stock and bond markets and deliver up recommendations. Dozens of reports are often available to individual investors who have an account with a full-service broker. Even if you're signed on with a discount broker, you'll have access to a lot of the same studies. At the same time, full-service brokerage firms use their research departments to generate stock and bond picks. So, if you like to get investment ideas served up on a platter, a full-service account may just be your ticket (see Figure 10.4).

Figure 10.4 A Full-Service Broker Is for You If . . .

- You'd like to get investment ideas from a multimillion dollar Wall Street or brokerage firm research team.
- You don't mind paying high commissions on stock trades.
- You'd like a salesperson or broker to call up with suggestions from time to time.
- You'd like someone's help in managing your money and your investments.

A brokerage account also comes in handy whenever it comes time to sell off an investment or cash in on a position. To cash out, your broker or discount brokerage will rely on the same connections it used to help you buy a stock.

Types of Brokers

Brokerage firms come in three main varieties. There are full-service brokers, like Merrill Lynch or A.G. Edwards. They offer a lot and charge a lot for it. Full-service outfits assign you a personal broker to handle your account. They'll offer up research brochures and throw in stock and sometimes bond picks to boot. They'll often charge you a healthy commission on any trades they perform for you as well.

Then, there are discount operations like E*TRADE or Ameritrade. The discount operations often don't have plush offices for visitors or brokers whose hand you can shake in person. They probably don't have reams of published investment research to pass out, either. What they can offer, though, is a very low commission on any trading you might do.

A third classification—the online brokerage—is a hybrid; it can be a full-service or discount outfit, provided it performs most of its business on the Internet. A barebones online brokerage will probably give you a rock-bottom price on any trades you make. An online company that offers up more perks, such as news stories or analysts' research and data, will probably charge more for its services.

THE FULL-SERVICE TREATMENT

Your relationship with a full-service brokerage firm starts when you open an account. If you have a broker in mind, you'll start working with him or her. If not, you will then be assigned a broker who becomes your investment adviser of sorts.

Often your broker will break the ice by doing many of the same things a financial planner does. He or she might look over your assets and liabilities, and make recommendations on how you might handle your finances. As time passes, you can expect regular calls from time to time with news about the stock and bond markets. Your broker will also offer up research studies for you to look at, recommend investments, and encourage you to look at certain trends and take advantage of them.

For all the tools at their disposal, though, full-service brokers are essentially salespeople. They have to generate commissions to eat, pay their bills, and keep an income flowing their way. Often enough, they're just following orders whenever they come calling with stock and mutual fund ideas. Brokers get a list of recommended stocks and investments from their research department analysts. Their instructions are to keep pretty close to that group of stocks, bonds, and the like. Should they convince you to follow up and invest, they'll make their money one of two ways. On a stock transaction, they'll take a commission—a fee for the trade. For a bond, your broker will set up a spread—the gap between a bid price, or what you pay and an asking price, or what the owner of the bond receives when you buy it. Your full-service brokerage will pocket much of that spread. In the case of a mutual fund that charges a sales load, they'll get a fee from the fund company. The fund company in turn will take a percentage of your investment. Therefore, some types of investments and transactions are squarely in your full-service broker's best interest, and others won't bring home a single strip of bacon.

As with many things in life, you get what you pay for. Sure, the full-service folks offer up a lot of perks, but their transaction fees for sales and purchases of company shares also tend to be high. You can expect a wide spread on bond purchases as well. And when it comes to mutual funds, your broker more often than not will recommend load funds, if only to guarantee some sort of sales income from your transaction. Figure 10.5 lists the attributes of full-service brokers.

Face to Face with Full Service

If you're thinking about a full-service broker, it's a good idea to sit down ask a few questions and get terms straight, beforehand. You'll need to

Figure 10.5   Full-Service Brokers

What they do:

Buy stocks, bonds, and mutual funds for you.

Review your finances, look over your goals, and make recommendations for the future.

Keep a detailed record of your account.

Keep you abreast of investment ideas and developments in the financial markets.

What you need to find out:

How much does this broker charge in commissions?

How many mutual funds does he or she have for you to invest in, and how many carry a sales load?

How much experience does he or she have?

How does he or she get investment ideas, and how have they fared over time in comparison to the S&P 500?

---

know what commissions your broker is making on trades. You'll want to know how many mutual funds he or she has available for you to invest in, and how many of them carry no sales load. Check our your broker's experience and qualifications.

Next, get some solid figures on the brokerage firm's track record in making market recommendations. Ask how the company's recommended list of top-ranked stocks has fared for the past 5 years, and check the figure against the Standard & Poor's 500. Lastly, you might inquire how many investment ideas does your prospective broker get from the company, and how many he or she happens to choose. Don't forget to check how his or her picks have done over time too.

How to Find One

There are a few ways to find a full-service broker. You can check the local Yellow Pages for the brokerage firms listed in Figure 10.6. Brokerage firms love one-on-one contact, "face-time" as you might call it. To keep in touch, most have branch offices scattered about the countryside, in cities and small towns, from the Atlantic to the Pacific. Chances are, there's one close to you.

A second avenue is to go online. The big firms—A.G. Edwards, Merrill Lynch, Salomon Smith Barney, and the like—have directories on the Internet that can dig up the branch office nearest you. Click on the site, put in a little information on your zip code or hometown and you'll find a listing in no time.

The third angle is perhaps the best. It's word-of-mouth. The recommendation of a relative, friend, work associate, neighbor, or anyone else who has a brokerage that has done a good job is a good launching point, with a built-in checkup of sorts. If a broker has been good to someone you know, chances are he or she will treat you equally as well. You'll also have a way to get the scoop on a broker before you sign a single check, and that's always a good idea.

Background Checks

It doesn't happen very often. And in all likelihood, the professional you deal with won't have a checkered past in the brokerage business.

That said, you'd be wise to look into the past of any broker you're considering to handle your investment account. Make a well-placed call to the industry's main trade group, the National Association of Securities Dealers, or NASD (800-289-9999, http://www.nasdr.com). The NASD has records of brokers who have run afoul of federal laws or who have had run-ins with clients over business.

Figure 10.6 Looking for a Full-Service Broker?

Here are a few suggestions. Each site lists brokers and will help you find a representative near you. You might also check the phone directory for local offices of these firms.

Brokerage Firm	Home Page	Branch Office Locator Page
Merrill Lynch	www.merrill-lynch.com	today.askmerrill.com/
Morgan Stanley Dean Witter & Co.	www.msdw.com	www.msdw.com/locator/index.html
Salomon Smith Barney	www.salomonsmithbarney.com	www.salomonsmithbarney.com/abt_sb/brnchloc.html
Paine Webber	www.painewebber.com	www.painewebber.com/indinv_frame.htm
Prudential	www.prusec.com	www.prusec.com/about_prudential/branch_locator.htm
A.G. Edwards	www.agedwards.com/index.fcgi	www.agedwards.com/welcome.fcgi?branches
Edward Jones	www.edwardjones.com	www.edwardjones.com/cgi/getHTML.cgi?page=/USA/entry/index.htm

NAME YOUR PRICE

Reading about brokers and planners, you might think the stock market is a combat zone where you have little control. Well, you might be somewhat relieved to know that you can name the price—the amount you're willing to pay for a stock or accept on the sale of shares. You can also dictate when your order to buy or sell stock is executed.

Many investors don't realize that the terms lie in the type of order you place with your broker. A market order, for example, is nothing more than instructions to your broker to buy or sell a certain number of shares at the best price currently available. If Intel is trading at $100 a share, and you place a market order to buy 60 shares, your broker or discount brokerage will probably complete the deal near that $100 mark.

Put in for a limit order, and you'll be exerting more say in the way your broker is doing the job. A limit order specifies the highest price you're willing to shell out for a stock if you're in the market to buy, or the lowest offer you'd be willing to entertain should you be selling. If the stock hits that price, then you can expect the order to buy or sell to go through. As an example, pretend that you've just placed a limit order to buy 10 shares of Bow Wow Dog Food Corp. at no more than $30 a share. If Bow Wow is at $31, your broker won't budge. The minute it's below $30, though, you're likely to see the limit order executed, at $30, $28, or $29—whatever the stock's price is at the time.

Finally, there's a stop order, which can limit your losses on a stock trade. A stop order tells your broker to sell shares or buy them the minute a stock crosses a price point. If you place a stop order for $25 on a purchase of IBM shares at a time when the computer company is fetching $30 a share, the minute the company's stock reaches $25 your broker will arrange to buy the stock for you.

Securities industry regulators in your state may have a list of unscrupulous brokers, too. To find the telephone number of your local watchdog, contact the North American Securities Administrators Association, or NASAA (202-737-0900).

DISCOUNT AND ONLINE BROKERS

On the surface of things, discount and online brokers don't seem to be bringing much to the table. There's no one assigned to shepherd you and your money around. There's no hand-holding and no one's around to draw up a set of financial blueprints for you. Often enough, there's no brokerage office to visit. There's no team of analysts covering different industries in the stock market and filing recommendations of company shares for you to purchase.

Instead, all—or most—of the financial shots are left up to you, the investor. It's your call to choose the stocks you want to buy. And its up to you to decide when to put in the order for shares of a mutual fund (see Figure 10.7).

There's one clear advantage to keeping things simple: a low price. By sidestepping all the trappings of a traditional brokerage—the offices, the research departments, even the teams of brokers and their salaries—the discounters keep their overhead at a minimum. That means an online operation can charge under $10 a trade, a pittance compared with some of the old-school brokerages, which might bill you $50, $60, or even $70 for the same service.

In some cases, despite the "discount" tag, online brokerages serve up a lot of perks or freebies. Take Charles Schwab, a firm that insists on calling itself a full-service brokerage, and rightly so. Schwab offers up access to stock screens, investment research from big-name brokerages, as well as stock market news. Most give you access to stock and fund quotes. You can place orders to buy or sell shares over the Internet (see Figure 10.8).

These days in the investment marketplace, low price is defeating perks handily. Online brokers may keep things simple, but it's becoming obvious that many individual investors would rather save dollars on commission than have a broker to call on the phone.

Online brokerage firms opened up 1.8 million new accounts for investors in the fourth quarter of 1999, alone, according to U.S. Bancorp Piper Jaffray, an investment bank. Almost 50 percent of all trades by individual investors were handled by online operators in the second half of 1999; as recently as 1998, the figure was 27 percent.

Just how hot is trading on the Internet? Consider this: In 1999, Merrill Lynch, a dyed-in-the-wool full-service brokerage firm jumped into the fray, announcing that it would serve up its own online service, with a basic charge of $29.95 for trades of U.S. company shares.

Figure 10.7   A Discount or Online Broker Is for You If . . .

- You read the financial press regularly.
- You have a good understanding of stocks, bonds, and mutual funds.
- You want to manage your money and your investments yourself.
- You'd like to save money on commissions.
- You have enough time to keep on top of the financial markets and your investments.

Figure 10.8 Discount or Online Brokers

What they do:

Buy stocks, bonds and mutual funds for you, at a low price.

Allow you the freedom to set your own financial goals and make investment choices.

Keep a detailed record of your account.

Provide perks such as market updates, free investment research, calculators, and investing guides.

What you need to find out:

How much are the company's commissions?

How many mutual funds does the brokerage offer and how many no-load funds are available to you?

How much is the minimum you need to open and maintain an account?

What is available in the way of calculators and other tools and guides?

In fact, nearly every big financial company around is hustling to get an online brokerage up and running. The reason: It seems an awful lot of people are looking to manage their own financial affairs and save money at it. Morgan Stanley Dean Witter has already joined the party, and Donaldson Lufkin & Jenrette set up shop on the Internet a few years ago.

Freedom

There are considerable advantages to working with a discount or online firm. For one, there's independence. You and you alone are at the helm of your account. You won't get cold calls from a broker hounding you to invest in shares of Mammoth Industries, Inc.

Consider, too, that you can check up on your account anytime of the day or night. Online brokers let you access your account statistics anytime you log onto the Web. You'll be able to track your investments and follow developments. There's no waiting for a broker to field your phone call and put you on hold; the lowdown on how your stocks and mutual funds are doing is there before your eyes.

Checking Out the Discounters

A growing number of people feel discount brokers or online brokerage firms make sense. To find out if you're one of them, think over a few things.

First, how much help do you need, and how motivated are you to dive into the books and learn more about investing and the financial markets?

Are you afraid of numbers, or worried that you might make a gaff? The more intrepid you are—or if you're open, even eager, to crunch numbers and examine stocks, mutual funds, and the like—the better suited you are to working with a discounter or online broker.

Consider self-control as well. Online and discount brokers have hacked the price of trading stocks so low, there's definitely the temptation to trade often. Leap in and out of a stock or two over the course of 2 months and its possible to still pay less in commissions that you would have to make one stock market purchase in the past. The problem is rushing in and out of investments can stack up some steep trading costs and pile on substantial taxes as well. If you make the move to discount or online to save, keep in mind that a little bit of willpower can help keep costs low, too.

Once you pass our brief exam, put your brokerage to the test as well. First, and foremost, you'll want to know what you're slated to pay for trades. No matter how thrifty a brokerage may be, it still should spell out how much you're paying for trades online or over the phone, in the case of a discount firm. You'll also want to check into account minimums. Some firms require that you open an account with a $2,000 balance, others more. Figure 10.9 lists some well-known discount brokers. Figure 10.10 is a list of the major online brokers. Some of these brokers fit both categories.

Take a tour online, kick around, and be sure to look for freebies. Online brokers serve up a smorgasbord of tools and helpful items. Start with market news and updates, which keep you informed about events and

Figure 10.9   Discount Brokers

Charles Schwab	800-540-9874
Muriel Siebert	800-USA-0711
Fidelity	800-544-3063
Quick & Reilly	800-533-8161
Brown & Co.	800-822-2021
Suretrade	800-909-6827
A.B. Watley	888-ABWATLEY
Dreyfus Brokerage	800-421-8395
TD Waterhouse WebBroker	800-934-4410
E*TRADE	800-STOCKS5
Scottsdale	800-619-SAVE
AccuTrade	800-494-8949

WEB SIGHTINGS
PLUGGING IN

There are a few spots where you can hunt for the discount or online that's best for you. Start with Figures 10.9 and 10.10 that list discounters and online outfits and their web addresses and/or toll-free telephone numbers.

WWW.GOMEZADVISORS.COM

Next, be sure to make a stop at Gomez Advisors (www .gomezadvisors.com). Gomez tracks practically every facet of e-retail, e-commerce, and e-finance for consumers, and rates online brokerages and banks. The Gomez site also includes contact information for e-brokers, company histories, and if that wasn't enough, a basic tutorial in investing and primers on how to choose a broker, too.

WWW. XOLIA.COM

Another site that has done exhaustive research on online and discount brokers is Xolia, a site that tracks e-commerce as well. Xolia is filled with web page after web page of information on the e-brokerage explosion. It has also collected up reviews of online firms from a host of different financial publications and has an exhaustive list of profiles of web brokers to boot.

WWW.SONIC.NET/DONALDJ/BROKERS.HTML

It could only happen on the Web. Brokerage enthusiast Don Johnson, known as Donald J on the Internet, has scanned, surveyed, studied, and gathered up commentary on discount and online brokers. Mr. Johnson is a former professor who has been an avid investor for almost 50 years. During that time, Johnson has learned a thing or two about brokers, much of which he's more than happy to share with web browsers.

At his Web address, you'll see Johnson's comments, comments of folks who have e-mailed him, and a digest of press pieces on discount and online brokers. You simply have to check it out to believe what's there. What's more, you'll find a ranking of discount brokers here, too.

Figure 10.10   Online Brokers

Here's a list of the biggest online brokers around with contacts.

Online Brokers (ranked by market share as of 12/99).

BROKER	WEB SITE	CONTACT NUMBER
Schwab	www.schwab.com	800-435-4000
E*TRADE	www.etrade.com	800-786-2571
TD Waterhouse	www.waterhouse.com	800-934-4410
Fidelity	www.fidelity.com	800-544-7272
Datek	www.datek.com	888-463-2835
Ameritrade	www.ameritrade.com	800-454-9272
DLJdirect	www.dljdirect.com	800-825-5723
Scottrade	www.scottrade.com	800-619-7283
Cybercorp	www.cybercorp.com	888-762-9237
Suretrade	www.suretrade.com	401-642-6900
MSDW	www.online.msdw.com	800-584-6837
NDB	www.ndb.com	800-417-7423

trends that affect your portfolio. Add to that the ability to plot your portfolio at the site and keep track of its ups and downs over time. See if the site offers up financial calculators, too. They're easy-to-use software that help you plan, plug in numbers from your own particular circumstances, and see scenarios come to life on everything from tuition planning to retirement. Some sites provide screening software to let you sift through the market or mutual fund choices. In addition, your online provider may publish tips and advice for individual investors.

ON TO THE FUTURE

Now that you've seen how the markets work, and know how to carve up your savings to get the best returns at the lowest risk, it's time to share your new-found knowledge with your kids. Believe it: learning how to keep track of their finances is not only a great way to beguile kids into doing their math homework, it's a skill that will make them confident adults and will help them make their way into the world as successful investors. Not bad, huh?

Chapter 11 has suggestions for teaching your children how to manage their money and look at stocks, bonds, and mutual funds without running away. Now, if only convincing them to eat their vegetables were just as easy . . .

11

HOW TO TEACH YOUR KIDS TO SAVE, INVEST, AND PROSPER

Now that you've become a knowledgeable investor, it's time to pass along what you know to some small folks who will someday soon need a leg up on the financial markets: your children. Investing and managing their money are simply skills they'll need the rest of their lives. But before you send your young ones off to gather up and compare stock quotes and price-to-earnings multiples, you'll need a strategy, a ruse of sorts to spark their interest and make learning the more complex aspects of investing fun and informative.

What begins as child's play has the potential to develop into grown-up successes. Great deeds that we all admire later are at some point based in simple, ordinary kid stuff; the games and little steps that are repeated again and again eventually become the best of habits. Those same small lessons help our children shape their lives and gain a sense of accomplishment.

One day your child may be carefully navigating his way through his ABCs sung in rhyme. Years later, those same alphabet games mature into well-organized, well-argued high school essays. In time, they're the stuff of great speeches, perhaps even a novel or a brilliant business report. Or, think how your preschooler started learning to count, slowly sticking one finger and then another into the air, repeating the numbers with as serious an expression as an accountant checking a tax form. It won't be long—maybe 12, 13, 14 years—when that facility with digits becomes the foundation for calculus or physics.

Along with numbers and the alphabet, investing and money management rank among the most important skills you as a parent can pass on to your children in today's economic environment. Although finances are not the only key to your son's or daughter's future happiness, the ability to save, invest, and plan life's steps will help guarantee success for any number of goals such as owning a car or buying a home.

The earlier you get your kids started in understanding the value of money and how to manage it, the better off they'll be in the long run. Studies show that children who are introduced to saving and investing tend to make better financial preparations when they get older. A report by B. Douglas Bernheim, an academic economist at Stanford University shows that adults who had a savings account as a child saved 108 percent more than their counterparts who didn't.

There's another bonus, too. While children are learning about stocks, companies, and the financial markets, they are also practicing mathematics and starting to understand how current events that steer the economy and politics both at home and abroad shape their lives. Finding the headquarters of McDonald's or Microsoft can be a geography lesson; a look at Ford Motor Company can be the launching point for a close look at the history of the automobile. Annual reports, chock-full of text and charts, are effective supplements to reading and math textbooks.

When it comes to teenagers, there's a word to explain another way of looking at investing and learning about the market: balance. The minute kids hit the magic age of 12, they undergo a miraculous transformation into consumers. Suddenly that cute little babbler is talking back and vacuuming up food, clothes, CDs, and video games with abandon. Teenage Research Unlimited, a Chicago company that tracks the spending habits of adolescents says your kids and his or her peers are funneling a whopping $141 billion into the economy to guzzle soda, munch away on fast-food burgers, buy computer games, or get the latest aerodynamic sneakers before friends can show them off. A taste of saving and investing can show kids there's another side to money other than littering it on countless store counters. And investing is one way to recoup part of the fortune your child is spending away on her favorite things (see Figure 11.1).

It doesn't hurt that the same money management lessons you're imparting will play a critical role in your son's or daughter's life. The day is

Figure 11.1   Your Kids Will Become Good Investors If You . . .

- Provide an earned allowance to help teach them the value of money.
- Show them how to save and set aside some of their income.
- Show them how stocks are a way to own a piece of companies that make the things they love.
- Link homework and lessons at school into stocks and the market.
- Set a good example yourself.

REALITY CHECK

You'd figure Duane Davis would be serious about teaching his kids Taylor and Duane II about stocks and mutual funds, especially since he's the head of a national investors' organization.

Well, the founder of the Coalition of Black Investors does have a plan, but at the same time, he's walking his children through the world of finance at a slow pace. Daughter Taylor, 6, and Duane II, now 4, get a lot of schooling in a variety of financial lessons, but Davis thinks he's had the most success with giving the kids a hands-on introduction to the bank and the stock market, bit by bit. "We try to get them involved a number of ways," he says. "We pay them to do chores, we let them punch the buttons at the ATM or fill out a deposit slip at the bank, and of course, we've started talking to them about stocks and owning shares."

From time to time, Davis also likes to buy his kids stock in companies with products they know. "They both own a few shares in companies like Coca-Cola and McDonald's, and whenever we're driving around, I ask them what companies do they see along the way that they own in their portfolios." Davis also coaxes his kids into looking at the paper or glancing over annual reports to discuss a little bit of what's happening with the shares they own. "My son adores Michael Jordan—in fact he's convinced that Michael's bound to make a comeback any day now—so we bought him a little bit of Nike. One time, not too long ago, when his Grandmom was putting on a pair of his store-brand socks, Duane stopped her and said, 'Put on the Nike socks, I own Nike and I want to help out.'"

Taylor's favorite toys, meanwhile are all made by Mattel, so Davis was sure to get her a few shares of the company. "It's not necessarily where I'll put most of their college savings, to be honest, but by buying them a few shares, they get to see how investing works and how it's important for them, too," he says.

That's also gotten the kids to ask some probing questions. "Taylor wants to know how rich we are, and just what is rich," Davis chuckles. "You know it brought up a pretty deep discussion . . . and what touched me about it was I think my daughter came away knowing that our family is rich in love first and foremost, and that money, while important, has its place."

fast approaching when your children will have to mull over options for a 401(k) or scratch their heads and wonder just how they'll ever get the money to put their kids in college. They'll have to balance checkbooks and rake together enough money for new cars, homes, or furniture. In all likelihood, they'll find out firsthand the inadequacies of Social Security and may even have to take care of you in your old age. In other words, the same obstacles, the exact responsibilities you wrestle with daily will soon be theirs. Make sure they'll have enough good sense to sort it all out and stay atop their finances.

There's no need to collar your kids or use ham-handed tactics to steer them in the direction of beneficial habits. And, even if your 3-year-old isn't already intrigued with the greenish-gray paper stuffing your wallet, he or she wants to know why you can't fill every request for Furbies, bicycles, and candy.

You're under close observation, too. Kids soak up every facet of your life only to amaze you with their imitation of you and your antics sooner rather than later. The same holds true for the way you handle cash and manage your finances. Whenever you fall behind on bills, every time you argue about finances, your kids will be close at hand to process what's going on. Lead by a good example and chances are your youngsters will be conscientious savers.

From there, the rest is easy. Puzzled about where to start? Well, look no further than a basic payment for help around the house—an allowance.

ALLOWANCES

The kids can't wait. They mind their p's, their q's, and anything else their parents want. They even try their best to stay out of trouble.

Children live for their allowance. Week after week, they know what they have to do—how many times to wash the dishes, when to cut the lawn or wash the car. Once the kids' version of payday rolls around, they have a new responsibility: making the money stretch to meet their needs. The candy bar, the dolls, the soda are all theirs for the taking—provided they have enough cash to cover the tab. It's a lot like the real world we deal with as adults.

There simply isn't a better way to get your kids to think about money than an allowance—a weekly salary of sorts. It teaches them how to generate an income with their work, and how to budget, limit their expenditures to what they can earn. And, it can also teach them to save.

Good habits get off to an early start, and savings is maybe one of the best to begin as soon as possible. And while there's no hard-and-fast guideline for how much of an allowance you should allot your kids, try to have them save at least a tenth of what they make.

Allowances make the most sense when your child reaches 5 or 6 years of age. At that point, most kids start to grasp how money set aside collects over time to become something bigger that can be spent on larger items.

How much is enough? Well, the experts have different advice on the matter. Some suggest that you give your kid a dollar for each year of age. A seven-year-old will get $7 dollars a week, a 10-year-old will pocket $10. If that seems extravagant, consider Plan B: a dollar amount that corresponds to their grade in school. That way, your 8- or 9-year-old in third grade gets $3 a week.

It's recommended, too, that you tie an allowance to the performance of chores. That way, your children will start to understand how effort or sacrifice help them out in the long run.

There are easy ways to make savings more of a game than a chore. For one, you can divide an allowance into change or dollar bills. Spending money can be stowed away in one jar; savings can go into a toy bank or another jar. Keep a running tab of each jar's contents, and your kids will be absorbing their first experiences with account balances.

Another idea is to actually open up a savings account for your kids, and to review monthly statements so they see how spending and saving both tap the same pool of money—their allowance.

In many cases, banks offer special accounts and savings programs for tikes. For some kid accounts, minimum balance requirements and fees are waived. And, if the local bank insists that you open a custodial account, remember to use your child's Social Security number so all interest earned will be taxed in his or her name—at an infinitesimally small rate.

INVESTING AS CHILD'S PLAY AND MORE

An allowance, though, is just a beginning. There's the heavy-duty stuff to wade through—investing. You might think stocks and the market are dry; so dull, in fact, that there's no way to interest your kids. Wrong. Even in this era of Nintendo, Pokemon, Playstation, and NBA trading cards, you'll be shocked how quickly most kids take to investing in the companies that produce their favorite things. Don't try to conquer the stock market in one sitting by scanning the Wall Street Journal. Let your kids warm up slowly. You'll discover that you won't need even half the coaxing you use to get them to eat green vegetables. Step 1 is easy. Start by looking at their favorite foods, their favorite clothing, recordings, or toys. Each of those items is made by a corporation, and many of the same companies have stocks that trade on the exchanges. For every bag of McDonald's french fries kids devour, a company with the same name and the ticker symbol MCD is logging a profit on the sales of fried potatoes and salt. Furbie's fortunes keep Hasbro (ticker symbol, HAS) steeped in profits. The cartoons on ABC are put out by Disney (DIS), which happens to own the broadcast company, too. There's a company—Nike (NKE)—that manufactures the sports apparel the All-Stars wear. Or, there's Toys "R" Us, the company that runs the store where they picked up their most recent board game or CD (see Figure 11.2).

It's easy to connect the product with its maker. Begin one Saturday by surfing the Web or heading down to the public library to research what companies make which items. Next you explain to your brood that it's possible to own a piece of the company that makes their favorite cheeseburger or sneaker. You might dredge up a copy of the daily stock results sheets in the newspaper and point out the ticker symbols to the same companies that ensnare parents' wallets.

Once your kids see a link between a stock and something tangible that interests them, you'll have them hooked. You'll also have a few learning games that might trick them into practicing things they have picked up in school. Multiply share price by the number of shares owned—you'll have the value of one holding. Take a company's earnings growth, multiply it by its current profits per share, and get a projection of next year's earnings. And the list goes on and on.

Don't overlook that tracking favorite companies and investing can teach your children some other excellent lessons. Looking up product and company histories can help your kids learn about the recent past. Help guide them either by using *Hoover's Guide*, which supplies a lot of background on large American corporations or by looking at company Web sites, which can be found on the Internet with the help of search engines such as Altavista, Excite, Yahoo!, or Ask Jeeves (www.askjeeves.com). Geography? Remember that companies, headquarters, factories, and markets often lie in

Figure 11.2   Kidstuff on the Stock Market

Your children's favorites—food, clothing, toys—trade on the stock market, too. Here are companies they'll find interesting.

PRODUCT	STOCKS (TICKER: EXCHANGE)
Nike sportswear	Nike (NKE: NYSE)
McDonald's hamburgers	McDonald's (MCD: NYSE)
Disneyland, Lion King, Winnie the Pooh	Walt Disney Co. (DIS: NYSE)
Toys, Pokemon, Star Wars figurines, Furby	Hasbro (HAS: NYSE)
Toys	Mattel (MAT: NYSE)
Coca-Cola	Coca-Cola (KO: NYSE)
Nintendo, Game Boy	Nintendo (NTDOY: Nasdaq)
Playstation	Sony (SNY: NYSE)

odd corners of the globe. Have your kids look through a company's annual report for locations around the world and then help them find spots from Manhattan to Timbuktu in the atlas.

Just as important, though, are the things your kid can pick up by learning about the trials of inventors, entrepreneurs, and other gung ho types who have led companies. Take perseverance, as an example. Alexander Graham Bell (whose work lay the foundation for AT&T and spin-offs such as Bell Atlantic and SBC Communications) worked dutifully in his lab until he discovered how to transmit the human voice over great distances. Then there's humankind's ability to adapt to change. Long before the antics of Donkey Kong, the Mario Brothers, or any number of other video game characters, Nintendo, the Japanese giant in the business, made playing cards. It wasn't until the 1970s that the company began to branch out and conquer the world living room by living room, television set by television set, computer by computer.

PARTING WITH REAL MONEY

Looking over the market is one thing. Letting your son or daughter dive right in is another experience, and one that's likely to win them over for good.

There are many ways to begin: Join a parent/child investment club or go it alone. There are two ways to do it yourself with minimal risk. One is to buy shares of a corporation yourself and designate a number—perhaps five for your kid. From then on, you have a project on your hands. Mornings, or perhaps once a week, you can scan the paper and follow your stock together.

The other is to enroll in a direct share purchase plan (DSP) or Direct Stock Purchase (discussed in Chapter 4). DSPs allow you to buy shares directly from a company with regular monthly payments. That allows you to purchase as little as a share a month, and accumulate shares over time. They'll also allow you to salt away a set amount every month—say $50—and will assign you fractional shares. That way, you needn't scrape up much money at all and won't be strapped with hefty commissions.

Whether you buy shares or enroll in a DSP, you and your son or daughter will be in for some nice perks. When it comes to illustrating key investment points to your kid, an annual report can go a long way, too. In many cases, it's loaded with colorful photography and slick graphics that can hook most anyone's attention—even a child's. On top of that, there is material aplenty you can use for impromptu lessons with your child, with the help of an encyclopedia or a trip to the local library. Take Microsoft, the software manufacturer. A trip through Microsoft's annual report can serve as the launching point for further exploration on topics ranging from the history of the computer to the location of Seattle, the company's home, on the map of the United States.

KIDDIE FUNDS

There are mutual funds that specifically target kids and help them become good investors. Some have Web sites that guide kids through the market. Others publish annual reports and newsletters that teach kids the difference between bonds, stocks, and the like. What's more, some of these same young investor funds have minimum initial investments low enough for many kids to foot (with a little help from Mom and Dad).

According to the Mutual Fund Education Alliance (MFEA), four fund companies have offerings tailored to children out on the market (see Figure 11.3). One of the best known, and most kid-friendly is the Stein Roe Young Investor Fund (SRYIX). Don't let the name fool you, however. By its charter, The Young Investor Fund aims to buy stocks of companies whose products affect the lives of kids. That's a broad enough definition to encompass Cisco Systems, General Electric, Citigroup, and America Online in addition to McDonald's and Mattel.

That kind of lineup might lead you to think that the Stein Roe fund is a growth stock fund. It is, with a twist. The fund runs a Web site that aims to teach kids the basics about investing while entertaining them. Young investors also receive a newsletter called Investment 101, with articles on what stocks are, why companies issue shares, and what companies are doing in the marketplace. It takes a minimum initial investment of $100 ($50 if you sign up for an automatic share purchase plan and pledge regular deposits each month to your account).

You might also opt for low-minimum mutual funds like USAA First Start Growth, which requires just $250 to open up a custodial account, and a

Figure 11.3　Funds for Kids

The following funds are tailored for you and your kids—they require low minimum initial investments and will take small investments later on, too. What's more, some offer reports and pamphlets that help children learn more about investing.

FUND	MINIMUM INITIAL INVESTMENT	MINIMUM SUBSEQUEST INVESTMENT
American Century Giftrust Fund	$ 500	$ 50
Royce Giftshares Fund	$2,000	$ 50
Stein Roe Young Investor Fund	$ 500	$100
USAA First Start Growth	$ 250	$ 20

Source: The Mutual Fund Education Alliance.

mere $20 if you sign up to have the fund tap another account electronically for deposits.

While USAA's fund has just two years under its belt, it has put up good numbers, with a 40.46 percent total return in 1998 and a 21.83 percent total return in 1999.

INDEX

283

Printed in the United States
1323100002B/49-166

9 780471 381846